ENCHANTED BY ETERNITY

ENCHANTED
BY
ETERNITY

RECAPTURING THE WONDER
OF THE CATHOLIC WORLDVIEW

WILLIAM J. SLATTERY, PhD
FOREWORD BY MARK WAHLBERG

Our Sunday Visitor
Huntington, Indiana

Nihil Obstat
Msgr. Michael Heintz, Ph.D.
Censor Librorum

Imprimatur
✠ Kevin C. Rhoades
Bishop of Fort Wayne-South Bend
September 25, 2024

The *Nihil Obstat* and *Imprimatur* are official declarations that a book is free from doctrinal or moral error. It is not implied that those who have granted the *Nihil Obstat* and *Imprimatur* agree with the contents, opinions, or statements expressed.

Every reasonable effort has been made to determine copyright holders of excerpted materials and to secure permissions as needed. If any copyrighted materials have been inadvertently used in this work without proper credit being given in one form or another, please notify Our Sunday Visitor in writing so that future printings of this work may be corrected accordingly.

Our Sunday Visitor Publishing Division
Our Sunday Visitor, Inc.
200 Noll Plaza
Huntington, IN 46750
www.osv.com
1-800-348-2440

ISBN: 978-1-63966-318-7 (Inventory No. T2965)
1. RELIGION—Christianity—Catholic.
2. RELIGION—Christian Living—Inspirational.
3. RELIGION—Philosophy.

eISBN: 978-1-63966-319-4
LCCN: 2024949879

Cover design: Tyler Ottinger
Interior design: Amanda Falk
Cover art: *The Garden of Eden*, by Thomas Cole, Alamy Images

PRINTED IN THE UNITED STATES OF AMERICA

*To the Crucified Hero, and to the Heroine who
stood beside Him, to whom I owe … all.*

*To Margaret, my mother, whose self-sacrificing
love has made dreams into realities.*

*To Paul Desmarais Jr., a friend on the journey through
the labyrinth since thirty-three years ago.*

People say that what we're all seeking is a meaning for life. I don't think that's what we're really seeking. I think that what we're seeking is an experience of being alive so that our life experiences on the purely physical plane will have resonances with our own innermost being and reality, so that we actually feel the rapture of being alive.

— *Joseph Campbell*, The Power of Myth

CONTENTS

FOREWORD

By Mark Wahlberg

I have friends from all religions and some from none, all of whom I respect and honor. They all know I'm Catholic, but they all agree that I would never try to jam my convictions down anyone's throat. Nevertheless, when you've found something really good, valuable, and useful, your instinctive reaction is to say, "Hey guys! Look at this! This just might work for you too!"

That's the way I feel about Catholicism.

I have made no secret about my troubled youth because the grace I received when I found God and turned my life around was so profound that I wanted others to see what was possible.

Once I started doing the right thing, good things started to happen in my life. And had it not been for that difficult start in life, I might have never discovered my faith and all the wonderful blessings that come with believing.

That's why my wife, children, and anyone else close to me know that prayer is how I start my day. Getting down on my knees in humility has given me the spiritual strength to stand up for the genuine, the good, and the beautiful in this world.

I want to do everything I can to build others up, to make a difference in their lives for the better. I want my life to be a Jacob's ladder for others to climb higher on the rungs of my experience, my outreach, and my faith. Especially young people — that's why I started my youth foundation: to help and — more importantly — inspire kids to dream big and reach those goals. I want others to find meaning, purpose, and hope through my work.

The ideas in this book resonate with the way I feel about the Catholic Faith. This book slam dunks why I'm proud to be Catholic — because real Catholicism is a tough, world-improving movement that is about both the forever-life and an urgency to make this life the best possible for everyone.

September 12, 2023

INTRODUCTION

The difference between ... post-Christian Western historians and their Christian predecessors is that the moderns do not allow themselves to be aware of the pattern in their minds. ... If one cannot think without mental patterns — and, in my belief, one cannot — it is better to know what they are; for a pattern of which one is unconscious is a pattern that holds one at its mercy.

— Arnold Toynbee

We are living in a rousing and tumultuous epoch — an unprecedented opportunity for us Catholics to begin the "long march through the institutions"[1] for the building of a new civilization of human flourishing. But for this to happen, we Catholics must begin to think *way* outside the box. In order to do so, we need to stop being *modern* and start becoming *ultramodern*. By "ultra," I do not mean "extremely" (as in "hypermodern"), but rather its meaning in Latin: "beyond," "outside the limits of," or "exceeding the range of."

Whether we realize it or not, we Catholics have been deeply influenced by modernity's failed worldview. By *worldview,* I mean the eyes through which we see all of reality — the deeply embedded patterns of thinking that we apply not now and then but constantly in daily living. A worldview is the stable, all-encompassing way a society or an individual not only looks at reality but feels reality. It is the pair of glasses through which you see the world around you. It is what you look *through* rather than what you look *at.* It is the window through which you gaze on the "real," the mirror in which you see yourself, the telescope through which you look at distant events. It is the set of givens, assumptions, and presuppositions through which you view the world. It colors what you mean by *God, universe,* and *human.* It answers the basic questions: Who are you? Who are we as a society? What is life all about? Where are we going? Why do we think the way we do? What time is it?[2]

One's worldview always takes the form of a story or myth. (The Greek word for story is *mythos.*) It is the story about the world, history, society — where we are, how we got here, and where we are going. Thus it is the ground of thought and behavior and therefore of lifestyle. In the light of this story, the individual (and society as a whole) separates true and false, right and wrong, the beautiful and the ugly, the important and the banal, in order to make decisions. Accordingly, worldview functions like a software that has been silently downloaded into the brain. Constantly working away in the background, it interprets new data entering through our senses. Everyone has a worldview, and that is why the recognition of worldviews in self and others is crucial to the search for truth, goodness, beauty, and for an optimal culture and civilization.

So, what exactly is modernity's worldview? Shaped by our understanding of history for the last three centuries, its core certainty can be expressed in a sound bite: *The eighteenth century is the turning point of world history.* The intellectual movers and shakers who laid the foundations for this attitude — such as Voltaire, Montesquieu, and Hume — declared that this was the most important century in the story of the human race, the beginning of an unstoppable march of progress, and therefore the salvation of humankind. They believed this was so, first, because of the promise of the scientific method, technology, and industrialization. Second, because it was the inauguration of a new world order founded on liberty, equality, and universal brotherhood, replacing monarchy with democracy and setting up the State as the protector of human rights. Humanity, it was believed, could now bring about a perfect society of peace and justice, and eliminate (or at least reduce) the impact of epidemics and sicknesses. The modern world would guarantee, through the power of education, science, capitalism, and materialism humanity's unending advance and the elimination of all forms of evil.

This is what most of the rulers of Europe and North America have believed from the eighteenth century up to our day. The ideology of the founders of the United States was an eclectic mixture of Protestantism, Deism, and Epicureanism in which God, if he exists, does not intervene in the world. Therefore, politics could be carried on without any practical reference to him, keeping only theoretical references, such as occasional public prayers on secular national holidays.

There is a telltale badge of this worldview on the back of the dollar bill. Above the pyramid is the phrase *annuit coeptis*, which means, "He has favored our undertakings." Underneath it are the words *novus ordo seclorum* ("a new order of the ages"). Both of these inscriptions appeared first on the Great Seal of the United States. The Great Seal's designer, the secretary of the Congress of the Confederation, Charles Thomson, said they alluded to "the beginning of the new American Era."[3] The founders of the United States of America along with the leaders of the French Revolution believed their countries were destined to provide the greatest hope of a new beginning, a new age, for the entire world.

The masses of people in the Western world, and more gradually in the rest of the world starting in the twentieth century, bought into this worldview. As did the majority of politicians (whether right-wing or left-wing, communists, socialists, democrats, conservatives, or liberals), even if in varying degrees and with notable differences.

The Postmodern Revolution and the "Great Reset"

My PhD specialization in alethic logic — the identification of hidden premises in worldviews — helped shape my conviction that we are now living in the midst of a new radical shift in thought patterns: the post-modern revolution. This revolution is a sweeping and uncompromising rejection of modernity's core certainty. Numerous intellectuals, both right-wing and left-wing, are alert to the fact that the modern worldview has not been able to build a civilization of human flourishing. Stress, pandemic levels of psychological addictions, environmental degradation, marriage and family breakdown, poverty, loneliness, and the menace of nuclear destruction leave no doubt in their minds about the fact. Things happened in the last three centuries that are largely unprecedented in history: genocides, concentration camps, and a cold-blooded, callous excusing of them for "rational" motives.

Postmodern intellectuals agree with Max Weber, the father of modern sociology, that the history of the modern era has been marked by the progressive "disenchantment of the world."[4] The sociologist Zygmunt Bauman points an accusing finger at the hidden menace of modernity, arguing that it was the convergence of characteristics unique to it — especially its technological know-how, valueless efficiency, rationalism detached from holistic humanness, instrumental reasoning, and managerial industrialism — that paved the way to the Holocaust.[5] As one of the fiercest critics of modernity, the leading postmodern philosopher Jean-François Lyotard bluntly stated regarding Auschwitz: "We wanted the progress of the mind, we got its shit."[6]

Postmodern intellectual elites — Jewish, Christian, agnostic, atheist, right-wing, left-wing, ecologists, feminists, physicists, microbiologists, and astrophysicists — at prestigious universities and in influential think tanks, largely off the radar screen for most people, are at work to build a new worldview. All of them, whether implicitly or explicitly, are calling for the "Great Reset."[7] They sense that we are living in an era of opportunity to inaugurate a "new world order."[8] We will first look at what is popularly seen to be the "right-wing" or "capitalist" proposal. I use the terms *right-wing, left-wing, liberal,* and *conservative* not because they are descriptive of these complex ideologies, but because they are the current popular labels.[9]

The most widely known right-wing proposal for a new civilization comes from the World Economic Forum that meets annually in Davos,

Switzerland. Made up of influential business leaders, politicians, scholars, trade unionists, and representatives of nongovernmental organizations (NGOs), members share the conviction that capitalism, democracy, and individualism are the way forward for humanity.[10] In 2020, the founder and executive chairman, Klaus Schwab, a German professor of business policy, coauthored with Thierry Malleret *COVID-19: The Great Reset*, a proposal for massive international economic and political change. He argued that a new automated society is coming into existence. Moreover, its birth has been accelerated by the need for social distancing provoked by the possibility of future epidemics like COVID-19. In his analysis, unless the world's leaders face up to this fact, they will expose the population to unprecedented hardships. Citing two Oxford University academics, he states that possibly "up to 86% of jobs in restaurants, 75% of jobs in retail and 59% of jobs in entertainment could be automatized by 2035."[11]

Schwab argues that high-tech has empowered the inauguration of a new type of world to which we must adapt. The coronavirus pandemic illustrates the urgency of this adjustment:

> We will continue to be surprised by both the rapidity and unexpected nature of these changes — as they conflate with each other, they will provoke second-, third-, fourth-, and more-order consequences, cascading effects, and unforeseen outcomes. In so doing, they will shape a new normal radically different from the one we will be progressively leaving behind. Many of our beliefs and assumptions about what the world could or should look like will be shattered in the process.[12]

Schwab and his coauthor Malleret sketch their proposal for the Great Reset as follows: "To achieve a better outcome, the world must act jointly and swiftly to revamp all aspects of our societies and economies, from education to social contracts and working conditions. Every country, from the United States to China, must participate, and every industry, from oil and gas to tech, must be transformed. In short, we need a 'Great Reset' of capitalism."[13] This reset is a project to *delete* present political-economic structures in order to build a *new* world: the ever-present goal of modernity.

As Paul de Man, a twentieth-century U.S. literary critic, writes, "Modernity exists in the form of a desire to wipe out whatever came earlier, in the hope of reaching at least a point that could be called a true present, a point of origin that marks a new departure."[14] This requires globalism: the bringing of Planet Earth into a single cultural, political, and economic unity. A reinvented capitalism and democracy would function as the vehicles to bring about a worldwide State under a single government. This, argues Schwab, will bring countless benefits, not least the end of Third-World poverty.[15]

Schwab, who was raised Catholic,[16] identifies three core benefits of the Great Reset, which International Monetary Fund director Kristalina Georgieva, in her keynote speech opening the Davos 2020 meeting, expressed as green growth, smarter growth, and fairer growth.[17] Three general strategies must be put in place: First, to "harness the innovations of the 'Fourth Industrial Revolution.'"[18] Second, to implement "stakeholder capitalism" — a structuring of businesses according to the needs of customers, employees, and local communities.[19] Third, because the nations of the world are interdependent for their survival, as the COVID-19 crisis has shown, a globalized Planet Earth will be best managed by a self-chosen group of governments, multinationals, and civil society organizations (CSOs) such as Amnesty International.[20] Schwab asks: "How will this expanded role of governments manifest itself? A significant element of new 'bigger' government is already in place with the vastly increased and quasi-immediate government control of the economy."[21] He forcibly argues against strong nation-states:

> The more nationalism and isolationism pervade the global polity, the greater the chance that global governance loses its relevance and becomes ineffective. Sadly, we are now at this critical juncture. Put bluntly, we live in a world in which nobody is really in charge. COVID-19 has reminded us that the biggest problems we face are global in nature. Whether it's pandemics, climate change, terrorism or international trade, all are global issues that

we can only address, and whose risks can only be mitigated, in a collective fashion.[22]

The Davos call for a "Great Reset" has impacted political leaders. U.S. President Joe Biden, New Zealand Prime Minister Jacinda Ardern, and Canadian Prime Minister Justin Trudeau have incorporated ideas based on the "Great Reset" in their speeches.

The left-wing proposal to birth a new world order does not have a single institute such as Davos expressing its worldview and agenda.[23] But it is everywhere, like an atmosphere, due to the presence of its ideology in universities, the mass media, and in politics. If one were to put a name on it, it would be either "Western Marxism," "Cultural Marxism," or "School of Frankfurt Marxism."[24] A rejection of classical Marxism-Leninism associated with dictators such as Lenin, Stalin, and Mao Zedong, its inspirational text was written by Antonio Gramsci (1891–1937), known as the "Prison Notebooks" because the thirty notebooks with three thousand pages of history and analysis were written during the imprisonment in Italy that led to his death. The young Italian formulated the new communist strategy by calling on Marxists to face the fact that the method of violent political revolution had failed in Europe and the Americas. Gramsci, convinced that classical Marxism's attempt to provoke conflict between workers and "capitalists" would not succeed in the comfortable bourgeois societies of Europe and North America, opted for a strategy faithful to Marx's dictate that man must decide whether or not his thinking is true according to whether or not it gives results. Looking at the influential Catholicism of his own native Italy, he knew that Marxists must begin the "long march through the institutions" if they wanted to triumph.[25] Every institution that shapes the patterns of thinking of the masses must be converted to the Marxist worldview: the mass media, universities, and schools from elementary levels to high school.

Inspired by Gramsci, whose philosophy was confirmed by the failure of the Marxist Revolution of 1918–1919 in Germany, Carl Grünberg founded the Institute for Social Research in Frankfurt in 1923.[26] Max Horkheimer became the director in 1930. Thinkers associated with it include Theodor W. Adorno, Erich Fromm, Herbert Marcuse, Walter

Benjamin, and Jürgen Habermas. Starting from the view of history laid out by Hegel and Marx, they cast new visions of a future civilization, often by subtly fusing insights from various disciplines, notably sociology and Sigmund Freud's psychoanalysis.[27] Indeed, the spread throughout the West of psychoanalytical thinking is due to this school, particularly Erich Fromm and Karen Horney, both followers of Wilhelm Reich. The outcome was a new social and political philosophy for achieving a new world order: "critical theory," the examination of society and culture in order to reveal, critique, and overthrow power structures that dominate and oppress.[28] This slammed capitalism with its mega corporations and monopolies, technology's applications in society, industrialization, and the destruction of personhood in the West. Since the 1970s, it has influenced the studies of law, literature, history, and the social sciences. Its foundational texts are Horkheimer and Adorno's *Dialectic of Enlightenment* and Marcuse's *One-Dimensional Man*.

Its influence has penetrated Western universities, birthing such disciplines as feminism, gender theory, and identity politics.[29] Herbert Marcuse, through his writings on repressive tolerance and his influence on Angela Davis and Rudi Dutschke, impacted the civil rights movement and the West German student movement.[30] From critical theory came critical pedagogy, a philosophy of education.[31] Based on Paolo Freire's 1968 book *Pedagogy of the Oppressed*, it seeks to bring about social justice through awakening critical awareness in students. Incorporating elements from the human and civil rights movements, postmodern theory, queer theory, feminist theory, and postcolonial theory, its ambition is to overcome all forms of oppression such as sexism and racism. Its trickle-down strategy to the masses through intellectuals such as Saul Alinsky has succeeded. Alinsky's 1971 handbook *Rules for Radicals* has influenced, among others, Barack Obama and Hillary Clinton.[32]

The most noticeable recent demonstration of the impact of critical theory came in 2020 during the massive social disturbance in response to the horrendously tragic and inexcusable murder of George Floyd. The various movements from #CancelRent to Defund the Police made political alliances a cornerstone of their strategy. As *The New York Times* op-ed writer Amna A. Akbar, a law professor who studies leftist associations, has remarked, the magnitude of the disturbance, its duration, and the interconnectedness of the groups fanning it is "far different from anything that has come before."[33] Moreover, climate change, racial justice, economic justice groups: "These movements are in conversation with one another, cross-endorsing demands as they expand their grass-roots bases. ... Each demand demonstrates a new attitude among leftist social movements. ... The people making these demands want a new society."[34]

The outcome of critical theory is a suspicion of Western civilization, its history and values in contemporary society. Through its influence a mentality of conflict marks the Western world: between generations, classes, and the sexes. We now live in a climate of suspicion because through critical theory the "masters of suspicion" — Freud, Marx, and Nietzsche — now influence key patterns in our thinking.[35] We are skeptical of the notion of truth and the possibility of certainty, imagining them to be the source of evil. We live in what Joseph Ratzinger called a "dictatorship of relativism which does not recognize anything as definitive and whose ultimate goal consists solely of one's own ego and desires."[36]

The outcome is that we now think about life as conflict. The new is always better than the old; "medieval" is the very worst of all societies; the State is the prime source of solutions to social problems and has rights even over the family. The only enemies are those who insist that change must be measured by the standards of the identity of man and the traditional understanding of marriage and family. Consequently, many politicians and intellectuals possess a confidence that enables them to dismiss or even crush such opposition with few qualms. And, most ominously, in the minds of the masses, this mentality is numbing any sense of life's deepest meaning.

Postmodernism's "Great Reset": Not Radical Enough

So, what to think of the right-wing and left-wing proposals? My reaction is the same as that of the physicist Niels Bohr, who, when the fellow scientist Wolfgang Pauli, after a lecture the latter had just given, remarked to him, "You probably think these ideas are crazy," replied, "I do, but, unfortunately, they are not crazy enough."[37]

They are not radical enough. By this I mean that neither liberals nor conservatives go to the roots of our contemporary problems. Both have starting points that are within the modern worldview that created them. Though both now see that all dimensions of reality are interconnected and that our crises are therefore intersectional, their analysis is flawed because their big picture of the universe and of humans is still that of the eighteenth century. It is the *machine* imagination of reality that dominates. Even the metaphors they use may be Freudian slips. For instance, the "Great *Reset*" is a machine-derived, electronic metaphor. Within this mechanistic cosmology there is no role for the immaterial (spiritual) dimension of the human and for the encoded blueprints for human flourishing to be found in both man and the biosphere. They are incapable of accepting this because they refuse to accept the reality of the universe as authored by an Intelligent Designer. Consequently, their strategies for their often-admirable goals are jeopardized.

If you want economy, politics, and education to the scale of the human, you must begin with a correct understanding of the universe and of man. After tackling why the universe exists and who man is, then you can lay out strategies for what to do and how to do it. Reality comes before action! To reverse the order is to beat your head against the wall. Moreover, even before cosmology and anthropology, you need theology: knowledge of the One who is the beginning and goal of the universe — its First and Final Cause. Modernity has a warped big picture. Jewish civilization and Christendom (the original shape of Western civilization), notwithstanding their shortcomings, did have the correct big picture, and this showed in their politics and economics which have given us the best of what we have today.[38]

Both liberals and conservatives view the universe and humans as sheer matter *practically*, even if not theoretically. Although they may give lip service to the Creator, they have made economics the criterion for building a society of human flourishing. This is because their ideologies are influenced by the father of capitalism, Adam Smith, whose economics triumphed largely for political reasons over the Catholic School of Salamanca.[39] Liberals and conservatives alike claim that, to ensure a successful economy, big government is essential. Therefore, in both Marxist-Leninist and capitalist societies, the human being is "man-for-the-economy": a cog in the machine of an economy largely controlled by the State and elites.[40]

Consequently, due to this economics-based starting point, neither wing proposes solutions addressing the deep relational causes underneath problems. For instance, both call for more free health care but do not tackle the need to eliminate the causes of so much physical and psychological sickness. Thus if either liberals or conservatives triumph, the outcome will be hypermodernity. As the cofounder of the U.S. Green Party movement and cultural critic, Charlene Spretnak, remarked:

> Our age is hypermodern, not so much because the tarnished ideologies of the modern worldview are still believed to be salvational, but because the conditions of modernity are now driven by the dynamics of the technosphere and the globalized economy. "Cyberspace" is hardly post-modern. What could be more disembodied, disembedded, and decontextualized? Surely the computer age is most modern, to use a term suggested by David Ray Griffin.[41]

Therefore, notwithstanding the difference in style and rhetoric between right-wing and left-wing, both are offering a remaking of modernity that is merely its prolongation: same business, new window dressing, new management. This is to be expected because both are historically merely *wings of the same modernity*. We even know the day of their birth as political terms.[42]

Ultramodern Catholics must be alert to the fact that it is not capitalism, communism, consumerism, industrialism, liberalism, or conservatism that is the problem, but the deep structure from which they all spring. Moreover, if we seek to find solutions by becoming a partisan of any of these "-isms," we will remain in the dead-end to which modernity has brought us.

We must exit the echo chamber of eighteenth-century thinking. Catholics sometimes feel themselves closer to modernity's left-wing because of its rhetoric about care for the poor and social justice; at other times they hear in conservatism echoes of their convictions about family, private property, and free enterprise. However, although strategically we may on occasion work with either, we need to be clear-minded about the fact that even if occasionally our goals coincide, our *ultimate goals, means, and methods* differ radically.[43] We Catholics heartily agree with Werner Heisenberg, the Nobel physicist, when he states: "I am firmly convinced that we must never judge political movements by their aims, no matter how loudly proclaimed or how sincerely upheld, but only by the means they use to realize these aims."[44]

We must build our own factories of the future on the foundation of our four-millennia-old worldview. Catholicism has its own blueprints for a new world order founded on our Judaeo-Christian biblical worldview. This fused with the most sophisticated expression of logic and reason gives us the culture and civilization of Christendom, the foundation of all that is praiseworthy in Western civilization — including the scientific mentality.[45] We must awaken to the fact that unlike both right-wingers and left-wingers, we actually have a track record of successful civilization-building. And what we did before we can do again because man's deepest needs remain the same, and the supernatural-natural tools of Catholicism still work.

Now is our opportunity! In the hunt for new solutions to our problems, countless intellectuals and the masses are opening themselves to new answers to the questions about who man is and what civilization should be like. Moreover, as we shall unpack in upcoming chapters, the roadblocks put in place by modernity to Catholicism — the materialistic interpretation of modern Newtonian physics (scientism) and the alleged theoretical foundations for skepticism — can be reduced to rubble by the explosive power of the ultramodern breakthroughs of quantum physics and other sciences.

Therefore, with deepened conviction, our top priority can be to rediscover the fascination of pure, organic Catholicism with its power to provoke a holistic lifestyle, culture, and civilization. That is the goal of this book. To achieve its end, I have organized it as follows: Chapter 1 will sketch why Catholicism is radically different when it is experienced without the warping contemporary worldview: because it imbues us with a deeply felt sense of connectedness to our deepest longings, to others, society, the biosphere, heritage, and to God, experienced as Creator-Lover-Rescuer. Chapter 2 will first sketch why both the masses and the intellectuals experience contemporary society as dehumanizing. Then, second, it will describe how in disciplines from healthcare to architecture and urban planning, thrilling new opportunities for resolving social and personal problems are appearing. Chapter 3 will sketch why our contemporary society has become dysfunctional and dehumanizing: the rupture of the connections that should exist between the scientific and humanistic disciplines, between individuals and community, and between people and their natural habitat. We will trace the origins of this deficiency to the new theory of how we understand reality and to the materialistic and scientistic interpretation of seventeenth-century Newtonian physics — both of which led to us reimagining the universe as a reality functioning as a complex machine, which became the model for economics, politics, education, the arts, and the sciences. Indeed, we began to think of ourselves as "biomachines" and subtly to treat each other as such. Chapter 4 will unpack why this new way of thinking was shaped by a crisis in European culture about the identity of God. This led to the undermining of the Catholic vision of the Deity as the Trinity, the Creator-Lover-Rescuer, reimagining him instead as the distant and terrifying powerful Absolute Being.[46]

Then we will outline the ultramodern Catholic worldview and lifestyle in three ways: first, by demonstrating how the chief insights of contemporary scientific breakthroughs support this worldview in chapters 5–8, second, by showing that its source is in the divinely inspired biblical vision in chapters 9–15, and third, by displaying how it harmonizes with universal human experience, especially our longings for holistic fulfillment, in chapters 16 and 17. By this threefold method, this book aims to make clear why this worldview has the power to change our way of thinking about every dimension of personal and social existence. My hope is that you, the reader, may discover Catholicism to be a way of experiencing reality that enraptures the ordinary and the everyday by disclosing the deepest dimensions of time and place.

Finally, I suggest two ways of reading this book. For those who want to discover the worldview of Catholicism and its biblical foundations immediately, I recommend you take the aerial tramway from the end of chapter 1 up to chapter 9 and the other peaks. However, I think that if you sweat it out by ascending on foot through chapters 2–8 you will have a far deeper appreciation of the panorama at your arrival on the heights — and you may even enjoy the climb.

CHAPTER 1

CATHOLICISM IS ABOUT REALITY, NOT RELIGION

Christianity, whatever else it is, is an explosion. … Unless it is sensational there is simply no sense in it. Unless the Gospel sounds like a gun going off, it has not been uttered at all.

— G. K. Chesterton, "The Theology of Christmas Presents"

"If Catholicism is only a 'religion,' then, to hell with it."

So thought the fifteen-year-old, freckle-faced Irish teenager as he stood one wintry day at the waterfront of his native Abbeyside on the Atlantic coast. The waves, pushed by the strong southwesterly winds, pounded the marina walls as relentlessly as the questions on his mind. "Does God exist? Is Christ divine? What difference does Catholicism really make?" Such were the doubts that had been rushing upon him since several months before.

"Does God exist?" At least I found the answer to that problem quite fast. Going through old books in the family library, I came across one written by a priest of the Society of Jesus presenting St. Thomas Aquinas's argument from design for the existence of God. "Wow!" was my teen reaction. And so I flung the temptations to atheism over the harbor wall into the Atlantic.

OK. So God exists. And he matters because he's eternal. And, yes, over the following months I grew in the conviction that the Lord Jesus is divine. And that the Catholic Church was founded by him. So, everything was solved — you would think.

Well, no. Something remained unanswered, and it rankled within me for decades.

I couldn't get my head around two conflicting realities: On the one hand, God matters, Jesus Christ is Lord, and Catholicism declares itself to be the messenger of the meaning about the ultimate purpose of reality; but on the other hand, in the modern world these three statements don't seem to matter. In education, politics, economics, and the arts, Catholicism and worldview are separated. Was schizophrenia rampant, or was I simply not seeing things right? What really puzzled me was not that the secular world felt like this but that the majority of Catholics I met, especially the most "religious" people and the "leading experts," seemed to think likewise.

My problem came from the following quirky way of thinking: Either all of reality should have a new sense because Jesus Christ is Lord, or, if it doesn't, then Catholicism simply doesn't make sense. I couldn't accept Catholicism as a mere "religion," a "faith," a "spirituality." I sensed that somehow its certainties should be like the sun, enlightening and warming everything. They should change all dimensions of life, encompass the cosmos, alter the telling of history, imbue the workings of science, politics, and economics, and inspire our urban planning. We should awake to the thrill of its liturgical rhythms and fall asleep to its existential cadences. It should be a game-changer in our decision-making — a worldview spontaneously fascinating our imagination, energizing our willpower, and shaping our lifestyle. I didn't want mere theory; I wanted an existential answer that would urge me onward in the face of obstacles.

I wanted a Catholicism that taught me to live heartily and to die meaningfully.

My intuition as a teenager was that Catholicism had to provide the answers not just for me, but for everyone. I had no interest in a "me religion" or a massage for my feelings. The grandeur of existence, the value of a lifetime, the beauty of nature — all shouted for an answer that would, within Mystery, explain the One who is the source of all and be for the benefit of everyone, both as individuals and as a society. It had to be an answer which, by giving my life an imperishable value, implicitly empowered it to benefit others and the world around me.

But that was not how others seemed to view Catholicism. Instead, it was seen as a private affair, part-time, and in a separate space. I got the impression that it was only about praying, Sunday Mass, and getting yourself "saved"; society could carry on independently. And Catholicism didn't enter into math, history, music, art, and science. The gut feeling I got from looking around me was that Catholicism for most people was a private set of convictions that had little to do with the "real" world.

Writing a book is like being overheard speaking to oneself. We Irish don't like talking about ourselves. Only after some hesitation did I decide to pen these personal reminiscences. In the end, I did so because I don't reckon myself as essentially different from you. Since you are reading this book, I reckon that your heart and mine are searching for the same answers. Therefore, my prayed ambition is that what follows may help you to see your lifetime's horizons in the sunlight of what I call "ultramodern Catholicism."

Long after the teenager had lost his freckles, the quest for an answer to this enigma continued to dominate my psyche. Something didn't seem to fit together; either there was a large, gaping piece missing from the jigsaw puzzle, or else I didn't know how to join the pieces. Everywhere I went, my antenna was always up, alert for a signal that would get me out of the maze. Yet I always had a sense that somewhere, there had to be an answer.

As a youth, this grew within me through my visits to the nearby monastery of the Cistercians of the Strict Observance (Trappists) in Mount Melleray. Some of my ancestors who had gone to France to be educated during the anti-Catholic persecution had entered the Trappist monastery of La Melleraie and had later returned to Ireland in 1832 as members of the abbey's founding group. Several times I cycled the fifteen miles to this mountain fortress in my native county Waterford to experience a place where I intuited I might find the secret of Catholicism.

Those bright-eyed, gaunt men who lived what seemed a superhuman lifestyle of prayer, silence, fasting, and hard work in the fields were evidently so convinced of Catholicism that they had staked their life's time on it. I still remember standing near one of the black-and-white-robed monks as he talked to visitors, wishing I could muster enough guts to ask him to disclose the mystery.

Flashes of Insight into an Unknown Catholicism

Growing up amid the last breaths of a Catholic Ireland in the 1970s, I had a few other flashes of insight into a Catholicism that was designed to shape society. It was springtime. I stood at the alert with my fellow Scouts for about two hours as the Corpus Christi procession wound its way through the streets. The town was at a standstill. At the end of the procession, in the square at the town center, a deep silence fell as the monstrance rose to bless the kneeling population. No wonder a similar experience in Livorno in 1666 had provoked the conversion of the Danish Protestant Niels Steensen, known to history as the father of modern geology.

As a high school student, I was also impressed by the fact that the Irish constitution of 1937 began with the following words:

In the Name of the Most Holy Trinity, from Whom is all authority and to Whom, as our final end, all actions both of men and States must be referred, we, the people of Éire, humbly acknowledging all our obligations to our Divine Lord, Jesus Christ, who sustained our fathers through centuries of trial, gratefully remembering their heroic and unremitting struggle to regain the rightful independence of our Nation, and seeking to promote the common good, with due observance of Prudence, Justice and Charity, so that the dignity and freedom of the individual may be assured, true social order attained, the unity of our country restored, and concord established with other nations, do hereby adopt, enact, and give to ourselves this Constitution.[1]

"In the name of the Most Holy Trinity!" I wondered — could the doctrine of the Trinity actually change the shape of society?

Another flash of insight alerting me to the fact that once upon a time a different type of Catholicism had existed came to me when I discovered how some of the leaders of Ireland's 1916 revolutionary movement had decided to go ahead with their failure-doomed act inspired by a sense of mystical union with Christ Crucified. "I see his blood upon the rose and in the stars the glory of his eyes."[2] So began the poem penned by one of the revolution's twelve leaders, shot by a firing squad on Easter Sunday, 1916, at the age of twenty-nine.

Occasionally, during my schooling, there were murmurs here and there that Catholicism was more than a "religion." I still remember the ever joyful, spartan Augustinian Father McCarthy, who taught me biology, physics, and chemistry, standing in the science lab, remarking how the biology of human reproduction pointed through its design patterns to a divine author. The English teacher, Mr. Breen, often drew out the impact of Catholicism on writers such as Gerard Manley Hopkins and Patrick Kavanagh, who seamlessly wove together existence and the Catholic ethos. And one day, a priest remarked while teaching Spanish that the reality of God should appear in the textbooks for learning Spanish.

Yes, and God should also be in geography, math, history, the sciences — and not merely as a wishy-washy add-on.[3] Either God matters or he does not; if he does, then he matters to everything, always. "I am the Alpha and the Omega, [the very beginning and the very end,] the One who is, the One who was, and the One who is coming: the All Powerful" (Rv 1:8, VOICE).

I wondered if there had ever been an era when people had experienced Catholicism as a game-changer. My studies of history in my teen years seemed to say that there had not been. I still recall the choice the history teacher gave my class when I was twelve: We could opt either for the study of the Middle Ages or the Renaissance. And how relieved I felt, after seeing the dreary images in my textbook for the former, that we would not be spending time on those "Dark Ages." In all my teen years, never did I hear a teacher speak of the grandeur of Christendom, the historical embodiment of Catholicism in a civilization. Why not?

"The Individual Is a Hostage of History"

Several times during my years in Rome and afterward, I have had an experience similar to that of the last Chinese monarch — a child — as portrayed in the movie *The Last Emperor*. The film's director, Bernardo Bertolucci, once stated that all of his creations had the same theme: "The individual is a hostage of history."[4] The film vividly symbolizes this conviction in the scene where the Chinese ruler as a young boy climbs to the top of the high wall surrounding the imperial palace and for the first time sees the world outside — only to discover that someone else is really ruling the country. In a similar way, I also have had a flash of insight: It is not Catholicism but someone else — a masked stranger — who rules inside the minds of Catholics; his name is modernity.

This intuition led me to five discoveries.

First, that I was living inside the mental walls built by modernity. Inside these walls, everyone thinks according to modernity's worldview.

Second, I discovered that the modern worldview as it exists today was constructed in opposition to the Catholic worldview as it had been synthesized from the eleventh to the sixteenth centuries during the era of Christendom. As philosopher Michael Allen Gillespie describes this change:

> Modernity came to be as a result of the displacement of religious belief from its position of prominence at the center of public life into a private realm where it could be freely practiced as long as it did not challenge secular authority, science, or reason. The authority of religion to shape private and public life thus was replaced by a notion of private belief and ultimately personal "values."[5]

Third, I learned that a revolution was rumbling, one in which avant-garde thinkers for the first time since the birth of the modern socio-political-cultural order in the sixteenth century had resolved to tear down not merely some of the walls of modernity's worldview but to detonate its very foundations.[6] Why? Chiefly because these intellectual elites — and, increasingly, through their influence, the masses — are dissatisfied with the contemporary quality of life. They have discovered that modernity hasn't been able to deliver on its promises to build a civilization in which humans can flourish.

Fourthly, I noticed during these years that modernism had also penetrated inside the walls of the Church. But here, too, a revolution was underway. During my years at the Gregorian, the Angelicum, and the Lateran, I studied one of the greatest hidden destroyers of the faith of millions of Christians in recent times: the skeptical arguments against the trustworthiness of the Bible. However, a new wave of biblical scholars are turning their backs on such skepticism. As a Jewish professor at Harvard remarked: "There have been immense discoveries in archaeology, epigraphy, and history. Whole civilizations have been discovered. Infinitely more is known about the biblical world now than in Wellhausen's time, *a fortiori* the era of the Talmudic rabbis, the apostles, and Church Fathers."[7]

Unlike their predecessors who interpreted the Bible through modern Kantian spectacles, these experts recognize that to understand these ancient texts, they need to travel back in time and get inside the Ancient Near Eastern mentality through which the Holy Spirit worked when the biblical books were written. Therefore, they study facts: history and archaeology. Excitingly, we are living in the era of the publicizing of the great archaeological discoveries, notably those of Ugarit, the Dead Sea Scrolls, and at Hag Nammadi. These have supported the new historical studies often called "Second Temple Judaism" led by such scholars as Oxford University's N. T. Wright and the University of St Andrew's Richard Bauckham, powerfully communicated to us on this side of the Atlantic by the St. Paul Center for Biblical Theology led by Dr. Scott Hahn. This has given us new insight into the sacred texts, new confidence in their reliability, indeed, an enthusiasm for the "springs of living water" (Rv 7:17). Like an underground river, these waters irrigate the landscape of this book.

Fifthly, though my professors made me alert to the postmodern worldview that was assaulting modernity, not one of them presented Catholicism as a movement with its own worldview, big picture, story, and metanarrative. Whatever they may have personally thought, the impression they gave was that Catholicism was merely one of the players on the field of modernity or postmodernity. Catholicism appeared as a spirituality, a "religion," a "faith." We Catholics were simply meant — at most! — to compete for a breathing space and to be thankful that we were tolerated.

To my thinking, this view of Catholicism as merely one more player on modernity's playing field is self-defeating; it results in a distorted and warped Catholicism, as limp as a dead rose's petals. What good could such a Christianity achieve for the world? Moreover, this view just doesn't fit with the facts of this thing called Catholicism — neither with the biblical texts nor with the self-description of the Church through the millennia. From Genesis to Revelation, all that the word of God had taught is emphatically unequivocal: "I am the way, and the truth, and the life" (Jn 14:6). Doesn't it follow, then, that the lived experience of Catholicism must be "You shall love the Lord your God with all your heart, and with all your soul, and with all your mind, and with all your strength" (Mk 12:30)? Doesn't that imply that all of our humanness and all that it touches is called to be gloriously transfigured by him? And, because he told us, "You shall love your neighbor as yourself" (Mk 12:31), doesn't it imply that we who have discovered the source of joy should ardently resolve to make it benefit all our fellow women and men, through beautifying all of culture, all of society? For Christ is Lord of all or not at all!

These five findings birthed my conviction that, in order to find and live real Catholicism, we must first break free of the gravitational pull of modernity's worldview. We must soar above its stratosphere to see reality from the different perspective of genuine Catholicism. We can achieve this by becoming alert to three realities: first, to the dramatic revolution in physics that broke out at the start of the twentieth century. Quantum physics destroyed the scientistic interpretation of Isaac Newton's discoveries, the chief foundation of modernity's materialistic worldview.

This stunned the scientific elite — Einstein, Planck, Heisenberg, Bohr, and others — leaving an intellectual vacuum in which, for the first time in centuries, scientists could no longer explain matter, time, space, and mind according to materialism.[8] Second, we can turn to the foundational texts of Catholicism, the biblical books, with a renewed enthusiasm for this complex, divinely inspired work of awesome literature whose first section is appropriately named "Beginnings" (*Genesis*) and whose final pages are called *Revelation*, which aptly means "Disclosure." Third, we can discover the civilization built by the blood, sweat, and tears of Catholics over a millennium: Christendom. Through these three perspectives, we can arrive at a new vantage point for a panoramic vision of genuine Christianity. We can move away from a faith shaped and colored by modernity into a faith that is truly *ultra*modern.

Organic, Alive, and Connecting You

Real Catholicism is organic. This is its chief characteristic. In this book, I use the term *organic* in three ways. First, by *organic* I mean a Catholicism that is pure, without any additives from modernity. It is classic, original Christianity in its pristine splendor. That is why we will travel back to the fifties — no, not the 1950s, but the AD fifties — to the era of the first Christians. There, we will see that they would not have recognized what Catholicism has become in the minds of us moderns: a "religion," a "spirituality," a "faith," and a moralism of dos and don'ts. The latter has led to so many of our contemporaries experiencing the call to relationship with God as a burden. How strange this is when we recall that the God-Man had said: "Come to me, all who labor and are heavy laden, and I will give you rest. Take my yoke upon you, and learn from me; for I am gentle and lowly in heart, and you will find rest for your souls. For my yoke is easy, and my burden is light" (Mt 11:28–30).

By contrast, when you discover classic Catholicism, what you will find is not a "religion" — a concept invented by the modern liberal State. William T. Cavanaugh in his ground-breaking book *The Myth of Religious Violence: Secular Ideology and the Roots of Modern Conflict* states: "The religious-secular distinction accompanies the invention of private-public, religion-politics, and church-state dichotomies. The religious-secular distinction also accompanies the state's monopoly over internal violence and its colonial expansion."[9] Nor will you find a "faith" — a modern concept invented by Immanuel Kant. The German philosopher Richard Kroner clarifies why: "Both [Luther and Kant] mean by faith a relation of man to God, not founded on objective facts but rather on our conscience; both mean a practical relation — that is, a relation which concerns primarily man's will in its moral aspect; both mean, therefore, something that affects a person as a person and not something that would satisfy the human intellect or reason in general."[10] Instead, through the lens of authentic Catholicism, you will find that it provides an insight into God because it is first an insight into reality in all its dimensions, even though conditioned by mystery. As C. S. Lewis remarked: "I believe in Christianity as I believe that the Sun has risen: not only because I see it, but because by it I see everything else."[11]

By *organic* I also mean that Catholicism is vitalistic — life-imbuing. It has a superhuman vitality capable of making us fully human and with the vision and energies to create a society of human flourishing. Why? Because the Catholic movement is an organism. In biology, an organism is a system composed of cells that functions in a unified way and is capable of self-movement; that is why it is living, with power for growth, reproduction, and progress. Catholicism as worldview and lifestyle flows from the living reality that makes it what it is: the Mystical Body of Christ. We are, as Saint Paul states, living in a new "geographical" dimension of reality: "in Christ" (2 Cor 5:17). This is a truth so important that he repeats the Greek equivalents of the term and related expressions 164 times.[12] We can jettison modernity's view of the Church as chiefly an organization with a bureaucracy and rituals. The Church is organically alive because she is the reality of all who are united to the God-Man so intimately that, analogously to a human body, they become a corporate reality: the Mystical Body of the God-Man.[13]

Mystical, as we shall explain further on, means "real," but real at the deepest level of what the ordinary is. It is therefore mysterious, that is, we know it is, but we do not fully understand *why* it is. What matters is that we become so united to him that you might say we become his contemporaries. We hear his voice, experience the revitalizing effects of his passion and resurrection, sense the effects of his "christifying" us — making us fully human by making us superhuman for the mission of acting as agents of world transformation.

This has been the intuition of the women and men throughout the millennia who have become enthralled with Catholicism and have entered the Church's gateways, often at great personal cost. One of them was the twenty-five-year-old Christopher Dawson, arguably the most original historian of the Church from the twentieth century. In an article entitled "Why I Am a Catholic," he describes the intuition provoking his decision as an insight into "sanctifying grace" (the classical term for the superhuman vitality imbued in us through the sacraments):

> It was by the study of St. Paul and St. John that I first came to understand the mental unity of Catholic theology and the Catholic life. I realized that the Incarnation, the sacraments, the external order of the Church, and the internal work of sanctifying grace were all parts of one organic unity, a living tree whose fruit is the perfection of the saints. … This fundamental doctrine of sanctifying grace, as revealed in the New Testament and explained by St. Augustine and St. Thomas in all of its connotations, removed all my difficulties and uncertainties and carried complete conviction to my mind. It was no longer possible to hesitate.[14]

Catholicism is organic because by its intrinsic dynamism, it is oriented to birthing an organic lifestyle, culture, and civilization. Because it is an organism — a multiplicity of cells harmoniously operating in unity — it is utterly relational. Therefore, Catholicism is all about connectedness. That is why it confronts modernity, which is disconnectedness, a worldview in which relationality is merely an added-on dimension to the way the cosmos, nature, and humans function. For moderns, reality can be explained atomistically by getting to know the parts of the wholes. And life can be lived merely by ensuring non-organic connections with stuff. For moderns, other people, the biosphere, and God are not organically necessary to the self but are nonessential add-ons. Modernity so downgrades relationships that it provokes what Ortega y Gasset calls "dis-society" — an Orwellian dystopia.[15]

In sharp contrast, Catholicism views relationships as intrinsic, innate, and basic to cosmic, social, and human flourishing. It is a vision of cosmic and human interrelatedness originating in a view of a relational God: the Trinity. That is why I will frequently use "Creator-Lover-Rescuer" instead of "God" throughout this book. "God" is the answer to *what.* "Trinity" is the answer to *who. For this is how we experience him! As the One who is ever creating and re-creating, ever loving, and ever rescuing!* The term *Creator* reminds us particularly of the First Person, the Father; *Lover* of the Third Person, the Spirit; *Rescuer* of the Second Person who became embodied in Jesus. However, any action of a divine Person in the creation or rescue of the cosmos is always a single shared action of the three divine Persons, in which each Person reveals the qualities unique to them in the Trinity, thereby disclosing that everything comes "from the Father," "through the Son," and "in the Holy Spirit." Could anything be more awesome? The connectedness in the depths of the Trinity murmurs in the landscape, echoes in the human psyche, shouts in the desire for friendship and love, and is encoded in the blueprints for a flourishing civilization. Catholicism's relational worldview, as we shall see, is one that finds support in the latest findings of ultramodern physics and the other sciences, which show reality as functioning optimally when its intrinsically relational dimension is respected.

Thus Catholicism is where you find a stunning combination of apparently contradictory realities — a combination that the human heart deeply aspires to. By living with the Church's organic vitality, you discover a freedom that makes you a rugged, one-of-a-kind individual, yet simultaneously identified with a greater whole (the Mystical Body of Christ) and, through it and because of it, with humanity. This freedom contrasts starkly with modernity's freedom, which is alienating, divisive, centrifugal, and dehumanizing.[16] The freedom of the "new man" (Eph 2:15) who is in Christ radically emancipates our powers of creativity. This creativity is inspired by the connectedness we feel with our Author, the biosphere, other humans, and our heritage. The "new man" is particularly eager to bond across the millennia to the earliest beginnings of our Jewish-Christian heritage in order to think way outside the box with radically new patterns of thought. The Spirit gave us these so that we might do all in our power to inaugurate advance signposts of the future heavenized Earth. Indeed, we affirm that this is our mission each time we pray: "Your Kingdom come … on Earth as in Heaven."

This is why the Jewish and Christian heroes and heroines of Catholicism through the millennia have always been restless spirits, anti–status quo individuals. Ceaselessly, they have burst through stagnant ways of living, constantly ascending the heights of the human spirit, ever searching for the unbounded exhilaration of what they now experience in the beatific vision. Simultaneously, they passionately assert the glory of the individual while, paradoxically, recognizing that this glory is fully possible only through union with the corporate reality of the Mystical Body of the God-Man.

The mission of ultramodern Catholics is therefore to create an organic civilization to replace the mechanistic, "machine" civilization of modernity. In this holistic view of reality, the Creator, humans, and the biosphere are interrelated within "Operation Genesis," the Trinity's ongoing involvement in cosmic and particularly in human history. For what ultimate purpose? For the creation at the Second Coming of the God-Man of "a new heaven and a new earth" (Rv 21:1) — an ecological civilization amid a heavenized world in which the Creator-Lover-Rescuer will be forever intimately bonded with humans.[17]

Longing to Meet the Artist

This relational worldview is *the* game-changer. Genuine Catholicism opens our eyes to see ourselves as made for relationships. It urges each of us to adopt a lifestyle that is organically and harmoniously bonded to our biosphere. It connects us to family, friends, forefathers, and heritage — all through our relationship with the Triune Creator-Lover. Indeed, our worldview weaves everything together into a unity through the threads of relationships, allowing us to envision reality as harmonious and symphonic. It has the organic unity of a work of music or art authored by a great, creative mind. It has the power to mesmerize us. And when we become fascinated by a work of art, we long to meet the artist. Through the years I have visited the galleries of Atlantic Ocean waves,

Alpine mountains, Mediterranean sunsets, summer-green fields in Ohio, the seductive blue hour before sunrise with its whispers of Heaven, and so many sublime people. And I'm longing to meet the Artist![18]

Consequently, because it provokes connectedness and the building of relationships, ultramodern Catholicism is a completely new way of living. The ultramodern Catholic lives out the worldview that buzzes in his brain, excites his emotions, and energizes him for action. This new way of living transfigures everything because we now view everything as connected to everything else. This explains why the mission of ultramodern Catholicism is to heal the psychic and social ruptures caused by modernity through reconnecting the natural with the supernatural. We will explore this in more depth in each chapter of this book, considering it theoretically, illustrating it historically, and exemplifying it practically.

By living a fully relational life, you live the fully human existence the Creator-Lover intended. The ecologist and cultural critic Charlene Spretnak, ten years after she had attended a talk by the nature writer Barry Lopez, still remembered his observation that "a bear taken out of its habitat and put into a zoo is still a form of mammalian life, but it's not a bear."[19] She continued:

> It's not a bear. It's not a human if its felt connections with the unfolding story of the bioregion, the Earth community, and the cosmos are atrophied, denied, and replaced. It's not a human if it can no longer experience awe and wonder at the beauty and mystery of life, seeing nothing but resources and restraints. It's not a human if it is socialized to be oblivious to the unity of life, so lonely that it is vulnerable to all compensatory snares. The only way we can recover a full sense of being is to develop awareness of the modern reduction and to cultivate a deeper participation in life.[20]

To these convictions, ultramodern Catholicism responds, "Amen." However, we are also convinced that this will come about in all its splendor when we connect ourselves to each other, nature, history, place, and time through the Lord Jesus, the Fully Human One, the true Renaissance Man who is "the image of the invisible God" (Col 1:15).

By seeing Catholicism as organic and relational, we will see it to be radically new. Indeed, it will forever be the only really new news around because it is organically connected to the absolutely new reality that has appeared in history: the Person of the God-Man. As Saint Irenaeus declared, "Know that he brought all newness by bringing himself who had been announced."[21] And he came to renew: "Behold, I make all things new" (Rv 21:5). And how he renews! "Thus, if anyone is in the Messiah, there is a new creation! Old things have gone, and look — everything has become new!"[22] The experience of Jesus through active membership in his Mystical Body will renew you and me, and it can renew civilization — as it did in the first millennium when it laid the foundations of Christendom, the Catholic civilization out of which grew the best features of Western Civilization.

Catholicism, true to its name (*catholic* means "universal"), is about every reality because it is about Reality itself. That is why it has the mission of inspiring lifestyle and civilization. Consequently, it is grittily materialistic, even if mystically so, because it aims to transform humans in our humanness so that we may creatively beautify the entire material world. And it is not an opinion but a sharp and deep conviction about how things should be put right. It is a subverter of status quo habits of thought, a pattern of thought in opposition to ideologies. In Catholicism's speech, whether in Bible or in liturgy, words like *freedom*, *liberation*, and *becoming free* recur frequently. With this spirit, gutsy Catholics birthed a new culture that became a new civilization: Christendom. But it all began with a worldview of which these Catholics were convinced. As the non-Catholic German writer Heinrich Heine once remarked, "People in those old times had convictions; we moderns only have opinions. And it needs more than a mere opinion to erect a Gothic cathedral."[23]

CHAPTER 2

THRILLING TIMES
TO BE ALIVE

The changes are so profound that, from the perspective of human history, there has never been a time of greater promise or potential peril. My concern, however, is that decision makers are too often caught in traditional, linear (and nondisruptive) thinking or too absorbed by immediate concerns to think strategically about the forces of disruption and innovation shaping our future.

— *Klaus Schwab*, The Fourth Industrial Revolution

Exciting new solutions and approaches are a sign of our times, in disciplines from healthcare, psychology, and education to economics, political theory, and the arts. Some of the breakthroughs are from the new sciences, such as psychoneuroimmunology and relational physiology.

Others have sprung up from new trends in old disciplines, such as homeo-pathic medicine.

Medicine, for instance, in its search to reduce epidemics of infectious diseases, has begun to discover the answer to the question that had baf-fled scientists for generations: How could millions of people carry the virus of a disease without developing its symptoms? Modernity's medi-cine with its view of the human being as a biomachine was silent on the matter. If one sought a solution according to the "germ theory" of Pasteur and others, disease-provoking microbes whenever present in the human body should provoke sickness. But recent discoveries have shown this is not so. Millions do not develop the symptoms because "our immune sys-tem, as it turns out, is highly relational. Whether it is robust or impaired depends not only on heredity, diet, and lifestyle choices (or opportuni-ties) but also on the condition of the relationships in our lives."[1] As an in-structor of psychiatry at Harvard University stated: "Connectedness is as much a protective factor — probably more — than lowering your blood pressure, losing weight, quitting smoking, or wearing your seatbelt. It's the unacknowledged key to emotional and physical health — and that's a medical fact."[2]

Moreover, counterintuitive though it be to the modern mindset with its view of the body as a machine functioning mechanically independent of man's spirit, the body's sicknesses can be prevented or healed, partially or totally, by methods other than surgery or pharmaceuticals. Based on scientific findings about the self-healing capacities man possesses when he is treated as an organic unity in which body and mind are recog-nized as working together inseparably as a single unit (a "bodymind"), and notwithstanding opposition from the "powder and pill and knife" old guard, nature-based therapies have often shown themselves to be ef-fective alternatives.[3] Obviously, the ideal is for us to open-mindedly use the magnificent achievements of scientific healthcare with these newly discovered treatments.

A striking example is the set of new proposals for preventing illnesses like dementia and Alzheimer's. In 2020, some 5.8 million Americans had Alzheimer's, more than half a million died because of the disease or its complications, and by 2050, experts calculate that the number of patients will increase to some 13.8 million.[4] In the face of the dominant medicine with its acceptance of mental deterioration as inevitable, the avant-garde relational physiology is calling for new approaches that would have been regarded as naïve and unscientific a few decades ago.[5] "Build relationships," they argue. Researchers have shown that even keeping in frequent touch with a few friends and holding a ten-minute conversation with another person each day does more to ward off dementia than classic practices such as doing crossword puzzles.[6] Breakthroughs in the new field of neuroimmunology claim that the immune system's role in the functioning of the brain for prevention of neurodegenerative diseases can be helped greatly by having and making friends, getting involved in volunteer groups, and strengthening family ties.[7] Such relationships quicken the mind and increase motor functions such as walking, because they offer an improved sense of well-being. Studies confirm this.[8]

Even healthcare providers and health insurance companies have begun to accept the new discoveries. As Spretnak notes:

> It is somewhat amusing, actually, to watch the medical profession, for instance, try to casually absorb the startling new relational findings by merely tacking them on to their usual way of regarding the human body — Oh, yes, here's one more prescription: socialize with friends to stay healthy — when, in fact, that single relational discovery alone challenges the most basic assumptions of modern medical science.[9]

Another breakthrough has occurred in stress management, which has improved the quality of life of millions. The latest wave of treatments, based on the discoveries in neurology, physiology, and psychology, and supported by the results of studies, urge us to live closer to nature. Simple lifestyle changes such as walking in green areas for a few minutes have proven effective for lessening anxiety and improving the health of those suffering from ailments ranging from asthma and intestinal problems to back and neck pains.[10] Allowing natural daylight to flood one's workspace fosters a serene mood, and even if you spend the day inside an office building, merely having plants and flowers nearby will boost mood and performance levels.[11]

Relational physiology is also solving problems created by some of modernity's methods of parenting and educating. Scientists now point out that a child's ability to learn requires more than merely turning up at school and getting "injected" with enough information to get through exams. Healthy relationships with parents and siblings affect even academic achievement. The more children are surrounded by affection in their childhood, the better their mental development.[12] Such human warmth helps to fight back against the pandemic of "attachment displacement disorder" among children and young people, due partly to excessive amounts of time spent in front of screens and texting.[13] In addition to human relationships, bonds with nature also impact our brain health. School gardens improve learning and mood by putting students in contact with trees, plants, and sunlight. Even a single immersive experience in nature can powerfully heal the psyche, as one teenager recognized: "For the past few months, I've found myself unmotivated. I almost felt a disconnection from myself because I couldn't take the time to think. When I sat down in nature to write this weekend, I found myself reconnected, my insides and outsides."[14]

The world of the arts is also experiencing changes in two ways: first, through a new understanding of the dynamism of creativity. Malcolm Gladwell, in *The Tipping Point* and *Outliers*, shows how creative and self-made people are achievers not only because of the qualities with which they were born but also due to those developed through friendships. In *The Empathic Civilization*, Jeremy Rifkin remarked:

> Empathetic moments are the most intensively alive experiences we ever have. We feel super-alive because in the empathic act, which begins with being embodied, we "transcend" our physical confines and, for a brief period, live in a shared non-corporeal plane that is timeless and that connects us to the life that surrounds us. We are filled with life, our own and others, connected and embedded in the here and now reality that our relationships create.[15]

Second, these changes are occurring through a shift in the content of arts such as urban design and architecture. Although still trying to break through status quo mentalities, some city planners and architects are designing neighborhoods that follow the principles of "organic architecture."[16] They give importance to fresh air by allocating space for trees and parks and take care to maximize the amount of sunlight entering offices.

In the area of criminal justice, instead of imprisoning offenders, some cities are discovering the benefits of the relational approach of "restorative justice."[17] Contrary to popular notions, it is not a soft-on-crime, wishy-washy ideology, but rather a way to ensure both justice and healing for criminals, victims, and society. It gives criminals the opportunity to face the harm they have done, ask forgiveness from the offended, and shoulder the responsibility by repairing the offense at least partially through community service. Compared to repeat offenders, among those who go through the typical imprisonment methods, the new restorative justice has a higher success rate.[18]

In economics, initiatives that would have been laughed at decades ago are now pioneering imaginative new solutions. Many emphasize a regionally centered economy, fostering the growth of local communities by promoting a healthy biosphere, ecology, wise energy use, and healthy agriculture. All of which helps, as the mission statement of one such group states, to "increase wellness and build community through equitable access to healthy food, thriving gardens, and urban green space."[19]

Why We Need These Breakthroughs

But why are all these breakthroughs needed?

These breakthroughs are needed in society because of the damage caused by the lifestyle unique to modernity and because of the ineffectiveness of modern solutions.

Take, for instance, contemporary lifestyle's damage to our health. We third millennials live longer than previous generations, constantly talk about our physical and mental condition, and yet, in some ways, have ended up less healthy than our grandparents. We live in a state of ongoing or recurring stress, which many accept — astonishingly — as the price to be paid for living in a "normal" society. Tragically, the outcome of intense levels of stress and other psychological problems is increasingly becoming suicide.[20] As of 2021, suicide was the second leading cause of death among young people aged ten to fourteen and twenty to thirty-four in the United States. Almost one in five high school students reports serious thoughts of suicide, and 9 percent have attempted it, according to the National Alliance on Mental Illness.[21]

Depression levels in the twenty-first century have reached epidemic levels, a fact confirmed by a national poll of America's eighteen- to twenty-nine-year-olds in 2021:

> Fifty-one percent of young Americans say that at least several days in the last two weeks they have felt down, depressed, or hopeless — 19% say they feel this way more than half of the time. In addition, 68% have little energy, 59% say they have trouble with sleep, 52% find little pleasure in doing things. 49% have a poor appetite or are over-eating, 48% cite trouble concentrating, 32% are moving so slowly, or are fidgety to the point that others notice — and 28% have had thoughts of self-harm.[22]

Gregg Easterbrook, in *The Progress Paradox: How Life Gets Better while People Feel Worse*, distilling the results of thirty years of research with the aid of the new science of positive psychology, shows why there is a causal link between the increasing levels of depression and the improving levels of material living conditions.[23] His work dismantles the myth that depression is linked to economic hardship. On the contrary, since World War I, rates of depression and economic well-being have increased simultaneously. As a result, many Americans are now on daily antidepression medication. David Herzberg in *Happy Pills in America: From Miltown to Prozac* explains how the spread of these "wonder drugs" is more than a story about psychopharmacology but rather points to a society of bare-knuckled marketing, political lobbying, and a callous mentality.[24] Obviously, a lot of people really do need this daily medication. Having to take such drugs isn't the problem but rather the sheer numbers involved, the methods involved in promoting them, and the closedmindedness to alternative therapies are at least complementary aids.

The effects are colossal on society. Even economically, "suicides and suicide attempts cost the nation almost $70 billion per year in lifetime medical and work-loss costs alone."[25] Moreover, as scientists point out, stress has highly damaging long-term effects, which can lead to brain deterioration and early aging. It weakens the immune system and our metabolism and decreases our fight-or-flight response to danger in emergencies.[26]

What is triggering such hitherto unregistered levels of anxiety? A convergence of causes within the fabric of modernity's lifestyle. Tension at work comes from the increasing pace of demands, which is now out of control for many. Countless individuals, for instance, feel pressured to constantly check for email messages — now at addiction levels — and ringing telephones.[27] Previous generations had found relief for stress in sleep. No longer. One 2016 study about the prevalence of chronic insomnia in adult patients visiting a family medicine outpatient department in a hospital states: "Various studies worldwide have shown the prevalence of insomnia in 10%–30% of the population, some even as high as 50%–60%."[28] The effects of insomnia — headaches, difficulty in concentrating, and irritability — go on to damage family and social life.

Serious psychological problems are on the rise, alarmingly even among children, teenagers, and college students. More than four million children in the United States (that's one in every fifty-nine kids) have one or more learning disabilities, such as attention deficit and hyperactivity disorder (ADHD), autism, or Asperger's syndrome.[29] Almost seven million people in the United States take antipsychotic medications to treat schizophrenia and other similar conditions.[30] The number of children and teenagers using these medications for difficulties such as mood swings has also increased.[31]

And it's not only mental health that is under assault, but also the body's immune system. Unprecedented are the threats to the body through toxins. Damaged bodily immunity combined with environmental toxins have led to increased rates of cancer: Cancer patients are expected to be 28.4 million cases in 2040, a 47 percent rise from 2020.[32]

The startling rise of levels of infertility — the average sperm count in Western countries today is less than half of what it was in 1950 — is attributed by experts to culprits from within contemporary lifestyle.[33] In the United States, "1 in 5 (19%) of married women aged 15 to 49 years with no prior births are unable to get pregnant after 1 year of trying [infertility]. About 1 in 4 (26%) women in this group have difficulty getting pregnant or carrying a pregnancy to term."[34]

To our bloodstream we unwittingly give entrance to industrial chemicals called PFAS, also known as "forever chemicals" because of their lasting effects in our bodymind. These are to be found in a vast range of everyday products including food packaging, clothing, and cosmetics. They provoke damage to the liver, thyroid, and other organs, increase the risk of cancer, harm the development of the fetus in pregnant mothers, and reduce the effectiveness of vaccines. Biomonitoring studies by the federal Centers for Disease Control and Prevention show that the blood of nearly all Americans is contaminated with "forever chemicals" which "can migrate into the soil, water, and air. Most PFAS (including PFOA and PFOS) do not break down, so they remain in the environment. Because of their widespread use and their persistence in the environment, PFAS are found in the blood of people and animals all over the world and are present at low levels in a variety of food products and in the environment."[35] A 2021 study of American women's breast milk for PFAS contamination detected toxic chemicals at levels nearly two thousand times higher than the level some public health experts advise as safe for drinking water.[36]

Obesity, due to junk food, is now an epidemic even among young people and children. Between 2017 and 2022, the obesity rate among adults aged eighteen and older increased 1.8 percent each year to thirty-three people per one hundred individuals. Children suffering from obesity are at risk for developing diabetes and other diseases.[37] But nowadays it is even difficult to improve the quality of the food we eat. Vegetables such as carrots, broccoli, kale, and onions currently have less calcium, iron, and vitamins than they did decades ago.[38]

Even the muscular and limb abilities of children's bodies are showing characteristics unknown in premodern societies. Team sports coaches of young children are noticing that children have more bodily awkwardness while playing, resulting in unprecedented levels of injuries, such as arm fractures. Because kids are spending more time motionless before smartphones and computer games, their bones are far weaker than those of prior generations who spent their childhood years developing sturdy bone structure through outdoor running, jumping, and rough-and-tumble exercises.[39]

Our eyes are also under assault. A National Eye Institute study found that nearsightedness increased 66 percent in the United States between 1971 and 1972 and 1999 and 2004. It also reported that about twenty million Americans (17.2 percent of the population over forty years of age) have a cataract in at least one eye.[40]

Problems Unique to Modern Lifestyle

These problems raise questions about modern Western society's capacity to foster a quality existence. Even more alarming, the problems have been intensified by the status quo solutions applied. For instance, in education, modernity's prophets have wreaked havoc on the psychology of children and teenagers. Just consider the theories of behaviorists such as B. F. Skinner and J. B. Watson, who recommended that parents avoid hugging or kissing their kids and instead treat them like adults. As the philosopher Mary Midgley has insightfully noted:

> This treatment (they said) was necessary because it was scientific and objective. It is interesting to notice that what made this approach seem scientific was certainly not that it rested on research showing the success of these child-rearing methods. ... Instead, the behaviorists' attitude seems surely to have been itself an emotional one, a fear of affectionate behavior as something dangerously human, something beneath the dignity of scientists. ... In order to escape these problems, psychologists stereotyped feeling in general as something "soft," something that was the business of the humanities, not the sciences.[41]

In the workplace, modernity applied the same distorting "solutions." Industrial titans such as Henry Ford applied a method often referred to as "scientific management" or "Industrial Taylorism." Its author, Fred W.

Taylor, "broke each job down into its individual motions, analyzed these to determine which were essential, and timed the workers with a stopwatch. With unnecessary motion eliminated, the worker, following a machinelike routine, became far more productive."[42] Remember that word: *machinelike*. As Midgley noted, it is "the philosophy of the conveyor-belt, the view that workers ought to be treated like any other physical component on the production-line. Any reference to their own point of view was seen as subjective and thus an illicit, unscientific distraction."[43] Already, in 1867, Karl Marx had accurately pointed out the effects of such a vision of work on our humanness, stating that its effect is to "distort the worker into a fragment of a man, ... degrade him to the level of an appendage of a machine, they destroy the actual content of his labor by turning it into a torment. ... *They transform his lifetime into working time*, and drag his wife and child beneath the wheels of the juggernaut of capital."[44]

At the end of this chapter, we are left with a number of puzzling questions about modernity. In the most sophisticated, scientific civilization in history, what are the causes behind so much needless suffering? What has fostered such baffling blindness to what we are increasingly coming to view as commonsense solutions? Why are some of the most recent scientific breakthroughs in areas such as medicine still meeting a most "unscientific" opposition? But even more alarmingly, why did the massive scientific powers of modern medicine and healthcare fail for so long to make these breakthroughs? Is there a single underlying macrocausal explanation, even if complex and multifaceted, that connects these phenomena? Finally, is there a reason why, at this precise moment in history, at the turn of the third millennium, the emperor's new clothes have been shown to be what they are by postmodern intellectuals?

CHAPTER 3

WHY THE STATUS QUO?

The witch said nothing at all, but moved gently across the room. … She took out a musical instrument rather like a mandolin. She began to play it with her fingers — a steady, monotonous thrumming that you didn't notice after a few minutes. But the less you noticed it, the more it got into your brain and your blood. This also made it hard to think. … After she had thrummed for a time … she began speaking in a sweet, quiet voice. "Narnia?" she said. "Narnia? I have often heard your Lordship utter that name in your ravings. Dear Prince, you are very sick. There is no land called Narnia."

— C. S. Lewis, The Silver Chair

Contemporary "innovations" in healthcare (such as recognizing the importance of relationships in the prevention of Alzheimer's) are actually not so new at all. Although many of these findings seem novel, their "newness" is due rather to our *re*discovering them. Many of these so-called advances in healthcare and education were simply common sense to our ancestors. And notwithstanding their common sense and their proven effectiveness, many of these solutions face intense opposition. It is also baffling that it took the most technological civilization in history so long to discover certain breakthroughs, such as homeopathic therapies. As Charlene Spretnak remarked:

> In recent years, however, the medical profession's general advice about staying healthy — eat nutritious food, get sufficient exercise, get a full night's sleep, avoid smoking, and wash hands often during cold and flu season — was joined by an incongruous addition: have friends and socialize often with them. Friends? This amended list seemed to me at first like one of those children's puzzles that ask "Which of these does not belong?" We were accustomed to hearing medical experts explain that illness results from quantifiable physical conditions, such as the malfunction of, say, the heart or the endocrine system, or the presence of a nasty bacteria or virus — but personal relationships? Moreover, we were assured that this new finding is now firmly established in 21st-century medical knowledge because it has been replicated in numerous well-designed scientific studies and published in prestigious medical journals. All of which left me wondering, "How is it possible that the vast analytical powers of modern medical research had missed this crucial fact for hundreds of years? And what else, by the way, have they missed?"[1]

The new solutions have to argue their way into our minds against deeply held status quo patterns of thinking. Chief among these is our way of seeing human beings as isolated and independently functioning. We view reality as existing in separate compartments: private life, social life, work, politics, science, economics, and religion. Modernity has carefully taught us to think like this from childhood. Everything and everyone is treated as a separate reality. Of course, the modern worldview doesn't deny that the biosphere, society, and people often interact, but it is convinced that they are not organically connected. By "organically," I mean that the connections are not of secondary importance but are necessary to people and society if they are to function as they should because of the relational nature of humans, the biosphere, and society.

Modernity views realities such as the human body, the ecological system, and society as so different from one another that we need different "logics" in order to understand their processes. Consequently, modernity has set up walls with barbed wire between different disciplines: the "scientific" method for the "hard sciences," the "humanistic" for the arts and "soft sciences" (such as sociology), and "faith" for "religion." The late Harvard paleontologist Stephen Jay Gould termed it the mindset of "Nonoverlapping Magisteria" (NOMA).[2] As early as the seventeenth century, Galileo was one of the first to popularize this view with his saying that the Bible is about "how one goes to heaven, not how the heavens go."[3] A similar way of thinking is termed "complementarity": Science and non-science may sometimes describe the same realities, but ultimately they are incompatible.[4]

Such compartmentalism rules in the minds of many Catholics today. We have a scientific mindset outside of the church building but a religious mindset inside. Politics is politics and faith is faith. Scientific research on projects such as human cloning and "religious sensibilities" are viewed as distinct compartments of life and must not be allowed to interfere with each other. Likewise, urban planning and architectural designing are done without reference to the human psyche's need for green spaces and natural daylight. In a similar way, industrial production organigrams turn the worker into "an appendage of a machine, destroy every remnant of charm in his work and turn it into a hated toil; they estrange him from the intellectual potentialities of the labor-process,"[5] dehumanizing him by arranging production processes so that humans function robotically.[6] Millions now execute rigidly defined jobs that have been standardized by the enforcing of protocols. These are destructive of personal expression, initiative, and human interaction, thus impeding the development of personality. In education, schools design curricula and schedules without attempting to strengthen child-parent relationships and without seeking to develop the two hemispheres of the child's brain, favoring instead left-brain analytic abilities useful for high-tech industry.

Living Like Machines Inside the Machine

Modernity has successfully taught us to apply the machine model to economics, politics, the arts, home, work, science, and religion. Machines function as separate things. They are things with mechanisms which, provided they are kept functioning according to their laws, keep running efficiently. Efficiency, of course, is what modernity is all about: short-term results and the satisfaction of material and immediate needs. Therefore, the modern mind separates and compartmentalizes. Even children have been distanced from parents because "our psychologists authoritatively conveyed to patients the Freudian notion that separating from core family relationships is the key to healthy maturation."[7] We have even polluted our air, rivers, soil, and oceans with toxic substances as if this would have no effect on our health. We think with a compartmentalized mind, unable to see the hardwired, intrinsic connections between all dimensions of reality. Accordingly, the scientists and megacorporations who are pushing for the creation of genetically manufactured humans are no longer viewed as extremists — because we have lost sight of what it is to be human.

The failure to see the connectedness derives from two chief causes: modernity's way of imagining the universe as a machine that can be explained by the way matter functions (materialism), and the modern theory about how we know reality, which denies that we are a bodymind unity but instead sees humans as a somewhat awkward combination of a material brain connected in a dysfunctional way to a material body, with the result that we do not connect with reality but only with our ideas about reality. The marriage of this epistemology with the modern way of viewing the universe (cosmology) birthed the contemporary dominant worldview.

The idea of the universe as a colossal machine began in the seventeenth century. Isaac Newton's laws of motion enabled scientists to predict the functioning of both the solar system and objects on Earth. This led philosophers such as Hobbes in *Leviathan* (1651) to compare the universe to a machinelike mechanical clock. Rapidly, the opinion spread that both the cosmos and everything in it functioned on the basis of mechanical laws. Since these laws regulate only matter, intellectuals began to think that any efforts to understand the universe need only reckon with concrete stuff (matter), in other words, all things that take up space by possessing volume. This led, first, to the birth of materialism as a method of analysis, which swiftly gripped the imagination of scientists and, through them, the general public. But second, over time, it became the cornerstone of a new worldview, which saw the universe as made up of only matter or, at least, as a reality that functioned as if that were all. This became the working hypothesis of scientists and thinkers such as Thomas Hobbes (1588–1679), Pierre Gassendi (1592–1665), Jean Meslier (1664–1729), and Denis Diderot (1713–84).

This was not a novel idea but merely a reheating of the ancient materialism of Democritus (c. 460–370 BC) and Epicurus (341–270 BC). By the nineteenth century, the dominant ideology had decided that physics was solely about matter, its variables, and the laws describing them. Therefore, it refused any role to the immaterial — that is, the spiritual). Consequently, the immaterial dimensions of reality — notably the human soul and the role of God in the functioning of the cosmos — were either denied or ignored as irrelevant and relegated to the realm of "religion."

Moreover, it was generally held with Democritus that everything was made up of atoms. From this conviction and from the opinion that there was nothing besides matter, scientists became convinced that the way to know how reality functions is by getting to know the atomic structure. Increasingly, they imagined that things functioned atomistically, though there was no experimental proof of this. It is important to note that the chief scientific breakthroughs came about from a gut feeling.[8] One thinker who pointed this out was C. S. Lewis. In his book *The Discarded Image*, he outlined the highly rational Catholic view of the universe as it was held in the Middle Ages. While unpacking it, he argued that any model of the universe, whether ancient, medieval, or Newtonian, is never strictly "scientific"; it owes a great deal to the intellectual atmosphere in which the scientific discoveries occur and in which the imagination plays its role. Moreover, the intellectual atmosphere does not exist in a protected bubble; instead, socio-cultural-political events also influence our "scientific" way of seeing.

Coinciding with the birth of modern science was the birth of a new theory about how we know reality: an epistemology. Along with the view of the universe as a nuts-and-bolts machine, modern philosophers, mesmerized by Newtonian physics and its powers for technological progress, re-evaluated both the content of our knowledge and its frontiers. The dominant modern mindset about how we identify the structure of reality is that of René Descartes (1596–1650).[9] He claimed that we can only have certain knowledge about those realities that are measurable, and which can be described mathematically because they are quantifiable. The rest of reality is merely the sum total of our own ideas which are not reality-based because our minds are incapable of seeing "underneath" the surface of things. Thus the reign of quantities began. Qualities such as colors, fragrances, and sounds, along with love, wonder, beauty, truth, and goodness, were subjective, and therefore nonreal. Thus they didn't have any practical importance for the scientific goal of controlling nature.

Cartesianism split our knowledge into the scientific and the nonscientific. By *scientific* is meant the "hard sciences" of biology, physics, and chemistry and their branches; by *nonscientific*, the "soft sciences" of the humanities and the arts. As a result, modernity reshaped the frontiers of knowledge. "Real" knowledge belonged to the hard sciences; all else was merely opinion.

Ultimately, the scientific imagination, by limiting itself to the knowledge obtained by experimentation, closed itself off from the supreme question: Why is there a universe instead of nothing? Modernity put a roadblock on man's journey to meaning.

Modern Myths

The second most influential philosopher of modernity, the grandfather of contemporary relativism, Immanuel Kant (1724–1804), "profoundly influenced by Newtonian mathematical physics,"[10] sought to construct an updated Cartesian view of human knowing. As a result, Cartesianism and Kantianism came to dominate in scientific research and ultimately in the general public's way of thinking.[11] A new philosophical view emerged: scientism, the opinion that the experimental method is the only objective standard for obtaining certain knowledge in all sectors of human, social, and political concern, and for making moral decisions.[12] It is important to note that scientism was not due to scientific discoveries in themselves but to philosophical theories about how the human mind connects with reality. Nobody ever discovered anything at the bottom of the microscope or at the end of the telescope that would support this attitude.

This scientific mentality has grown today to the status of a faith in the power of scientific techniques to solve all problems. Indeed, anyone critical of the limits and risks of technological applications is regarded as backward. This ideology asserts, in a nutshell, that modern science is the sole way to reality and the unique judge of truth. It is an ideology: a particular set of prejudgments about reality functioning in a certain way that has been made into a normative frame of reference. When nowadays we speak of "science" (in phrases like "science says"), we are usually not referring to scientific facts but to "science" as a prejudgment, a prejudice about reality — *scientism*. The interweaving of scientism with rationalism and chronological snobbery asserting that the "modern" is the only correct answer has led to science becoming the dominant myth of the modern world. The British philosopher Mary Midgley, in her insightful book *The Myths We Live By*, remarks:

> We are accustomed to think of myths as the opposite of science. But in fact they are a central part of it: the part that decides its significance in our lives. So we very much need to understand them. Myths are not lies. Nor are they detached stories. They are imaginative patterns, networks of powerful symbols that suggest particular ways of interpreting the world. They shape its meaning.[13]

In this myth, the universe as a machine has become the model for how we imagine almost everything around us. Even our choices of metaphors betray us when we describe ourselves as "living machines" or speak of "genetical engineering," "bio-engineering," "microbial cell factory," "genes as code," and "biological chassis." The trend-setting French architect Le Corbusier (1887–1965), whose real name was Charles-Édouard Jeanneret, wrote, "A house is a machine to be lived in."[14] As Mary Midgley notes: "We still often tend to see ourselves, and the living things around us, as pieces of clockwork: items of a kind that we ourselves could make, and might decide to remake if it suits us better."[15]

We cannot overestimate the importance of the metaphors with which we think. The cognitive linguist, George Lakoff, and the philosopher Mark Johnson, show that metaphor "is not just a matter of language, that is, of mere words … human thought processes are largely metaphorical" because metaphor is a basic mental mechanism. We all have "metaphors we live by."[16] Without our ever noticing them, our metaphors shape systematic ways of understanding our physical and social experiences and ultimately our worldview.

Another metaphor which quietly patterns our thinking is the atom (from the Greek *atomo*, meaning "indivisible"). The imagined atomistic structure of reality became so deeply embedded in the modern mind that we now focus on seeing things not as wholes but as parts that merely happen to be wholes — and such wholes are a fact of little importance for science. The first discipline to adopt this way of viewing reality was physics, which came to define itself as the branch of knowledge that seeks to discover, describe, and make available for technology the functioning of these tiny, infinitesimal components. Consequently, we tend to think that, as Mary Midgley remarks, "The right way to understand complex wholes is always to break them down into their smallest parts." Moreover:

> We have come to think that truth is always revealed at the end of that other seventeenth-century invention, the microscope. Where microscopes dominate our imagination, we feel that the large wholes we deal with in everyday experience are mere appearances. Only the particles revealed at the bottom of the microscope are real. Thus, to an extent unknown in earlier times, our dominant technology shapes our symbolism and thereby our metaphysics, our view about what is real.[17]

The myth of the machine and its atomistic structure became the basis of modernity's big picture of reality. It was a predictable outcome. Because science can describe and predict everything from planetary movements to the gears of precision instruments, it was inevitable that scientists and the general public would come to picture everything as working like a machine in the absence of a strong alternative. This imaging starts with God, whom Deists viewed as the watchmaker who had set up the mechanisms of the watch of the universe and then abandoned it. However, Isaac Newton did hold the opinion that, like a watchmaker, God had to occasionally intervene and tinker with the mechanisms of the universe to ensure its working order. Humans also came to be imagined mechanistically. And because machines have no freedom but are predetermined, human free choice was imagined to be merely an appearance (the ideology known as *determinism*).[18]

By the early twentieth century, a nonrelational view dominated our way of thinking. The modern mind gave little importance to the connections between the bodymind and our environment, the individual and society, and even between the individual's own past, present, and future. Such connections were seen as marginal. In the machine universe, all was made up of matter and energy functioning by material cause-and-effect laws. We discover the causal mechanisms by identifying the smallest units of composition. Thus the modern scientific mindset ignored, first, the importance of understanding realities as wholes (holistically), and second, their place within the whole of the universe.

The model of the machine has been applied to managing everything from the human bodymind to society, education, healthcare, and economics. The results have been, in one way, dazzling — indeed blindingly so: smartphones, space shuttles, starscope monoculars, sequencing of a human genome, laparoscopic surgery, low-band 5G, Low Earth Orbit (LEO) satellites, and the internet. Mesmerized, we assumed that by applying the same methods with the same underlying materialistic presuppositions, we could make progress in child-rearing, relationships, and in everything human. Just treat the human as a biomachine, and we are on the road to Paradise.

In ordinary, everyday thinking, we no longer look at people and things as wholes with identities with the same vividness as our premodern ancestors did. We no longer view each reality, especially each person, as a unified, integrated whole, but as a hodgepodge of parts. Moreover, due to the influence of Darwinism, we assume that we are the outcome of laws of random natural selection with nothing that makes us unique as humans.

A Subtly Dehumanizing Mindset

This view is noticeable everywhere today. In healthcare, for instance, doctors look for quantifiable, measurable symptoms when a patient turns up in their office. The role of emotions on the psyche, of contact with one's biosphere and with one's roots, is only beginning to appear in some places on the diagnostic list. In education, schools and universities have become places of airtight specialization, graduating students who, to quote the Austrian zoologist Konrad Lorenz, "know less and less about more and more, until they know nothing about everything."[19]

Because we presume that we only know the surface features of reality, we are convinced that the only certain knowledge we can have about our humanness is that provided by the experimental sciences. Neither can we know the purpose of the universe. The outcome is that we breathe in skepticism (or, as it is often called, relativism) daily. In whatever colors it takes, skepticism is the world's "flight from reason."[20] One of the most influential shapers of our contemporary way of thinking about reality, Friedrich Nietzsche, described it well: "There are many kinds of eyes. Even the sphinx has eyes — and consequently there are many kinds of 'truths,' and consequently there is no truth."[21] G. K. Chesterton recognized that relativism is "the work of the sceptic [who] for the past hundred years has indeed been very like the fruitless fury of some primeval monster; eyeless, mindless, merely destructive and devouring; a giant worm wasting away a world that he could not even see; a benighted and bestial life, unconscious of its own cause and of its own consequences."[22]

Relativism sees truth as purely subjective, giving rise to its clichés: "your truth" and "my truth." These act like an immunodeficiency syndrome threatening to abolish our humanness. For, as Chesterton said, "A man was meant to be doubtful about himself, but undoubting about the truth."[23] The ultimate consequences of relativism could not be grimmer. As one of the intellectuals who best understood the modern outlook, C. S. Lewis, once concluded: "Out of this apparently innocent idea [that values are subjective] comes the disease that will certainly end our species (and, in my view, damn our souls) if it is not crushed; the fatal superstition that men can create values, that a community can choose its 'ideology' as men choose their clothes."[24] It threatens to bring about the "abolition of man" and the creation of the "Un-man."[25]

Modernity's politics, economics, education, and lifestyle rest on the shaky foundation of our inability to see the connectedness of all dimensions of reality. The three most influential shapers of our way of thinking about politics, Rousseau, Locke, and Hobbes, taught us that society is really a mixum-gatherum of loners, a "dis-society" in which the presence of others is an add-on to one's existence.[26] Thus moderns don't feel the bonds between themselves and their family, birthplace, and nation with the intensity and naturalness of the Catholics of Christendom.[27] We live in an empty, generic space rather than in a definite, meaning-filled place.

This affects our social and political life in many ways. Politics is now about maintaining the social contract that restrains "the will to power"[28] among individuals, who compete against each other knowing that it is a matter of the "survival of the fittest"[29] in a world where "man is a wolf to man."[30] It is all about coercing individuals to behave in such a way that they will not step on each other's toes. Economics is the science that determines politics and is directed exclusively to the physical survival of humans; all other nonmaterial ways of achieving happiness are ignored. Thus consumerism reigns blatantly in both the right-wing and left-wing states. In economics, the machine model is evident in both right- and left-wing economic theories. Right-wing capitalism (which is not the same as free-enterprise economics[31]) has a charmingly naïve faith in the "hidden hand" of the market allied with big government to empower the economy to succeed and bring well-being to the population.[32] Left-wingers have an equally strong belief that government control of the means of production will guarantee economic progress.

As regards nature and the ecosystem, well, modernity didn't say much about it, but its actions sure spoke loudly. One of modernity's founding fathers, Francis Bacon, rejected the ecological vision of Catholicism's Christendom, which had "left Nature herself untouched and inviolate."[33] He declared that if this vision were not destroyed, we would be destined "never to lay hold of her and capture her."[34]

Moderns live on top of nature, not in it. Industrial decision-making seeks only to maximize production levels without taking into account the effects of toxic substances on the biosphere. We refuse to see ourselves in a two-way relationship with nature, and as a result, ecological disasters have followed. A report of the European Environment Agency from 2021 states:

> In 2017, air pollution emitted from large industrial sites in Europe is estimated to have cost society between €277 and €433 billion. This is equivalent to about 2–3% of EU GDP, and is higher than many individual Member States' total economic output that year.[35]

The British Lancet Commission on Pollution and Health in its 2023 report on the global impact of environmental pollution presents alarming statistics:

> Pollution is the largest environmental cause of disease and premature death in the world today. Diseases caused by pollution were responsible for an estimated 9 million premature deaths in 2015 — 16% of all deaths worldwide — three times more deaths than from AIDS, tuberculosis, and malaria combined and 15 times more than from all wars and other forms of violence. In the most severely affected countries, pollution-related disease is responsible for more than one death in four.[36]

Due to modernity's nonrelational, mechanistic style of urban planning, many humans now live in cement neighborhoods, cut off from green spaces, and without regard to creating a sense of fellowship. What matters most is efficiency and use of space to the maximum — all, of course, for the sake of economic efficiency. Architecture in modernity has become dehumanizing, incapable of fostering human health, family bonding, neighborhood relationships, and contact with nature.[37]

I suspect that modernity's machine-view of the human being has also made us more prone to impatience and anger. Because we expect everything to work with the perfection of a machine, we carry over this mindset into our relationships. We have unrealistically high expectations of spouses, children, parents, friends, and even casual acquaintances or perfect strangers whom we encounter in shops and on the street.

Subtly, modernity's worldview has even changed the importance we give to what our five senses tell us. Because Cartesianism has formed us to think of our sensations as mere figments of our imagination, our experiences are partially numbed. We don't fully enjoy the colors of fiery sunsets and speckled trout in glittery lakes; the smells of honeysuckle sweet, and the riot of fragrances in wonderland-green spring meadows; the sounds of babbling brooks and the chirring of grasshoppers. Modernity shouts to us, "Quantities and numbers are what matter — not the intangible and the beautiful." The French poet Charles Baudelaire, in his essay "The Painter of Modern Life," sensed this: "Modernity is the transient, the fleeting, the contingent; it is one half of art, the other being the eternal and the immovable."[38] Moreover, for modernity, artists, poets, and musicians are pretty add-ons at the edges of society. For Christendom, they had vitally necessary roles at the center of civilization.

This has downgraded our sense of beauty. It has also redefined the mission of artists, musicians, and other creators, who now think they can impose their arbitrary ideas and tastes on reality. Moreover, creative young people are cut off from the sources of genius because they have been educated to think that in order to be successful, they must function like machines: independently. They must be free of all that would restrict self-expression, including the heritage of the great artistic tradition of the millennia, nature's nurturing patterns and rhythms, and the genius of place and time. Thus they become prime illustrations of what the Canadian philosopher Charles Taylor, author of *A Secular Age*, calls "the buffered self"[39] of modernity: the mind-enclosed self in which the frontiers are barricaded against others, mind against body, and each of us against nature. The result in the arts has been well described by the German philosopher Oswald Spengler, author of *The Decline of the West*:

> [Today] we find a pursuit of illusions of artistic progress, of personal peculiarity, of "the new style," of "unsuspected possibilities," theoretical babble, pretentious fashionable artists, weight-lifters with cardboard dumb-bells. ... What do we possess today as "art"? A faked music, filled with artificial noisiness of massed instruments; a failed painting, full of idiotic, exotic and showcard effects, that every ten years or so concocts out of the form-wealth of millennia some new "style" which is in fact no style at all since everyone does as he pleases. ... We cease to be able to date anything within centuries, let alone decades, by the language of its ornamentation. So it has been in the Last Act of all Cultures.[40]

The final outcome: shriveled humans. The modern world has become like the girls' boarding school as described by the South African intellectual Olive Schreiner:

> Of all cursed places under the sun, where the hungriest soul can hardly pick up a few grains of knowledge, a girl's boarding-school is the worst. They are called finishing schools, and the name tells accurately what they are. They finish everything but imbecility and weakness, and that they cultivate. They are nicely adapted machines for experimenting on the question "Into how little space can a human being be crushed?" I have seen some souls so compressed that they would have fitted into a small thimble, and found room to move there — wide room.[41]

CHAPTER 4

THE FACE OF MODERNITY'S GOD

―――――――

The originality of Christianity lies not in its so-called monotheism, but in the gigantic nature of its God, the creator of both heaven and earth: it is a gigantism that is alien to the pagan gods and is inherited from the God of the Bible. This biblical God was so huge that, despite his anthropomorphism (humankind was created in his image), it was possible for him to become a metaphysical God: even while retaining his human, passionate, and protective character, the gigantic scale of the Judaic God allowed him eventually to take on the role of the founder and creator of the cosmic order and all that was good: this was the very role attributed to the supreme God in the pale deism of the philosophers.

— *Paul Veyne*, When Our World Became Christian

Terry Eagleton, author of *Culture and the Death of God*, recognizes a crucially important driving force behind contemporary patterns of thought: "The history of the modern age is among other things the search for a viceroy for God. Reason, Nature, Geist [Spirit], culture, art, the sublime, the nation, the State, science, humanity, Being, Society, the Other, desire, the life force and personal relations: all of these have acted from time to time as forms of displaced divinity."[1] This is why we must define with utmost precision what we mean by the word *God*.

As the spokes extending from the hub, what we mean when we say *God* influences the meaning we give to the universe, time, space, matter, the human person, society, and lifestyle. Steven D. Smith, in his book *Pagans and Christians in the City*, states that "God" provides "identity-forming beliefs about what is meaningful, valuable, important, good and bad, right and wrong."[2] As historians and sociologists have demonstrated, all societies have had a "God" in this sense. Secularized moderns are no exception. Modern secularism is as much a "religion" as pre-Christian paganism. It is a worldview in which theories about "God" can be tolerated as private opinions but may never be allowed to influence the ordinary social and political activities of a state except inasmuch as they prop up its policies.

However, this tolerant attitude with regard to "God" has met with opposition in recent decades from what is known as the "new atheism" ideology led by Richard Dawkins, Sam Harris, Christopher Hitchens, and Daniel Dennett, collectively referred to as the movement's "Four Horsemen." It assaults not so much the existence of God as the very thought of a personal God. "God" is regarded as the antihuman and consequently both formal education (schools and universities) and informal education (social media) should strive to persuade people of its harmful effects. Christopher Hitchens describes this view in his book *God Is Not Great*:

> I think it would be rather awful if it was true. If there was a permanent, total, round-the-clock divine supervision and invigilation of everything you did, you would never have a waking or sleeping moment when you weren't being watched and controlled and supervised by some celestial entity from the moment of your conception to the moment of your death. ... It would be

like living in North Korea.[3]

Tracing this widespread disillusionment with Christianity to its source reveals a cultural revolution that occurred over the course of five hundred years, from the fourteenth century to the end of the twentieth. During that time, "God" underwent a revolutionary change inside the minds of Westerners. Almost imperceptibly, the Catholic notion of God as the Creator-Lover-Rescuer (founded on the Bible and Tradition) was replaced with modernity's worldview, which sees "God" as an all-powerful but distant and uninvolved, transcendent, faceless reality — someone to be feared.

The most important cause of this shift was the philosophy of nominalism, whose most influential thinker was William of Ockham (c. 1287–1347). Nominalism states that we can only have certain information about concrete, individual things that exist in space and time. Abstract objects and universals such as humanity, beauty, and truth only exist within our perception and are merely names or labels we put on them. For instance, individual people are really human, but "humanness" does not exist; it's only a label I use in my attempt to find a common meaning for all of these individuals. In sharp contrast, realism as upheld by Catholicism affirms the existence of universals because they are necessary for meaning, understanding nature, and can be demonstrated as being present in multiple places and times.

Nominalism, in its attempt to understand God, no longer gave importance to his "abstract" qualities and instead focused on his all-powerful will. It concluded that God is the terrifyingly powerful One who can act arbitrarily, establishing right and wrong without any limitations defined by a metaphysical order in reality that we can discover through reason. As Michael Allen Gillespie argues, "Moreover, this God could never be captured in words and consequently could be experienced only as a titanic question that evoked awe and dread. It was this question … that stands at the beginning of modernity."[4] This is because William of Ockham rejected the Catholic synthesis of reason and Divine Revelation, undermining the rational foundations of theology. He contradicted Catholicism's insistence, especially in the work of Aquinas, that we can know with certainty, through our reason, God's existence and divine qualities such as his goodness and justice.

And because Christendom was built on the foundations of theology, cracks began to appear in the walls of civilization. Thus Ockham initiated the shattering of the superstructure of Christendom's society, which led to a collective trauma for Westerners over the past five hundred years.[5] Indeed, one of the world's leading mathematicians, Edward Frenkel, has been interpreted as affirming that Cartesianism — a child of Nominalism — and our resulting disconnectedness from reality are effects of our "collective childhood trauma."[6]

What nominalism in the fourteenth century began, Martin Luther (1483–1546), the father of Protestantism, popularized unwittingly, and René Descartes, the father of modern philosophy, perfected. Nominalism thus functioned as the hidden ideology behind the revolutionary process that destroyed the civilization of Christendom. Luther, who had been educated by nominalists, was filled with their stark notions of a terrifying divinity, notwithstanding his frequent references to the love of God.[7] Gillespie writes, "God's power is so profound and inexplicable that it would destroy the man who sought to comprehend it. God thus conceals his majesty — he is a hidden God, a *deus absconditus*. This was the God that so terrified the young Luther, the omnipotent and transrational God of nominalism. In Luther's later thought, this God is superseded although he is never truly eliminated."[8]

Descartes made "God" irrelevant for intellectuals. According to his mathematics-driven philosophy, the Divinity certainly exists, but he makes no difference to the way nature functions. Gillespie argues, "As Descartes puts it, whether or not God exists, nature operates in much the same way and in either case we must use the same mathematical means to understand it."[9] Descartes believed that we could understand reality through the methods of math and science without the need to refer to God's existence and action. He considered God as sheer willpower and viewed humans as essentially beings with power. While God's willpower is infinite in reality, that of humans is infinite in aspiration.[10] Therefore, Descartes wanted humans to overcome the gap between the human and the divine by scientific control of nature so that, like the Creator, they might become, in a sense, all-powerful. "What is crucial for Descartes," writes Gillespie,

> is the rational application of the will to the mastery of nature. Descartes believes that his method and *mathesis universalis* [an assumed universal science modeled on mathematics] will make this possible. Humans are therefore Godlike but they are not yet God. To become God, to master nature utterly and dispossess God entirely, one needs Cartesian science. This finally is the answer to the problem with which Descartes began his philosophizing: if the fear of the Lord is the beginning of wisdom, then wisdom is the means by which the Lord is captured, disarmed, dispossessed, and subsumed within the citadel of reason.[11]

One after another, the most influential philosophers of modernity replaced the Catholic God with their own version of the "modern God." Spinoza (1632–77) viewed him as an impersonal, unthinking cosmic presence. Fichte (1762–1814) considered him as the moral order: "The living and efficaciously acting moral order is itself God. We require no other God, nor can we grasp any other."[12] Hegel (1770–1831) concluded that human self-consciousness is the self-consciousness of the Absolute, that is, God.[13] By the late nineteenth century, Nietzsche (1844–1900) became aware of the outcome: the practical "death of God" in the minds of millions and the end of Christianity as the framework for civilization.

Disconnecting God from Everything

The change of meaning of *God* over the centuries had occurred almost imperceptibly for the masses because the "God" of modernity often masked himself as the Christian God. Within "official Christianity" — a term coined by Søren Kierkegaard (1813–55) — there was no change in the approved language. All the same words were used: *faith, religion, Creator, creation, Jesus, Father, Spirit, salvation, Heaven*. But the intruder had denuded them of their original Christian meanings and replaced them with a new significance.[14] New spiritualities grew up alien to the mindset of the first Christians. The truths that had illumined the minds, fired the imaginations, and warmed the hearts of our forefathers had been numbed. One can apply Samuel Taylor Coleridge's description to what happened to the experience of Catholicism's core certainties: "Truths, of all others the most awful and mysterious, yet being, at the same time, of universal interest, are too often considered as so true, that they lose all the life and efficiency of truth, and lie bed-ridden in the dormitory of the soul, side by side with the most despised and exploded errors."[15]

The Trinity came to be theoretically acknowledged on paper but practically irrelevant in the lived experience of Christians. Jesus was seen as someone to be trusted but often with a sentimentalizing warping of his reality; the Eternal Father was seen as the behind-the-scenes angry figure to be feared; and the Spirit hardly registered on the radar screen for most believers. And because the Triune nature of God is the basis for the certainty that God is love, a new way of conceiving one's relationship with God overshadowed the hearts of Christians. Christianity became increasingly a religion of duty, a matter of fulfilling obligations to the powerful deity, often impelled by fear. Modernity in that sense marked the second Fall of humanity. The original provocation for the first Fall at the beginning of history had been Satan's success in convincing the first humans to distrust God. As a result of this distrust, humans began to sense that God is in competition with humanity. Modernity only deepened this sense of God and humans as competitors.

Over time, we came to see the Creator as the disconnected, uninvolved, distant, irrelevant, and even dangerous "God." Yes, of course, he could always intervene, and fervent Christians prayed for his interventions. For most people, however, the atmosphere in which these prayers were made had changed from the summer warmth of the first millennium of Christianity to winter coldness. In the three hundred years from the early 1700s to our century, as millions of Europeans and North Americans adopted the emerging modern worldview, they either formally abandoned the following of the God-Man or remained merely nominal Christians. Even many of the constant churchgoers no longer had the mindset of their Catholic forefathers who had converted the West and had sent the spires of Gothic cathedrals shooting into the skies of Europe. "God" increasingly became an idea, something isolated from the universe. Even at the end of the thirteenth century, insightful minds such as Meister Eckhart (1260–c. 1328), the Catholic mystic, already saw it happening and cried out in alarm: "They want to see God with their own eyes, just as they see a cow; and they want to love God just as they love a cow."[16]

Disconnecting God and the universe led to the unraveling of the connections between human activity — politics, economics, the arts, education, healthcare, architecture — and God's biblical blueprints for world transformation. Moderns were convinced that because God is so distant and uninvolved, it is up to humans to get on with the business of running this world and improving it through technology. Things must and can be made to run efficiently. Since the "Boss God" is uninvolved, modernity's elites — most conveniently — can now take exclusive charge, without any risk of interference, in order to organize politics, economics, the sciences, and the arts as they think best. Our modern ambitions can run the show; there are no divinely encoded messages in the natures of things to point to divinely determined purposes. Even Christians began to act "as if God did not exist"; they became convinced that this is how the world should function.[17]

What has been the result of modernity's revolution? A "disenchanted world," according to Charles Taylor, one of the most important contemporary analysts of modernity.[18] Christianity has become a thing inside the mind; it is now a "religion," a "faith," a "spirituality." No longer is it what it was once upon a time in Christendom: the source of connectedness, embeddedness, and embodiment. The Catholics of that era experienced Catholicism as a belonging within the Mystical Body of the God-Man. It inspired them with pride in their heritage. It gave them a sense of closeness to society and nation, which were felt as natural extensions of the family. Because of Christianity, they felt themselves within a meaningful universe, bonded as loving stewards to all living organisms from the highest mountain peaks to the deepest ocean trenches. Modernity's God had exiled the God revealed by Our Lord Jesus Christ — the power-sharing God who works through and with humans — to the backstage of people's minds. The Catholic God had become "an unknown God" (Acts 17:23) of the Areopagus. As a result, we today are disconnected loners in a dis-society[19] — disconnected from God, from one another, and from the world around us. Indeed, it can be argued that the contemporary epidemic of loneliness is due to modernity having cut us off from deeply bonding relations with others, our birthplace, our ancestors, our heritage, our nation, and even the Earth — because it has cut us off from the living Triune Creator-Lover-Rescuer who is the relational God.

Former U.S. surgeon general Vivek Murthy, writing in the *Harvard Business Review* in 2017 about work and loneliness, noted, "During my years caring for patients, the most common pathology I saw was not heart disease or diabetes; it was loneliness."[20] This is a modern phenomenon, as Dr. Alison Hulme, senior lecturer in international development at the University of Northampton, explains: "Loneliness is a much more modern phenomenon than you might think. Well into the 17th century, the words loneliness and lonely rarely appeared in writing. In 1674, the naturalist John Ray compiled a glossary of infrequently used words — it included loneliness. Fast forward to today and we're in the midst of a loneliness pandemic."[21] This loneliness is one of the causes threatening to create a hellish world, as one of the scientists of Silicon Valley, nicknamed the "Sage of Cyberspace," remarked: "I think mankind is a species hell-bent on building artificial intelligences to overcome human loneliness."[22]

The Unprecedented God of the Christians

The French historian Paul Veyne, an agnostic, stated that the chief reason why Christianity conquered the Roman Empire was the "gigantic nature of its God."[23] Unlike the gods of the Greco-Roman religions and the philosophical god of Plato and Aristotle, the Christian God was not one more object in reality alongside humans and the galaxies. He was Creator! When we say God is "Creator," we are not saying that he is one half of the big picture facing the other half of the universe. He *is* the Big Picture! There would be no big picture without him. There would be no "reality" without him. He alone *is*, and because the Creator *is*, everything else *is*. He is the source of the "is-ness" of everything: of the universe, of every human, thought, desire, footstep, breath; of each ocean wave and morning dawn; of the budding rose and the falling leaf. There would be no existence without him — which means there would be nothing — literally "no thing." He is in the air we breathe; in the seasons of time and of life; at the core of our humanness and at the origin of the universe.[24] In this instant as you breathe, read, think, you are doing so because, in the words of Pope Benedict XVI, "Each of us is the result of a thought of God. Each of us is willed, each of us is loved, each of us is necessary."[25] God is he who keeps reality from becoming nonreality. The philosopher Herbert McCabe expressed it in an analogy: "As a singer sustains her song over against silence — and that too is only a feeble metaphor, for even silence presupposes being."[26]

In the Christian worldview, the cosmos continues to exist because it is being created in every instant by its Author. He alone is the Necessary One, the "I AM WHO AM" (Ex 3:14, Douay-Rheims [DRA]), the First Uncaused Cause of the cosmos, the all-perfect, the only self-sufficient reality. He is the One whose identity is "is-ness," the boundless one, the ultimate purpose of the cosmos and everything in it. And therefore he is the transcendent One who is necessarily immanent to the universe. This means that he is present and operating within it. He is not outside the universe but is active everywhere within it, though not in any way pantheistically identified with it. He is omnipresent because of his action in every cosmic reality, conserving it in existence and in its identity. And, because the action and the identity of God are the same, wherever he is in action there he is also present.[27] Moreover, humans are made in the image of the Creator. Through creative humans, our Creator wants to beautify all dimensions of the biosphere and culture, according to the patterns encoded in nature and in the divinely disclosed biblical texts, as we shall unfold in future chapters.

This notion of God — the ultramodern, truly Catholic understanding that will be explained throughout the rest of this book — differs sharply from modernity's understanding of "God." And since our notion of God decides our notion of self, society, time — everything! — the way we understand who God is matters deeply. Instead of an opposing reality who impedes us from running ourselves and the world, and even from enjoying existence, the Christian God is the power-sharer versus the powerful one; the Father versus the Boss; the Lover versus the Tyrant. He is the Creator of our humanness and therefore of our characteristic quality as humans: freedom, which empowers us to love and find joy.

But to truly grasp this and begin to understand God in this way requires a revolution in our way of thinking. Instead of thinking about God solely with the left brain as modernity has educated us to do, we need to train ourselves to think about him holistically, with the two hemispheres of our brain, as indeed Augustine, Thomas Aquinas, Bonaventure, and all the great Jewish and Christian prophets and sages of the ages have done. Yes, of course, we can rationally demonstrate the fact of God with the help of Saint Thomas's five arguments from change, efficient cause, possibility and necessity, gradation, and design. Yet, the starting point for these arguments is an attitude of the whole person —including intelligence, emotions, senses, decision-making ability, sense of trustfulness, and open-mindedness — looking out at the world. As the neurologist and psychiatrist Iain McGilchrist has urged:

> This helps illuminate belief in God. This is not reducible to a question of a factual answer to the question "does God exist?," assuming for the moment that the expression "a factual answer" has a meaning. It is having an attitude, holding a disposition towards the world, whereby that world, as it comes into being for me, is one in which God belongs. The belief alters the world, but also alters me. Is it true that God exists? Truth is a disposition, one of being true to someone or something. One cannot believe in nothing and thus avoid belief altogether, simply because one cannot have no disposition towards the world, that being in itself a disposition. ... Truth and belief, once more, as in their etymology, are profoundly connected.[28]

The more we allow the Creator-Lover-Rescuer God to act in us, the more we will participate in the divine nature and become deified, thus becoming maximally human. Consequently, we will be empowered to work to bring about the end of the machine civilization in which we are living. We will be inaugurators of an organic, for-life, holistic civilization, one functioning on the basis of the natural relationships encoded by the Creator into the cosmos.[29] This Catholic view of the universe has received validation from a most unexpected source: the most recent breakthroughs in quantum physics, astrophysics, microbiology, visual perception, and pure mathematics. To these we will now turn our attention.

CHAPTER 5

FEELING AT HOME AS YOU GAZE ON THE NIGHT SKY

Even in your world, my son, that is not what
a star is but only what it is made of.

— *C. S. Lewis*, The Voyage of the Dawn Treader

To begin to understand ultramodern Catholicism, we must look at the star-filled night sky and sunstruck ocean waves as if we were seeing them for the first time. We must begin to see facts as wonders. Only then will we truly even desire answers to the mystery of twinkling stars, rustling grass, and cooing pigeons, to skin-tingling, eye-widening, and heart-throbbing moments, to why we become bewitched by moonlit lakes and mesmerized by the soft symphony of rippling waves. Even more fascinating is why the mysteries of friendship and love enthrall us. Might there be meaning to it all? Is creation possibly seeking to speak to us of purpose, where time is headed, who its Author is, and what he's like?

Catholicism is unique in its answers to these questions because its answers are not "spiritual" and otherworldly, but earthly and this-worldly. They begin and finish with the concrete, real world around us — with matter, space, and time. We are mystical materialists because we say that matter matters, that body matters as well as soul, and that landscapes and seasons matter to their Author. We are convinced that everything is interconnected, and that the Creator has acted and is acting to bring all to completion through cocreators who live and act with his sense that this world matters. As Chesterton remarked, "A mystical materialism marked Christianity from its birth; the very soul of it was a body."[1]

But before I unfold this worldview, let me alert you that it will probably sound weird to your modernized ears. Not because it is bizarre, but because its view of the universe as destined to be the homeland of the Creator-Lover and humans clashes with the two dominant ways of thinking about reality: first, the materialistic view of the universe as a massive machine in which an impersonal "god" is not involved; second, the cosmos as identified with the divine.

As regards the first view, why should we think that our seventeenth-century notion of the universe as a machine is more relevant than the ancient Jewish and Christian view of it as home and Temple? Why should we imagine that our "modern" (but actually our reheated third-century BC Epicurean-Deist ideology spiced up with the "scientism" of an uninvolved "god") is more relevant than the biblical portrait of the passionately involved Lover? Because we have smartphones, a 5G mobile network, and laparoscopy? Nothing that Copernicus spied through his telescope, nothing that Pasteur squinted at through his microscope, nothing unfolded from Einstein's equation $E = mc^2$ contradicts the sophisticated biblical mindset. But, as we shall unpack in this and the upcoming chapters, everything that Max Planck (1858–1947), the "father of quantum mechanics," Werner Heisenberg (1901–76), the "father of quantum physics," and contemporary astrophysicists and microbiologists have discovered strengthens our assurances about the biblical worldview. These recent discoveries have led some of the world's scientists to thunder in unison with Psalm 150: "Praise him!" For instance, Enrico Medi (1911–74), an Italian physicist — in the process of being canonized, wrote his "Hymn to the Creation":

> O you mysterious galaxies, you send light but you do not understand; you send flashes of beauty but beauty you do not possess; you have immensity of greatness but greatness not calculated. I see you, I calculate you, I understand you, I study you and so do I discover you. I penetrate you and I gather you. From you, I take the light and I make science of it; I take the motion and I make wisdom from it; I take the sparkle of colors and I make poetry of it; I take you — O stars! — in my hands and trembling in the unity of my being, I lift you above yourselves and in prayer I hand you to that Creator whom, only through me, you stars can adore.[2]

The same scientist stated: "Do we wish then to share in the song of the galaxies? If I were Francis of Assisi I would say: O galaxies of the immense heavens, give praise to my Lord, for he is all-powerful and good. O atoms, O protons, O electrons, O bird-songs, O blowing of the leaves and of the air, in the hands of man, as a prayer, sing out the hymn which returns to God!"[3]

This is the reason for these chapters on the ultramodern scientific breakthroughs which have revealed a vastly different view of the universe to that dominant in the past three centuries. By recognizing the revolution ushered in by quantum physics and discoveries from astrophysics to microbiology, we will throw overboard any chronological snobbery whereby we think that just because we are modern, we can reject the biblical worldview. We will discover that, in reality, the "modern" worldview is no more modern than Stonehenge and that, stunningly, the biblical worldview is "ultramodern."

In this chapter, we will explore the more easily understandable — and alluringly beautiful —implications of recent discoveries in astrophysics. Then, chapter 6 will sketch the discoveries of microbiology and other sciences, which show complex functionality and intelligent design patterns throughout nature, providing experimental evidence for purpose and meaning in the universe. Chapter 7 will unpack the breakthroughs of quantum physics, the "big bang" theory, and Einstein's theories that have left modernity's materialism and scientism in rubble and reopened the way for us to confidently recognize that the scientific worldview and the Catholic worldview mutually reinforce and are vitally necessary to each other. Chapter 8 presents why the foundations for contemporary skepticism and relativism have been utterly destroyed by the revolutionary new understanding of how we understand reality. The statement by the "father of quantum theory," Werner Heisenberg, has come true: "We may have to learn at the same time a new meaning of the word 'understanding.'"[4]

Why Your View of the Universe Influences Your View of God — and Everything Else

To get right answers, you need right questions. No questions are weightier than "Why am I?," "Where am I?," and "What time is it?" Only by answering these can you solve "Where should I be going?" But when we use a GPS to position, time, and navigate ourselves as individuals, we do so *within the universe*. The answers to the cosmic questions must come before those about our individual identity and destiny. The poet F. W. H. Myers recognized this. A friend once asked him, "What is the thing which above all others you would like to know? If you could ask the Sphinx one question, and only one, what would the question be?" After some silence, Myers replied: "I think it would be this: Is the universe friendly?"[5]

The answer to this query was given a long time ago by the Author of the universe in Genesis. But for three centuries, our minds have been unable to understand it because of the monovision of the ideology that bossily assured us that the cosmos is sheer stuff, an immense machine, and, moreover, one that is headed nowhere special. But the momentous ultramodern discoveries in physics have shown this opinion to be based not on scientific facts, but on scientistic interpretation. Therefore, as we examine the exciting new view of the universe as a vast window unto the Creator, let us remain alert to the fact that our view of the cosmos shapes the deepest thoughts of our psyche. The Lithuanian intellectual Oscar

Milosz expressed it well: "Unless man's concept of the physical universe does accord with reality, his spiritual life will be crippled at its roots, with devastating consequences for every other aspect of his life."[6] For as we see the night sky, so we think in daylight and so we shape lifestyle, society, and our biosphere. Philosophers point out — and historians of civilization confirm — the mutual mirroring of our images of universe, man, and society with our image of God. As we see creation — the cosmos, the biosphere, humanity — so we see God, and so we see ourselves![7] As Iain McGilchrist remarked: "Goethe wisely wrote, however, that 'we are, and ought to be, obscure to ourselves, turned outward, and working upon the world which surrounds us.' We see ourselves, and therefore come to know ourselves, only indirectly, through our engagement with the world at large."[8]

If nowadays we talk about man as a *biomachine*, want to *upgrade* our brain like a *computer*, *hack* our lifestyle like *software*, *map* our *genome*, and *engineer* society, it is due to the seventeenth-century Newtonian vision of the cosmos as machine. And if we are suspicious of *absolute* truths, it is in no small way the effect — unintended by Einstein, who deplored relativism — of the general and specific theories of relativity. Cosmology has decisively influenced culture from ancient to medieval to modern times. Modernity's cosmology emptied the universe of all meaning beyond the materialistic. We now live inside a windowless universe. It thus deprived us of the intuition of the dimension of the sacred which Rudolf Ott defined as the experience of the "awe-inspiring mystery" (*mysterium tremendum*).[9] When you eliminate the sacred, the resulting vacuum is what we call the *secular*. The secular (from the Latin *saecularis*, relating to an epoch of time) is exclusively about time. By excluding eternity, it disconnects us from meaning, which is timeless — eternal. This disconnectedness is the hallmark of modernity's worldview: between time and eternity, cosmos and cosmic purpose, the biosphere and humans — and humans and the Divine Author. Religious studies scholar Huston Smith notes:

> The world, once an "enchanted garden," to use Max Weber's memorable phrase, has now become disenchanted, deprived of

purpose and direction, bereft — in these senses — of life itself. All that which is allegedly basic to the specifically human status in nature, comes to be forced back upon the precincts of the "subjective" which, in turn, is pushed by the modern scientific view ever more into the province of dreams and illusions.[10]

The outcome is inevitable: "So a meaningful life is not finally possible in a meaningless world."[11] Impossible because modernity blinded us to the connections between the dimensions of reality when it shattered the cosmos-Creator relationship. But modernity as a worldview is now dead — even if news of its death is taking time to spread — because of the new physics, microbiology, and what we shall immediately examine, discoveries in astrophysics.

"Go Out on Any Starry Night and Walk Alone for Half an Hour"[12]

When we moderns look at the starry sky, we are overwhelmed by the imagination of apparently infinite space, as C. S. Lewis described in a 1956 lecture:

> You can lose yourself in infinity; there is indeed nothing much else you can do with it. It arouses questions, it prompts to a certain kind of wonder and reverie, usually a sombre kind, so that Wordsworth can speak of "melancholy space and doleful time" or Carlyle can call the starry sky "a sad sight." But it answers no questions; necessarily shapeless and trackless, patient of no absolute order or direction, it leads, after a little, to boredom or despair or (often) to the haunting conviction that it must be an illusion.[13]

We see the *facts* of the universe, but we do not see meaning, order, or purpose. We feel that we have "to give a meaning — or at least a shape — to what in itself had neither."[14] But we sense our meanings to be mere make-believes. If, however, during a starlit walk, you gaze on the night sky through the *biblical* worldview, recovered in its key features and intensified in its meaning by recent findings of quantum physics, astrophysics, and microbiology, you will be seeing what our Christian forefathers saw, and you will understand why they had stars in their eyes, why they were in love with the universe, why they felt it as *home*. For they saw it as a designer-made universe, one with "built-in significance" imbued with wisdom and goodness because authored by *the* Lover.[15] "The achieved perfection was already there. The only difficulty was to make an adequate response."[16] Lewis asked his audience to perform this experiment:

> Go out on any starry night and walk alone for half an hour, resolutely assuming that the pre-Copernican astronomy is true. Look up at the sky with the assumption in your mind. The real difference between living in that universe and living in ours will then, I predict, begin to dawn on you.
>
> You will be looking at a world unimaginably large but quite definitely finite. At no speed possible to man, in no lifetime possible to man, could you ever reach its frontier, but the frontier is there; hard, clear, sudden as a national frontier. And second, because the Earth is an absolute center, and Earthwards from any part of this immense universe is downwards, you will find that you are looking at the planets and stars in terms not merely of "distance" but of that very special kind of distance which we call "height." They are not only a long way from the Earth but a long way above it.[17]

From the perspective of contemporary astrophysics, the ancients were wrong or ignorant on many points in their description of the physical universe, such as its mechanics, the structure of the subatomic, and, most glaringly, the placement of Planet Earth at the physical center. However, even though their picture of the material universe has appeared to moderns in the past four centuries to be crude and primitive, contemporary astrophysicists and microbiologists have confirmed its key features to be accurate, even if from a perspective that would have dazzled — and delighted — the minds of our Catholic ancestors.

You Are Living at the Center

The implications of these recent scientific discoveries can be summed up in three conclusions.

First, you are living on what Guillermo Gonzalez and Jay W. Richards call "the Privileged Planet."[18] The "Copernican Principle"[19] of modernity is often referred to as the "principle of mediocrity" in cosmology and astronomy because it holds that Earth is an insignificant, average planet whose features and evolution are nothing unusual in the universe. It smiles at the naivete of believing that Earth is at the "center." This has deeply conditioned our way of thinking about everything on the planet, including humans, as we now view even ourselves in this light. As Stephen Hawking eloquently remarked: "The human race is just a chemical scum on a moderate-sized planet, orbiting around a very average star in the outer suburb of one among a hundred billion galaxies."[20]

Of course, it is true that the Earth spins around the sun and the Milky Way is not in the physical center of the universe. There likely are many other galaxies in which there *might* exist the conditions for complex organic life. However, in a deeper, far more significant way than our ancestors imagined, recent scientific findings are pointing to the fact that Planet Earth is at the "center" of the universe. This is because we understand "center" not as mere geometrical position but as positioning that is privileged: "In a sense, we are nestled snugly in the 'center' of the universe not in a trivial spatial sense but with respect to habitability and measurability."[21] In both the infinite Newtonian universe and the finite expanding big bang cosmos there is no physical cosmic center, but there most certainly can be a position that is so advantaged due to the convergence of privileging factors that we can call it the "center." This is exactly what contemporary astrophysicists and microbiologists are discovering. The evidence that shows Planet Earth to be no mere speck in a vast cosmos is growing. It is no ordinary planet circling an ordinary star in one of the two hundred billion galaxies. Its makeup and its place within the cosmos is unique and purposeful. Amid the vastness of the Milky Way, Earth has been positioned with remarkable precision not only for bringing forth life, but also for scientific discovery.

How is our planet privileged for bringing forth life? Not only is

Earth's biosphere fine-tuned for this, but the stars and planets around Earth give the impression that someone "programmed" them for the same purpose. Gonzalez and Richards reveal many stunning factors that converge for making our planet suitable for human life:

> A large stabilizing moon, plate tectonics, intricate biological and nonbiological feedback, greenhouse effects, a carefully placed circular orbit around the right kind of star, early volatile elements — providing asteroids and comets, and outlying giant planets to protect us from frequent ongoing bombardment by comets. It depends on a Solar System placed carefully in the Galactic Habitable Zone in a large spiral galaxy formed at the right time. It presupposes the earlier explosions of supernovae to provide us with the iron that courses through our veins and the carbon that is the foundation of life. It also depends on a present rarity of such nearby supernovae. Finally, it depends on an exquisitely fine-tuned set of physical laws, parameters, and initial conditions.[22]

It is remarkable how Earth's atmosphere with extreme selectiveness allows the entry of the right type of light, excluding dangerous wavelengths of UV and gamma, making our environment perfect for human breathing. Likewise, carbon, oxygen, and water "just happen" in the right proportions. Water, a liquid that behaves in a way that is different from most other liquids, has quirks that make it the perfect liquid for multicellular organic life. Scientists have not found the precise combination of chemicals and minerals on Planet Earth anywhere else, and some of them argue that the more we discover about the universe, the probability increases that this combination is unique. Moreover, the size of Planet Earth, its distance from the sun, and even its geological history filled with extinctions caused by ice ages, asteroids, volcanic explosions, and continental shifts, have all played their role in allowing the birth of intelligent bipeds.

Second, Gonzalez and Richards unfold why our place in the cosmos is not only unique because it is habitable but also because it looks like it has been designed for humans to be discoverers.[23] The scientific evidence continues to increase for the fact that Earth's environmental features along with its location in the solar system and the Milky Way galaxy make "our planet strangely well suited for viewing and analyzing the universe."[24] Whoever authored the Earth seems to have wanted humans to be explorers, discoverers, and scientists because its features "allow for a stunning diversity of measurements, from cosmology and galactic astronomy to stellar astrophysics and geophysics. ... Earth offers surprisingly good views of the distant and nearby universe while providing an effective platform for discovering the laws of physics."[25] Many of the unique features of Planet Earth demonstrate this: the fact that we can see the stars at night, that our moon's gravity stabilizes Earth's rotation, that we can see total solar eclipses and marvel at rainbows. Each of these has led to scientific breakthroughs. For instance, eclipses enabled the testing of one of Einstein's predictions in general relativity.

Nowadays, we have more reasons for asserting that we are at the "center" precisely because we know we are not at the physical center. If Earth had been positioned near the galactic hub, "The light from surrounding stars could well have blocked our view of intergalactic space. Perhaps astronomy and cosmology as we know these subjects would never have developed."[26] Moreover, as biochemist Michael Denton notes, "Were we positioned in the center of a galaxy, we would never look on the beauty of a spiral galaxy nor would we have any idea of the structure of our universe. We might never have seen a supernova or understood the mysterious connection between the stars and our own existence."[27]

Now, as we gaze on the night sky with the naked eye or through a telescope, we delight in the reversal of the implication of a vast, expanding universe. Instead of feeling ourselves insignificant, we sense the Voice by which "all things were created, in heaven and on earth, visible and invisible" (Col 1:16) murmuring to us: "Discover! Explore! Travel!" The grandeur of humans, the splendor of our intelligence, the responsibility of a mission spelled out in our sacred texts has been clarified by contemporary astrophysics and astrobiology.

Likewise, humans live not only in a privileged position but at a privileged time.[28] Due to the fact that nowadays we can look farther and farther into space, we are simultaneously looking backward in time. The

Hubble space telescope has shown us galaxies nine billion light years away, which means we see them not as they are "now" but as they were nine billion years ago. Through the phenomenon of background radiation, we have not only the information to affirm that the universe had a beginning but also "a sort of cosmic 'Rosetta stone' on which is inscribed the record of the Universe's past history in space and time."[29]

As physiologist, chemist, and biologist Lawrence Henderson has argued, the convergence on Planet Earth of favorable factors for *both* the specific type of life that is human *and* the development of complex technologies is wildly improbable.[30] Why is Planet Earth so fine-tuned not only for survival but also for us to be able to marvel at wonders such as stars, eclipses, and rainbows and to make scientific discoveries? It need not be so. It could have been set up otherwise. All of this "is evidence of a cosmic conspiracy rather than a mere coincidence."[31] There is colossal evidence that "the myriad conditions that make a region habitable are the best overall places for discovering the universe in its smallest and largest expressions."[32] It is also the best place for getting to know the Author.

It is becoming increasingly evident that he is keen for us to discover him, to get to know him, to enter into relationship with him through this planet, solar system, and Milky Way. Moreover, all these discoveries disclose that the mysterious Author acts like a Father, doing all in his power to encourage his children to grow, learn, become. As one learns of these new findings in astrophysics, quantum physics, and microbiology, one has the uncanny sensation that the Author spent billions of years designing a universe for the sake of a little planet and a strange race of bipeds.

Seeing the Heavens — Not Space

Contemporary physics confirms Catholicism's convictions about the nature of the deepest levels of space and time. Even though our spiritual ancestors had a primitive *picture* of the physical universe, their metaphysical explanation for the physical and their answers to the why and final purpose of everything cosmic has been found to harmonize with contemporary scientific breakthroughs. It is important to remember that modernity has merely a cosmography (a physical description of the measurable dimensions of the universe), whereas Catholicism has a cosmology[33] — a rational explanation for the universe in all of its dimensions. In Christendom's cosmology we find "the medieval synthesis itself, the whole organization of their theology, science and history into a single, complex, harmonious mental Model of the Universe."[34] It gives importance to the reality of Nature and its laws that operate as the internal "drive" with which each reality achieves its identity — something quantum physics has discovered and needs in order to explain the behavior of subatomic quanta. It also affirms both a "final standard of size" and an order in the cosmos — dimensions that have also been discovered by quantum physics, ultramodern astrophysics, and microbiology.[35] On the basis of what our Christian forefathers could see with the naked eye and because of the biblical worldview, they were convinced that their vantage location was indeed privileged — a conviction that contemporary astrophysicists and microbiologists now share. Theirs was (and is) a view of the night sky that both "abashes and exalts the mind."[36] It is not only large and seemingly infinite as it appeared to moderns but "a whole of finely graded parts."[37] Poetically, one can assert that "everything descends from the circumference with a steady diminution of size, speed, power and dignity."[38]

On one level of thought, when our Catholic forefathers gazed on the night sky, they thought of the concentric spheres circling their privileged planet. But on another level — one that would have been explicit to the era's intellectuals but felt by everyone — these concentric circles symbolized the deepest meaning of the cosmos as an ordered reality with three "planes" of existence. These planes could be pictured imaginatively as according to levels of "height."

The first and "highest" plane is the *eternal* plane, characteristic of the Creator. Although distinct from the cosmos, it interacts with it because creation is not an event in the past but is ongoing in each and every instant. As Meister Eckhart wrote: "God makes the world and all things in this present now."[39]

The second plane is the *aeviternal*, where God's "eternal time" interacts with our clock time.[40] It is the plane of reality where the earthly, physical, material realities exist in a way not limited by the quantifiable, material limits of the earthly plane. It is where "Nature" in and of itself with its ideal universal forms (as recognized by Plato) exists; where everything exists as it comes forth from the mind of the Creator in the cosmogenetic act. It is here we find the natural laws, the ideal or form of every reality, whether a living organism or a nonliving reality. It is where the divine ideal for you as an individual exists.

On the third, "lowest" plane of existence is the earthly, physical universe with Planet Earth at its center, as characterized by the limits of space, time, and matter. This is the world we experience through our senses: the everyday reality of smells and bells, sights, touches, and tastes. But this lowest plane is intimately connected with the highest plane through the intermediate aeviternal plane of existence.

In order to understand this aeviternal, intermediate plane, we need to remember that the biblical texts and Catholic Tradition affirm that everything in existence has had two births. It asserts both the "*with-time*" and the *timeless* authoring of all cosmic realities by the Creator.

First, "with-time": Genesis portrays the Creator authoring time ("In the beginning") together with space ("heaven and earth") and gradually bringing all living and nonliving realities from the chaotic, raw material (symbolized by the "formless void") of the "big bang" to the identifiable realities we experience around us. Therefore, implicit to this authoring of the cosmos is the authoring of the identities of all the realities in the cosmos in aeviternal time. These identities become real and enter everyday, Einsteinian spacetime when their potentialites become real ("actual") through the ongoing creative action of the Creator, who gives each reality its being through secondary causes in created realities, whose causal effectiveness relies on God's working in and through them. One could say that all the cosmic realities are "incubated"[41] in the aeviternal spacetime plane until they enter the physical world as *realities*.

Second, the timeless authoring of all: "He who lives for ever created the whole universe" (Sir 18:1). Before the Creator authored the universe into existence, he authored it and every reality within it *in his mind* before the "big bang." This means that the absolute origin of everything from stars to humans to ocean waves is not within space and time but rather within the eternal "time" of the Creator. Everything that exists has had a double birth: first, in the divine birthing by the Creator in his thought, and second, when everything is born in time and space, in what popular parlance calls the "real world."

Accordingly, as Henry Stapp, the mathematical physicist, remarked: "Everything we know about Nature is in accord with the idea that the fundamental process in Nature lies outside space-time but generates events that can be located in space-time."[42] This is why recent breakthroughs in astrophysics, microbiology, and quantum physics have shown us that the universe is bigger than that imagined by modernity. The Austrian mathematician and philosopher Wolfgang Smith concludes, "Thus the cosmos as such cannot be confined within the bounds of Einsteinian space-time."[43]

The three planes of the eternal, the aeviternal, and the Einsteinian spacetime are united in a certain sense organically in much the same way as the organic unity of the human mind, soul, and body. This is not to be understood pantheistically. The eternal plane interacts with the everyday Einsteinian spacetime plane through the intermediate aeviternal plane where the ideal forms and meanings of everything exist. These are the cosmic, natural, human, and social orders. Everything we see around us points beyond itself to these ideal forms and meanings. Therefore, as Wolfgang Smith states, everything is *symbolic*.[44]

This is also how the ultramodern mind sees the cosmos. Indeed, we no longer see *space* but *the Heavens*. This is the conclusion of the hero in C. S. Lewis's *Out of the Silent Planet*. Ransom, who has been kidnapped and placed inside a spaceship headed to the planet of Malacandra, begins to reflect on the meaning of the vast expanses of outer space that he sees through the windows:

> He had read of "Space": at the back of his thinking for years had lurked the dismal fancy of the black, cold vacuity, the utter deadness, which was supposed to separate the worlds. He had not known how much it affected him till now — now that the very name "Space" seemed a blasphemous libel for this empyrean ocean of radiance in which they swam. ... No: space was the wrong name. Older thinkers had been wiser when they named it simply the heavens — the heavens which declared the glory.[45]

CHAPTER 6

A DESIGNER-MADE UNIVERSE

The eternal mystery of the world is its comprehensibility
… the fact that it is comprehensible is a miracle.

— *Albert Einstein*, "Physics and Reality"

The modern scientific mentality was born in Catholic Christendom and not elsewhere. Scientific discoveries had been made in many other civilizations, but it was the Catholic worldview that activated the experimental mindset in Western Europe. Catholicism is convinced that the universe is authored by a Creator who, as supreme intelligence and goodness, did so rationally, freely, and motivated by love. Therefore, the cosmos is designed and ordered in such a way that we can glimpse the Author through his work. Through observation, experiment, and reason, we can detect *design* in nature and thus infer the need of an intelligent designer.

Our four ways of knowing reality work together harmoniously. These are universal experience through our senses, physics (the foundation for all other sciences), a metaphysics based on what our senses know, and certainties disclosed to us by the Author of the cosmos (Divine Revelation). These four branches of knowledge are four different windows enabling us to have a panoramic vision of the Creator and reality. Catholicism uses all four, providing a "progressive" or multifocal lens with which to see reality. In this one lens we have near, middle, far, and depth vision. Thomas Aquinas developed the explanation for this realism, and it empowered Catholic intellectuals such as Robert Grosseteste (c. 1175–1253) and Roger Bacon (1220–c. 1292), who laid the foundations for the modern scientific mentality. These men asked the ultimate question: Why is there something rather than nothing? Then, from the question marks which nature proposed to them, they developed the chief branches of modern science.[1]

However, proponents of nominalism, as well as Descartes, Kant, and other philosophers, rejected the synthesis. This led to the belief that only physics and math could give us knowledge that is certain. The outcome is the dominant contemporary mentality, which states that we know brute facts but not their ultimate meaning and purpose because we have no way of finding a connection between the designs in nature and a possible divine designer. As the atheist biologist Richard Dawkins has stated, the universe "has precisely the properties we should expect if there is, at bottom, no design, no purpose, no evil and no good — nothing but blind, pitiless indifference."[2]

However, many of the recent scientific breakthroughs have left this ideology in rubble for two reasons: First, they have discovered highly sophisticated design patterns in even the grain of sand on the ocean shore. Second, they have recognized that these design patterns are possible only because of a supreme intelligent designer.

Since the middle of the twentieth century, scientists have increased their knowledge of biological systems. A biological system is two or more organs working together to form organ systems such as the nervous system, the digestive system, or the blood-clotting cascade. These systems are made up of parts that necessarily need each other; if any one of them were missing, the system would stop functioning. They are therefore irreducibly complex. Michael Behe, the biochemical researcher and professor at Lehigh University who coined the term "irreducible complexity," has identified many irreducibly complex biological systems at *the molecular level*, such as the bacteriophage T4, the chromosomal theory of inheritance, the recognition of inborn metabolic errors, hormones, and the mechanism of the nervous impulse.[3] Each one of these is "a single system which is composed of several well-matched, interacting parts that contribute to the basic function, and where the removal of any one of the parts causes the system to effectively cease functioning."[4]

Because certain biological systems with many interacting parts would not function if one of them were removed, they could not have evolved according to the theory of Darwinian natural selection. They cannot be the outcome of slow, gradual, unguided processes. Successive small alterations from earlier less complex systems through natural selection cannot explain them. Gradualism is not an explanation. Behe uses the example of a mousetrap: Remove any part of it, and it just won't work.

Behe and others argue that the Neo-Darwinian theory of evolution cannot explain *the origin* of any form of life, not even the simplest living cell. Indeed, Darwin never intended to explain the origin of any living reality, but merely to explain how new living forms come from simpler preexisting ones. The highly specified design patterns in humans, animals, and other living realities cannot be explained by Darwinism. The key reason is one stated by Darwin himself, a modest man who intensely disliked the "Darwinism" of his cousin Herbert Spencer (who coined the term "survival of the fittest"):[5] "If it could be demonstrated that any complex organ existed which could not possibly have been formed by numerous, successive, slight modifications, my theory would absolutely break down."[6]

Intelligent Design and Its Designer

The 1998 complexity specific information theorem (CSI), popularly known as the intelligent design theory, authored by the mathematician William Dembski, is a powerful *mathematical probability theory* for a designer-made universe, proposing an intelligent cause as responsible for specified complex forms of life.[7] It adds the persuasive power of math to the biological discoveries of irreducible complexity to prove the fact of intelligent design and, by inference, the existence of an intelligent designer. Unfortunately, colossal resistance from the status quo Darwinian mentality has not allowed it to impact the general population, notwithstanding the first-class mathematicians and scientists supporting it.[8]

Dembski distinguishes *complex* information (e.g., the positions of the grains of sand on the seashore) from *complex specified* information (CSI), for example, the rational arrangement of the grains of sand in the form of a sandcastle engraved with the words, "Built in AD 2023." The American mathematician asserts that we can detect a design in nature by ruling out explanations based on natural regularities or haphazard chance.[9] He defines design as "the purposeful or inventive arrangement of parts or details."[10] Where you detect a complex event or reality that matches a preexisting pattern (called a *specification*), you have discovered an event or reality that is not caused randomly or regularly by natural forces without intelligence but is designed. This presupposes an intelligent cause, a designer. Wolfgang Smith explains it as follows:

> Let us suppose that an archer is shooting arrows at a wall. To conclude that a given shot cannot be attributed to chance ... one evidently needs to prescribe a target or bulls-eye which sufficiently reduces the likelihood of an accidental hit. What is essential is that the target can be specified without reference to the actual shot; it would not do, for example, to shoot the arrow first, and then paint a bulls-eye centered upon the point where the arrow hit. ... What counts, as I have said, is that the target can be specified without reference to the shot in question. In Dembski's terminology, the target must be "detachable" in an appropriate sense.
>
> Consider a scenario in which the keys of a typewriter are struck in succession. If the resultant sequence of characters spells out, let us say, a series of grammatical and coherent English sentences, we conclude that this event cannot be ascribed

to chance. An exceedingly unlikely and indeed "detachable" target has been struck, which however was specified after the event. In general, the specification of a target requires both knowledge and intelligence; one might mention the example of cryptanalysis, in which specification is achieved through the discovery of a code. What at first appeared to be a random sequence of characters proves thus to be the result of intelligent agency. The fact is that it takes intelligence to detect intelligent design.[11]

Dembski's argument can therefore prove false on a mathematical basis, by using CSI as an invariant factor, the Darwinist claim that irreducibly complex natural organisms, such as the bacterial flagellum, are possible by chance. This argument proves intelligent design and does not require that we check out all possible alternative explanations for the outcome.[12]

It is impossible for evolutionary algorithms to bring highly specified complex organisms into existence. Evolutionary dynamisms can transfer the information, shuffle the content, produce variations on an existing archetype (as in microevolution), but they cannot produce it (as in macroevolution).[13] Wherever there is CSI, there is the hallmark of an intelligent design. Intelligent design (ID) is evident not only in biology, but also in physics and chemistry whose laws are finely tuned for the existence of life.[14]

Dembski's presentation of the highly complex specified information in the genome of any living organism as due to a "Great Designer" arguably supports the view of evolution proposed by the popes from Pius XII to Benedict XVI and by the majority of Catholic theologians. There is no official position of the Church on evolution beyond what Pius XII stated in his 1950 encyclical *Humani Generis* about the fact that there is no intrinsic opposition between the biblical worldview and the theory of evolution, provided Catholics recognize that God is the Creator, and the individual human soul is directly created by him and is not the outcome of merely material forces. The Catholic scientist who led the Human Genome Project, Francis Collins, expresses the majority opinion among Catholic theologians today, which is "theistic evolution" — the position that "evolution is real, but that it was set in motion by God," that evolution occurred as microbiologists describe it, but according to the divine design patterns.[15]

Cardinal Joseph Ratzinger affirmed that evolutionary theory and the Catholic doctrine of creation belong to two realms of knowledge which are complementary:

> We cannot say: creation or evolution, inasmuch as these two things respond to two different realities. The story of the dust of the earth and the breath of God, which we just heard, does not in fact explain how human persons come to be but rather what they are. It explains their inmost origin and casts light on the project that they are. And, vice versa, the theory of evolution seeks to understand and describe biological developments. But in so doing it cannot explain where the "project" of human persons comes from, nor their inner origin, nor their particular nature. To that extent we are faced here with two complementary — rather than mutually exclusive — realities.[16]

Evolution is a complex concept, and our knowledge of it is dependent on three factors that are ever developing: first, the discoveries of microbiologists (such as those of Michael Behe), which are presented in this chapter; second, the correct scientific interpretation of these findings, such as that presented by Dembski; and third, the correct metaphysical interpretation. As Catholics, open-mindedness is our hallmark.

Seeing Realities and People as Wholes

This has important implications also for how we seek to know reality. It means that the modern approach to understanding — by dissecting it into its parts, going down to its smallest components to know what a thing is — does not work. Dembski's theorem confirms an implication of quantum physics: "One is led to a new notion of unbroken wholeness which denies the classical [scientistic] idea of analyzability of the world into separately and independently existing parts."[17] This "unbroken wholeness" requires that we know realities as complex *wholes*. The experimental sciences (such as physics) only allow us to know the mathematically quantifiable dimensions of realities and are therefore incapable of enabling us to know reality, which is composed of qualities as well as quantities, and which has been designed as a complex whole.[18] This means that we have a new way of understanding *everything*.

For instance, the human being: Modernity sought to know him by isolating him in his parts and then allocated to the different sciences the task of knowing more and more about less and less.[19] Now in some ways this has given magnificent results, as for instance in medicine. But in other ways it has been disastrous. Because it relegated feelings, intuitiveness, goodness, and beauty to the bottom of what is important in the human (since these are qualities and therefore not knowable but merely imagined), this led to us viewing ourselves and each other differently. We didn't see each other as wholes, and so we didn't treat each other holistically. And that has had very practical effects, as I have previously noted. Now, thanks to ultramodern scientific breakthroughs, we can look at the universe with fresh eyes freed from modernity's cataracts.

Both astrophysics and microbiology have confirmed what our biblical worldview always insisted upon: We live on a "privileged planet."[20] As the Nobel Prize–winning physicist Charles Townes stated: "Intelligent design, as one sees it from a scientific point of view, seems to be quite real. This is a very special universe: it's remarkable that it came out just this way. If the laws of physics weren't just the way they are, we couldn't be here at all."[21] Even some leading atheist intellectuals, such as Thomas Nagel, recognize that, as so many ultramodern scientific discoveries have pointed out, the cosmos is no mere chaotic conglomeration of material "atoms" combining with or repelling each other. Rather, it is a *whole* with an intrinsic purpose capable of bringing into existence embodied intelligences —that is, humans — through purpose-driven processes of evolution in sharp contradiction to blind, purposeless, chaotic Darwinian evolutionism.[22] "It is no longer legitimate simply to imagine a sequence of gradually evolving phenotypes," states Nagel, "as if their appearance through mutations in the DNA were unproblematic — as Richard Dawkins does for the evolution of the eye."[23] The philosopher goes on to recognize that life can't be a fluke:

The inescapable fact that has to be accommodated in any complete conception of the universe is that the appearance of living organisms has eventually given rise to consciousness, perception, desire, action, and the formation of both beliefs and intentions on the basis of reasons. If all this has a natural explanation, the possibilities were inherent in the universe long before there was life, and inherent in early life long before the appearance of animals. A satisfying explanation would show that the realization of these possibilities was not vanishingly improbable but a significant likelihood given the laws of nature and the composition of the universe. It would reveal mind and reason as basic aspects of a nonmaterialistic natural order.

Nagel reasons that a rational explanation for the universe must include a teleological explanation. *Teleological* means beginning from the end and reasoning backward, explaining why and how things are based on their purpose or end — in other words, everything happens for a reason. The atheist philosopher recognizes that "in addition to physical laws of the familiar kind, there are other laws of nature that are 'biased toward the marvelous.'"[24] Nagel's statements have led Douglas Axe, a professor of molecular biology, to pose a key question:

Why does Nagel not allow himself to acknowledge that God is at the very center of this plausible picture? Here again, I admire the frankness of his own account. Atheists of the Dawkins variety like to pretend that scientific progress has made God less plausible. They love that conclusion. What they lack is an argument to support it. Nagel refuses to play that game. He's an atheist because he dislikes the thought that he comes under God's authority, which I suspect is true of most atheists, including Dawkins. Nothing intellectual or scientific in that. Just very human. ...

My guess is that this cosmic authority problem is not a rare condition and that it is responsible for much of the scientism and reductionism of our time. One of the tendencies it supports is the ludicrous overuse of evolutionary biology to explain everything about life, including everything about the human mind.[25]

The intelligent design in cosmic realities confirms what St. Thomas Aquinas once stated: The identity of every thing is due to the Creative Designer as its *exemplary* cause. By this he meant that every reality's identity exists first as a pattern in the mind of God, like a painting in the thought of the artist, a sculpture in the imagination of the sculptor, or music in the thinking of the composer. The pattern is of the reality in its integrity.[26] But the Creator-Designer is also the *formal* cause. The form of a reality is what makes it intelligible: It is "the embodiment of the maker's or artist's idea in the object produced, thereby giving the being its meaningfulness, structural features, and objective capacity to awaken aesthetic pleasure."[27] In other words, in a loose sense, it is what provides something with its identity. This combination of the exemplary and formal causes in everything transforms the cosmos into a vast stained glass window through which the light, goodness, beauty, and creativity of the Creator-Lover constantly pour.

These recent scientific breakthroughs, together with Dembski's mathematical argument for design, confirm what Catholicism has always asserted: that the cosmos and all within it is no mere anarchic outcome of the convergence of energies and subatomic particles without purpose or pattern. We live in a cosmos with identifiable realities, from humans to quarks, stars, species of plants, fauna and flora, animals and birds, and each has an identity that could not possibly have come about as the result of mere blind, haphazard chance spilling chaotically out of a "big bang." Our blurred vision of reality due to the cataracts caused by modernity has come to an end, and wonder reawakens in our mind.

CHAPTER 7

QUANTUM PHYSICS AND THE "BIG BANG" GOD

Both religion and science require a belief in God.
For believers, God is at the beginning; for physicists,
He is at the end of all considerations.

— *Max Planck*

As the twentieth century dawned, the future was bright indeed for the future of mathematical physics, which was regarded as the master key to unlocking reality's secrets. Since Isaac Newton's *Principia* (1687), mathematical physics had gone from success to success. But just at the moment when many scientists were convinced that the materialistic understanding of reality would guarantee unstoppable progress, several bombs exploded one after the other inside the building of physics. When the smoke cleared, all that was left of materialism and scientism was rubble. Stunningly, the culprits were all scientists, and their bombs were not philosophical speculations but scientific breakthroughs. These findings began the counterrevolution to modernity's revolution against the Christian worldview and civilization embodied in Christendom.

The first assault was on the Newtonian view of the universe, which was held to be infinite and static — a vast, empty void where objects such as the planets and stars move predictably, like "clockwork." There is no central point or edge to the cosmos because of the balancing effect of the forces of gravitation throughout the infinite vastness. Everything about it can be precisely calculated because it is ruled by fixed laws that can be formulated in mathematical principles; thus there is no need for metaphysics and still less for "religion."

The revolution broke out in 1905 when the twenty-six-year-old Albert Einstein published the special theory of relativity, which focused on the relationship between time and space in the absence of gravity. In 1915 he issued his general theory of relativity, introducing his explanation of how mass and energy warp spacetime: Massive objects like planets, due to their mass, curve the fabric of time and space around them, creating what we call *gravity*. Therefore, contrary to what Newton believed, time and space are not absolute but are instead entangled and can be warped by energy and mass.[1] Consequently, as the American physicist Stephen M. Barr explains, the implications of Einstein's equations[2] present in the first version of his general theory of relativity are that "time and space themselves had a beginning,"[3] that the universe is not eternally static but is dynamically ever expanding or contracting. Einstein was initially deeply disturbed by his own discovery. However, his perplexity was resolved by Alexander Friedmann, the Russian meteorologist and mathematician, and Georges Lemaître, the Belgian physicist and Catholic priest. These scientists, building upon the idea of an expanding universe, discovered the solutions to the Einsteinian equations, describing a universe in expansion. It was especially Lemaître who, by connecting these to the astronomical observations of Hubble and Humason, proposed that "all the matter in the universe was originally concentrated into an incredibly dense 'primeval atom' that exploded to produce the world we see"[4] — the basis for what has become known as the "hot big bang" theory. The "big bang" in the opinion of most contemporary physicists marks the beginning of both the material universe and with it the beginning also of time. This is due to the fact that, in the Einsteinian theory of special relativity, space and time are relative and are inextricably linked.[5] There was no time before the big bang.

Einstein's theories and the big bang were a massive assault upon the dominant modern worldview. They contradicted the Newtonian physics which, based upon Euclidean geometry and Galileo's doctrine of absolute time, had mesmerized the general public with the image of the universe as an eternally existing reality that was sheer matter ruled by unfailing laws — like an immense factory that had always been around, self-regulating, self-contained, and having no need of any reality "outside" it.[6] Almost subconsciously, this machine model had captured our imagination and changed our way of thinking about ourselves and our way of doing everything from healthcare and politics to education and urban planning.

When Father Lemaître first disclosed his discovery, the majority of physicists were stunned and bluntly expressed their disbelief. Their reactions can be summed up in that of the German physicist Walter Nernst: "To deny the infinite duration of time would be to betray the very foundations of science."[7] Many scientists sensed that in the big bang theory they were hearing echoes of a long-forgotten text from an ancient book, "*In the beginning* God created the heavens and the earth" (Gn 1:1, emphasis added). They had a sense of ominous foreboding that, after three hundred years of exile, the God of the Judaeo-Christian worldview was returning to the halls of science — with a bang!

Dizzying View of Space and Time

The second revolutionary assault on the Newtonian worldview was on modernity's view of the fundamental level of reality, the subatomic. It broke out in physics with quantum theory (also known as quantum physics) which, as Professor Barr states, "is not so much a theory *in* physics, as an entirely new theory *of* physics."[8] Quantum physics is the study of the structure and behavior of matter and energy at the most fundamental level of reality as it manifests itself in its mathematical dimensions. It arose out of the discoveries grouped together and known as "quantum mechanics": mechanics, the branch of applied math dealing with motion, and quantum (plural, *quanta* — from the Latin word for "how much"), the smallest measurable unit of energy. Scientists began thinking of matter as measurable "packages" of energy known as *quanta*. Quanta happen naturally: This is the way that nature herself delivers and measures out energy to us. Quanta cannot be broken down into smaller units. Atoms are amazingly tiny: "If an apple is magnified to the size of the earth, then the atoms in the apple are approximately the size of the original apple."[9] But the quanta are even tinier. For instance, light with a certain frequency will produce energy in quanta known as "photons." If you are outside on a sunny day, your eye absorbs about 250 million quanta of light each second.

Quantum mechanics began in 1900 when Max Planck discovered "the quantum of action," or Planck's constant. Swiftly, by around 1960, Niels Bohr, Max Born, Werner Heisenberg, Wolfgang Pauli, Louis de Broglie, John von Neumann, Erwin Schrödinger, John Bell, and Richard Feynman made other key discoveries of the new physics. A *new* physics: *That* was the problem. Its discoveries could fit with Newtonian *physics*, but they could not in any way fit with the associated Newtonian worldview of a machinelike universe that seemed, in the opinion of the majority of scientists, to fit the implications of the Newtonian laws.

Why not? It is chiefly because classical physics was based on the assumption that the cosmos, besides being eternal, is sheer naked matter made of infinitesimally tiny, indecomposable particles: atoms. Interrelating on the basis of attraction or repulsion, these "parts" bring into existence "wholes." However, contemporary physicists discovered that the quanta behave like lawless revolutionaries, in a way totally unlike the realities on the scale that we can see. This deepest level of reality is mysteriously fluidlike. Sometimes it behaves as if it were clumps of matter like subatomic golf balls, other times like ocean waves. Quantum physicists often describe the wave-particle duality as *wavicles*. This has a perplexing implication. It means that quantum particles can be found anywhere, but we have zero certainty of finding one of them in a particular place. That is not the way things behave in the scale of reality of our everyday life. If you build a house on a certain street, you're not going to wake up tomorrow to discover it's at the other side of the city!

Even more mind-boggling, physicists have discovered that a quantum particle may be found *in many places at the same time*! This is going to impact our lifestyle because it will empower technologists to revolutionize the way computers work. Our contemporary non-quantum computers function on the basis of trillions of switches built into microchips that calculate the information we request. But the quantum computer (already existing in a primitive form at Google and IBM research centers) uses quanta to calculate. Because such a quantum can be several things simultaneously until we request the info from it, it may be "on" or "off" or anywhere in between. This means that they can do many calculations simultaneously at a speed thousands of times faster than that of our present computers. Scientists have also proven that pairs of quantum particles can be entangled with each other, even if they are on different sides of the city. In 2022, researchers from the Ludwig-Maximilians University and the Saarland University proved entanglement between two particles separated by 33 km (20.5 miles) of fiber optic.[10]

The chief discovery that perplexes physicists is that these quanta, depending on how they are measured by physicists, simultaneously have the characteristics of particles (tiny bits of matter) and waves. A wave is a disturbance traveling through space transporting energy from one location (its origin) to another without transporting matter — like waves traveling on water. This "wave-particle duality" is the way electromagnetic waves like light function. Up to the twentieth century, physicists thought that light consisted of either waves or particles. In 1906, J. J. Thomson was awarded the Nobel Prize for showing that electrons are particles. But in 1937, his son, George P. Thomson, received the same award for proving the electrons to be waves! This baffled and continues to baffle theoretical physicists because a particle in Newtonian physics is defined as a tiny, *localized* object that is *material* because it has *volume* (an amount of space) and *density* (ratio between mass of matter and the volume of something). However, waves, according to that definition of matter, are *nonlocal and nonmaterial because they have neither volume nor density.*

The breakthrough discovery in 1964 by the Irish physicist John

Stewart Bell confirmed what physicists are now calling the "principle of nonlocality."[11] Known as Bell's theorem, it has marked a milestone in the history of science. "The quantum revolution that's happening now, and all these quantum technologies — that's 100% thanks to Bell's theorem," remarked Krister Shalm, a quantum physicist at the National Institute of Standards and Technology.[12] Henry Stapp called it "the most profound discovery of science," one that brings us to the deepest level of the physical universe that is detectable by physics.

Not only does it prove the wave-particle paradox, but it also subtly implies that the physicist must think in a new way in order to know quantum reality, because the measurement statistics of a multiple-part quantum system cannot be explained by the classical local realistic theory of knowing. "Local realism" is based on the conviction that a thing is changed materially only if it is touched, that is, only by material contact mechanisms. This requires that it be *matter* and that it be *located* in a particular place. But Bell's findings contradicted this axiom. He showed that interactions and connections occur "between events that are too far apart in space and too close together in time for the events to be connected even by signals moving at the speed of light."[13] Experiment after experiment has confirmed Bell's theorem that quantum particles can bizarrely "know" and correlate the behaviors of two such separate quanta apparently *simultaneously* and *instantaneously*. The classic double-slit experiment, which shows that light and matter can fulfill the apparently incompatible definitions of Newtonian physics for both particles and waves, demonstrates nonlocality. In 2022, the Nobel Prize in Physics was awarded to the physicists Clauser, Aspect, and Zeilinger, whose experiments with entangled photons confirmed nonlocal action to be real by showing that nonlocality could explain the coordination between particles.

Therefore, Bell's theorem subtly undermined the sense of "local realism" characteristic of Newtonian physics, whereby scientists held that the universe behaves like a machine functioning on the basis of material cause-effect connections, which act as laws that determine outcomes. Quantum physicists discovered to their consternation that quanta behave *non-deterministically* and therefore *unpredictably*. According to the mainstream Copenhagen interpretation of how a quantum behaves, before it is measured by a physicist it is *in action* in *all the locations* inside what is known as a "wave" *simultaneously*. But when the physicist measures it, the quantum is *localizable*: It is in a particular location. It is always pointlike without any spatial extension. Because a wave is nonlocal — it is distributed across space and time — and a particle is localized in a particular place and moment, precise knowledge at the quantum level of both position and velocity is impossible. It is only because of the act of observation of the physicist that the quanta (which act like a wave when not observed) collapse (*decohere*) and behave like particles, thus enabling the physicist to obtain partial information. Physicist Dan Hooper writes:

> Imagine an electron. It's described by a wave function that peaks sharply at two places, which we will name locations A and B. Now, let's assume that the shape of the wave function covers locations A and B equally, and to the same extent. In this case, if an experiment is carried out to measure the location of the electron, there would be a 50% chance that it would be found at location A and a 50% chance that it would be found at location B.
>
> This example may seem identical to a coin flip, which presents two equally likely outcomes. However, such a comparison would fail to take into account something important about the role probability plays in quantum mechanics.
>
> When a coin is flipped and covered, it's possible to liken it to the electron mentioned above. It could be heads or tails. The crucial difference is that at the moment the coin is covered it's already configured itself to either heads or tails, we just don't know it yet. Whereas, the electron in the above mentioned experiment, is simultaneously present in both locations A and B.
>
> This experiment illustrates that even if we know everything about the electron, even if we know the exact shape of the electron's wave function, there is still a 50% chance that it would be found at location A, and a 50% chance that it would be found at location B. So, the universe isn't behaving deterministically.[14]

Therefore, because of the non-localized way of functioning of quanta, the physicist cannot determine both the position and the speed of an electron. Consequently, *uncertainty* is now characteristic of the way physicists work and think about scientific thinking. This was formulated as the "uncertainty principle" by Werner Heisenberg in 1927. It accepts the fact that quantum realities are nonlocalized and therefore physicists can never have certain information about their positions and velocities because it is impossible to locate the particle without collapsing the wave function. In the act of measuring something at the quantum level, the physicist "collapses" (destroys) the superposition of the quantum, preventing it from being particle and wave at the same time. Thus Heisenberg explained, "The more precisely we determine the position [of an electron], the more imprecise is the determination of velocity at this instant, and vice versa."[15] Quantum objects which are present at all possible times in all possible locations can only be localized at a particular location and time *probabilistically*.

This factor of uncertainty destroyed one of the chief pillars of modernity's view of how the universe functioned. Newtonian physics asserted that all events can be explained by cosmic laws, which always have a unique outcome for given initial conditions. This became a pattern of thought known as *determinism* and it birthed the characteristic attitude of moderns to knowing and knowledge.[16] This ideology even led some philosophers to assert that all events, including human thoughts and choices, are determined by preexisting causes.

However, by the indeterminism of quantum physics we don't mean merely that chance and probability have roles to play in scientific experimentation, as for instance when we flip a coin. What bothered Einstein and so many others is not *practical indeterminism* (how we must include probablism in our scientific methods) but *real indeterminism* encoded into the fabric of nature and the universe and therefore into the laws of physics.[17] Einstein described this new picture of the universe as "spooky."[18] He was right; it is weird! It means that, generally speaking, the physicist does not know what *will* happen but only what *might* happen because, at the level of quanta, the universe is apparently free from the laws that regulate realities on the scale we experience in everyday existence. How can we harmonize this with the real, everyday world we live in where things either happen or don't happen at a particular place and time?

The majority of scientists for whom it was and is business as usual just accept this paradoxical situation. After all, for technological applications and ordinary, everyday cause-and-effect explanations such as gravitational pull, the old physics still functions. But when engineers build laser appliances, they are like cooks preparing a delicious meal with a recipe they don't fully understand because they don't know how all the ingredients function and interact to make the food so tasty. Their attitude is that of David Mermin, often misattributed to Richard Feynman: "Shut up and calculate!"

But the elite of the scientific world have a different attitude. One cannot exaggerate how the need to deal with uncertainty unnerved, even alarmed, Einstein, Planck, Bohr, Gödel, Schrodinger, Heisenberg, and others. They were stunned to find that they were dealing with an unimaginable substratum of reality — one that resulted in them no longer understanding why the universe functioned the way it does. Their materialistic and mechanistic view of the universe was now in rubble. In the materialist worldview held by Einstein and others, the cosmos, although a highly complex machine, is one that behaves in a completely predictable manner.

Until his death, Einstein held that if quantum mechanics were accepted without connecting it to the worldview of Newtonian physics, it would mean that there would be "spooky action at a distance."[19] He remarked, "All my attempts to adapt the theoretical foundations of physics to these new notions failed completely. It was as if the ground had been pulled out from under one with no firm foundation to be seen anywhere upon which one could have built."[20] In a letter to Max Born, he furiously penned these words: "I find the idea quite intolerable that an electron exposed to radiation should choose of its own free will, not only its moment to jump off, but also its direction. In that case I would rather be a cobbler, or even an employee in a gaming-house, than a physicist."[21] In another letter, he added: "Quantum mechanics is very worthy of regard. But an inner voice tells me that this is not yet the right track. The theory yields much, but it hardly brings us closer to the Old One's secrets. I, in any case, am convinced that He does not play dice."[22] To which Bohr supposedly sharply replied, "Don't tell God what to do!"[23] Nevertheless, Bohr was clear-minded about the new situation in which physicists found themselves: "Those who are not shocked when they first come across quantum theory cannot possibly have understood it."[24] Elsewhere, he added: "Anyone who can contemplate quantum mechanics without getting dizzy hasn't properly understood it."[25] Professors Rosenblum and Kuttner summed it up neatly: "Classical physics explains the world quite well; it's just the 'details' it can't handle. Quantum physics handles the 'details' perfectly; it's just the world it can't explain."[26] The Nobel Prize–winning physicist Richard Feynman summed up the attitude of his peers:

> I think it is safe to say that no one understands quantum mechanics. In fact, it is often stated that of all the theories proposed in this century, the silliest is quantum theory. Some say that the only thing that quantum theory has going for it, in fact, is that it is unquestionably correct. Do not keep saying to yourself, if you can possibly avoid it, "But how can it possibly be like that?" because you will go down the drain into a blind alley from which nobody has yet escaped. We have always had a great deal of difficulty understanding the world view that quantum mechanics represents. At least I do, because I'm an old enough man that I haven't got to the point that this stuff is obvious to me. Okay, I still get nervous with it. … You know how it always is, every new idea, it takes a generation or two until it becomes obvious that there's no real problem. I cannot define the real problem, therefore I suspect that there is no real problem, but I'm not sure there's no real problem.[27]

Almost feverishly, the scientific elite has been working to find a big picture coherent with quantum mechanics. In 1927, at the famous Copenhagen conference, Niels Bohr, in opposition to Einstein, who clung to modernity's mechanistic model of reality, concluded that "there is no quantum world. There is only an abstract quantum description."[28] Most physicists sided with Bohr, who had received the Nobel Prize in physics in 1922, and this became known as the "Copenhagen interpretation."[29] The result is that nowadays, most scientists work with the technological abilities of quantum mechanics aware that they haven't a clue about the underlying reality. As the philosopher Alfred North Whitehead remarked with British irony, physics had become "a kind of mystic chant over an unintelligible universe."[30] Or, as the American physicist Nick Herbert quipped: "One of the best-kept secrets of science is that physicists have lost their grip on reality."[31]

Nevertheless, there are still theoretical physicists who refuse to accept the apparent contradiction between reality at the level of subatomic particles and reality as experienced in the "real world." They are seeking to discover a "theory of everything" (ToE), a hypothetical, all-encompassing, coherent framework that links together all dimensions of the universe. The outcomes include "multiverses." Such quests have also led to colossal financial investments, such as the effort to reconcile Einsteinian physics with quantum physics by finding the so-called "supersymmetry" particles. This effort led to the construction of the costliest item of scientific equipment in the history of humanity, the Large Hadron Collider (LHC) in Geneva. The world's highest-energy particle collider required approximately a budget of nine billion U.S. dollars as of 2010 — and still it has not achieved its chief goal. Indeed, its experiments have not only failed to find evidence of supersymmetry but have even ruled out the simplest supersymmetric models.

Still, the majority of quantum physicists are able to go about their task of applying quantum mechanics to high-tech inventions pragmatically and successfully. This is largely due to the physicist Werner Heisenberg, who, in 1925, when he was twenty-four years old, authored the mathematical formulation of quantum mechanics. His wife, Elizabeth, remarked, "With smiling certainty, he once said to me, 'I was lucky enough to be allowed, once, to look over the good Lord's shoulder while he was at work.' That was enough for him and more than enough."[32]

Quantum theory, as formulated in mathematical formalisms by Heisenberg, provides a workable explanation for quantum mechanics. Newtonian physics had been able to describe the functioning of macroscopic realities which have relatively tiny velocities compared to the speed of light. By contrast, because of Heisenberg's discovery, scientists can describe and explain, at least in a way sufficient for technological application, the functioning of microscopic subatomic particles. It is now the best description of how the sub-atomic world works: "Quantum electrodynamics is the most precisely tested theory in all of science."[33] Now influential for about a century, its successor, superstring theory, requires its principles to function. In its application in technology, it has been wildly successful, becoming the key to the functioning of everything from hard drives to lasers to high-speed quantum computing, robotics, and mobile phones connected to satellite technology.

The Involved Creator

Nevertheless, the fundamental "spookiness" of quantum mechanics noticed by Einstein remains — and, indeed, has increased in recent decades. Most scientists are unable to fit together the picture of subatomic reality with that of the real world of everyday existence, largely due to their mindset. This is characterized first by either an antimetaphysical bias or by a sheer absence of knowledge about metaphysics; second, by a split-mind (subjective-objective separation) theory of how we know reality (the Cartesian epistemology); and, third, by ignorance of the Platonic-Aristotelian tradition that reached its greatest synthesis in St. Thomas Aquinas's metaphysics.

But, nevertheless, the majority of scientists do have their own implicit metaphysics: positivism. The dominant philosophy behind modernity's scientism holds that only the statement that is capable of logical, mathematical, or experimental proof is true. Consequently, it rejects metaphysical reasoning and such certainties as the fact of God, the identity of the human, and the nature of marriage. Heisenberg, who won the Nobel Prize in Physics in 1932, recognized the omnipresence of this simplistic "scientific" positivism, and he despised it: "The positivists have a simple solution: the world must be divided into that which we can say clearly and the rest, which we had better pass over in silence. But can anyone conceive of a more pointless philosophy, seeing that what we can say clearly amounts to next to nothing? If we omitted all that is unclear, we would probably be left completely uninteresting and trivial tautologies."[34]

The metaphysics of Plato, Aristotle, and, above all, Aquinas is realist and universal because it is founded upon man's spontaneous experience of reality. Thus the scientists who are epistemological realists and have studied the great philosophical tradition of the West are in the vanguard of the effort to resolve the quantum enigma. As I unpacked in my book *The Logic of Truth*, metaphysics affirms that the logic with which one experiences and lives daily existence can also make sense of the subatomic world and can conclude in a coherent understanding of reality.[35] Moreover, this philosophical tradition is compatible with the biblical worldview. This theory of how we connect with reality is in line with common sense, understood not as folk wisdom but as the infrastructure of how the mind knows. This is what is attracting some contemporary scientists to St. Thomas Aquinas. One of them, Walter Freeman, a cognitive neuroscientist and pioneer of neurodynamics, has pointed to Thomism as the philosophy of cognition most compatible with neurodynamics:

> The core Aquinian concept of the unity of brain, body and soul/ mind, which had been abandoned by mechanists and replaced by Brentano and Husserl using the duality inherent in representationalism, has been revived by Heidegger and Merleau-Ponty, but in phenomenological terms that are opaque to neuroscientists. In my experience there is no extant philosophical system than that of Aquinas that better fits with the new findings in nonlinear brain dynamics.[36]

Werner Heisenberg was also knowledgeable of the Aristotelian-Platonic-Thomist tradition. In his late teens, while hiking in the Bavarian Alps, he read the *Timaeus* of Plato. "My mind was formed by studying philosophy, Plato and that sort of thing."[37] An avid reader, he remarked that of all the many authors he had studied, Aquinas was the most open-minded. In his work *Physics and Philosophy* Heisenberg wrote, "The older concept of soul for instance in the philosophy of Thomas Aquinas was more natural and less forced than the Cartesian concept of the 'res cogitans.'"[38]

This metaphysical mentality enabled Heisenberg to discover connections between the subatomic level of reality and what we perceive through our senses. Faced with the enigma of quanta, he had two key insights: First, the quanta are configurations of reality. He wrote, "I think that on this point modern physics has definitely decided for Plato. For the smallest units of matter are, in fact, not physical objects in the ordinary sense of the word; they are forms, structures or — in Plato's sense — Ideas, which can be unambiguously spoken of only in the language of mathematics."[39] Second, he viewed the quanta as realities-in-the-process-of-becoming: "In the experiments about atomic events, we have to do with things and facts, with phenomena that are just as real as any phenomena of daily life. But the atoms or elementary particles themselves are not [as] real. They form a world of *potentialities or possibilities*, rather than one of things and facts."[40] Elsewhere, the Nobel Prize–winner stated: "The probability wave ... means a tendency for something. It's a quantitative version of the old concept of *potentia* in Aristotle's philosophy. It introduces something standing in the middle between the idea of an event and the actual event, a strange kind of physical reality just in the middle between possibility and reality."[41]

Wolfgang Smith has developed Heisenberg's remarkable insight. Due to his knowledge of Thomistic metaphysics,[42] he has proposed "potentiality" and "actuality" ("real-existingness") as two dimensions belonging to everything. Every reality possesses a potentiality or capacity to exist and an actual existence; at one point it is a potential reality, at another an actual, fully achieved one. Both are *real* states of the same reality. Both depend on a movement that transforms them from capacity-*for*-identity to full *existing-at-this-moment* identity. Aristotle gives examples: The lush, golden cornfield is potentially present in the seed buried in the soil; the human being is potentially present in the tiny zygote.[43] The sculpted statue is potentially present in the marble block.

According to Smith, when physicists speak of "particles" and "waves" of the quanta as if they really existed, it is because the substratum of reality discloses itself in this way due to the measuring of the substratum by the technological instruments. Physics "sees" the invisible level of subatomic reality through instruments — never by direct perception. Consequently, ultramodern physics is a science of measurement that can only tell us quantities. Therefore, neither the particles nor the waves are *real, actually existing* things; rather they are "a sub-existential-domain."[44] Thus Smith confirms Heisenberg's intuition: This level is not real; the quantum particles are something "mid-way between being and nonbeing,"[45] "in the middle between possibility and reality."[46] He agrees with Heisenberg that they are indeed reminiscent of "Aristotelian potentiae";[47] the subatomic world beyond our experience is a world of possibilities that does not have qualities as we experience them in everyday reality.[48]

Smith applies Aristotle's theory of hylomorphism, developed by Aquinas, which holds that every physical reality is a combination of matter and form. Matter is the primal, undifferentiated dimension from which particular, differentiated, identifiable —that is, having an identity — realities originate. He explains how quanta are the "matter" or chaotic, unshaped, formless potential realities that become identifiable "forms" (identifiable things with a recognizable identity in the world around us). But the physicist does not see the quanta in their integral reality, that is, as they are in nature, but merely their mathematical features that become evident to him through his scientific experiment. Here is the explanation for the wave-particle duality and several other perplexing features of quanta.

To the question, "What is it that *causes* the potentiality to become a reality?" Professor Smith answers that it is the intervention of a causality that is both "outside" and "inside" spacetime — that is, it is transcenden — giving "is-ness" to a raw, undefined potentiality. In other words, it gives it its existence and essence, making it into an identifiable particular reality.[49]

This transition from the subexistential plane to the existential plane, from potentiality to reality, can only be explained, as Max Planck (the "father of quantum mechanics") implied in a 1944 speech, by acknowledging that the Creator's action in creating the cosmos *is an ongoing creation, an action that is ever-occurring*:

> As a man who has devoted his whole life to the most clear headed science, to the study of matter, I can tell you as a result of my research about atoms this much: There is no matter as such. All matter originates and exists only by virtue of a force which

brings the particle of an atom to vibration and holds this most minute solar system of the atom together. Since there is neither an intelligent nor an eternally abstract force in the whole universe ... [which] moves of itself ... we must assume behind this force the existence of a conscious and intelligent spirit. This spirit is the matrix of all matter. Not the visible, transient matter is real, true, manifest ... but the invisible, immortal spirit is the real thing! However, since spirit cannot exist as such, but every spirit belongs to a being, we are compelled to presume the existence of spirit-beings. Now since even spirit-beings cannot exist out of themselves, but have to be created, I do not shy away from calling this mysterious creator the same as all cultures of the earth have called him in previous millennia: God![50]

The importance of this insight cannot be overestimated. In order to understand why, it is important to underline that matter and form *are made for each other*. They unite as an identifiable reality that exists in the real world due to what Aquinas called "the act of coming into being." Smith calls this an act of "vertical causality,"[51] distinguishing it from horizontal causality, which itself requires vertical causality in order to function.[52] Horizontal causality is causality within time and space, for example, energy from sunlight causing a chemical reaction that breaks down the molecules of carbon dioxide and water, reorganizing them to produce sugar (glucose) and oxygen. By contrast, vertical causality is in itself instantless but is *instantaneous* in its causing: It is transcendent. Because it *transcends time and space*, it is therefore in a dimension that cannot be reached by even the most sophisticated instruments of ultramodern physics. It occurs in an "ultra-physical" level of reality, beyond the capacity of the experimental sciences to register its presence by measurement. Therefore, only a metaphysical (literally, "beyond the physical") explanation can account for it. It is the causality inserted into nature by its author that is necessary for the identities of things — what Saint Thomas calls their "substantial form."[53] A substance is a reality that is something existing *in itself* and not merely as a feature of something (e.g., a rose or a mountain versus the rose's *redness* or the mountain's *height*). The "substantial form" is, as the *Dictionary of Scholastic Philosophy* states, "the intrinsic incomplete constituent principle in a reality which actualizes the potentialities of matter and together with the matter composes a definite material substance or natural body."[54] It is "that by reason of which matter is a definite thing, a 'such,' a 'this' by which it has its own specific powers and properties; therefore it is the first (ultimate), actual (real), intrinsic, proper (specific) principle by which a natural substance is *what* it is."[55]

For instance, what makes a person human is his substantial form as a psychosomatic whole (a bodymind) whereby he is and functions as a free, reasoning animal. The *cause* of your existence as a human being with all the qualities that make you *what* and *who* you are is what Saint Thomas calls the *actus essendi*, "the act of being," the "perfection of all perfections."[56] He explains that the act of being is the action by which anything in the cosmos has "is-ness" because it receives it from the one reality that is sheer reality, the *one necessary reality* that does not *have* existence and reality but *is* existence and reality — that which "we call 'God.'"[57]

Therefore, our reality is due to the fact that we are *created* realities. To create is to give being, and anything that is has being and exists because it has received the gift of its "isness" from the Creator.[58] God's act of creating is "the primitive existential act which causes [a thing] both to be and to be precisely that which it is."[59] Both existing and existing *as a definable reality* are due to the Creator's ceaseless causing "to be" and "to-be-this-or-that." What Saint Thomas's metaphysics demonstrates, quantum physics now points to. As Bruce Gordon, the philosopher of science, states:

> The mathematically describable regularities of nature are thus active expressions of God's perpetual faithfulness (Psalms 33:4; 119:90; 2 Timothy 2:13). God is the one in whom we live and move and have our being (Acts 17:28), the one who is before all things, and in whom all things hold together (Colossians 1:17). From our standpoint within time, then, there is no distinction to be made between creation and providence, since reality, in toto, is continually realized through divine action (mental causation) as an expression of *creatio continua* [ongoing creation]. God's

design of reality is continuously woven into the very fabric of existence.[60]

This has astounding implications for the rediscovery of the meaning, purpose, and identities of realities — especially of man! It means that every cosmic reality that *is* owes its *isness* — which includes both its existence and its characteristic qualities — to the act of creation, which is not an event in the past but an ongoing action of God in the present. The Creator "fills all in all" (Eph 1:23). His creation is ongoing, here, now, in the present. God is the verb in the universe, in the biosphere, in your life! What is said about the authoring of the universe is also to be affirmed about everything within it: It is the outcome of a vertical causality (the divine creating) acting through horizontal causes but transcending them. It gives realities from babies to stars to redwoods their *isness* along with their identity and characteristic power to operate.[61] In his book *Quantum Glory*, Phil Mason writes: "God saw ... God said. God continues to see and God continues to speak. He holds the entire universe together with the word of His power. God speaks to what He sees."[62]

John Archibald Wheeler (1911–2008), one of the twentieth century's most renowned theoretical physicists, who invented the term *black hole* in 1967, studied the implications of the relationship between the *observed* experiment and the *observer* (the scientist performing the experiment). In quantum physics it is only when the quanta packets of energy are being interfered with by the observing of an observer that they "collapse" into a particular material state. It is only when the observer sets up his experiment in a particular way, asking specific questions, that he sees light either as a "wave" or as a composition of "particles." Only then do they become identifiable and measurable. Wheeler concluded that an "Observer" was essential for the existence of the universe itself, because only such an observer could give it reality. Physicist Paul Davies and astrophysicist John Gribbin explain in their book *The Matter Myth*: "Wheeler has actually gone so far as to suggest that the entire Universe only exists because someone is watching it — that everything, right back to the Big Bang some 15 billion years ago, remained undefined until noticed. This raises huge questions about what kind of creature qualifies as being alert enough to notice that it exists, and collapses the cosmic wave function."[63]

Quantum physics has removed the four-hundred-year-old road-blocks to the recognition that we live in a mysterious, more-than-material universe. First, in order to explain the connection between the quanta and the realities we see all around us, quantum physics has led to a *new understanding of reality*. We will unfold this in chapter 9. Second, it has led to a revolution in how we view the human mind. Davies and Gribbin reject the Cartesian notion of the human mind as "the ghost in the machine — not because there is no ghost, but because there is no machine."[64] Third, when quantum physicists finally broke through to the ultimate level of material reality, they discovered bewilderingly that in order to explain its way of functioning, they could only do so by going outside of the ideology of materialism. They had to reinstate the teleological dimension of reality — the dimension of purpose and therefore *ultimate meaning* in the universe.

The famous astronomer Fred Hoyle, who for much of his career was a committed atheist, by the time of his death asserted, "There is a coherent plan for the universe, although I admit I have no idea what it is." He stated further: "A common sense interpretation of the facts suggests that a superintellect has monkeyed with physics, as well as with chemistry and biology, and that there are no blind forces worth speaking about in nature. The numbers one calculates from the facts seem to me so overwhelming as to put this conclusion almost beyond question."[65] The atheist theoretical physicist Stephen Hawking once remarked, after he had stated that a theory in physics is "just a set of rules and equations": "What is it that breathes fire into the equations and makes a universe for them to describe?"[66] Quantum physics has pointed us toward the answer: the God of Genesis.

CHAPTER 8

NEW MATH AND RESTORED WONDER

In the history of science, ever since the famous trial of Galileo, it has repeatedly been claimed that scientific truth cannot be reconciled with the religious interpretation of the world. Although I am now convinced that scientific truth is unassailable in its own field, I have never found it possible to dismiss the content of religious thinking as simply part of an outmoded phase in the consciousness of mankind, a part we shall have to give up from now on. Thus, in the course of my life I have repeatedly been compelled to ponder on the relationship of these two regions of thought, for I have never been able to doubt the reality of that to which they point.

— Werner Heisenberg, "Scientific and Religious Truth"

The theory of René Descartes about how we know reality broke down the bridge between us and the real: We now hold the opinion that we do not know realities but only *our ideas* of them. The meaning of the universe, our life's time, the existence of God, the soul, life after death, the nature of love and marriage, the purpose of society —all our opinions about these are supposedly subjective. Cartesianism is a major contributor to contemporary skepticism and relativism and to the division of knowledge into the "hard sciences" (clustering around physics and math) and "soft sciences." Even committed Catholics find it challenging to avoid the mental atmosphere this creates, sapping the experience of Catholicism of conviction, enthusiasm, and energy. Before we unfold the ultramodern Catholic worldview, we must show why the most recent discoveries in science support realism, and that the "soft" sciences are just as "hard," even if in a different sense. We must be convinced that *we do connect with reality.*

As an epistemologist who specialized in a contemporary alethic logic, I was aware of both Aquinas's arguments for realism as well as the counterarguments of modernity's leading thinkers, notably Descartes and Kant.[1] It was therefore a sheer delight to discover that a hardheaded scientist, James J. Gibson, a Cornell University professor of psychology, as the result of fifty years of *experimental* research, had concluded that this realism is also the valid *scientific* conclusion to the question of human knowing.[2] He inaugurated what he called "the ecological theory of visual perception,"[3] developing what he called an "ecological approach" to the study of visual perception, according to which humans connect with their environments directly, without bridges of "ideas" or mental images. This contradicted the dominant contemporary theory of knowing, in which the eye is a glorified camera providing us with retinal and mental images which are then processed by the brain to give us knowledge.

As Wolfgang Smith recounts, Gibson declared that "the very notion that 'the eye sends, the nerve transmits, and a mind or spirit receives' needs to be radically modified. In the final count, perception is to be conceived as an act, not of the body, nor of the mind, nor indeed of the two operating in tandem, but of the mind-body compound, conceived holistically as a single entity."[4] Gibson showed that our sensing of realities is not a sum of parts. Nor can our sensing be split into stimulus and response. Most importantly, his experiments led him to reject the notion that we merely perceive an *image* of the reality sensed, whether we understand the image as existing physiologically in the brain or psychologically in the mind. What is perceived, Gibson found, is not a picture of the reality but the reality as it is in the world outside of our mind. Therefore, the conclusion of his ecological theory of perception is that in normal circumstances we see realities, not images.[5]

In other words, there is no "inside" our mind cut off from the inside-identity of the reality. We know the *whole* reality and not merely its measurable, mathematically definable quantities. Gibson showed that we do not see merely the surface features of things, which are then organized by the brain to give the *impression* of a whole; rather, we see *whole realities in their wholeness*, in their identifiable features constituting them as realities different from other realities. With the fullness of our humanness, we "sense," "intuit," "feel" the world around us, grasping both the qualities *and* the quantities of realities.

Thus Gibson resolved the problem recognized by Sir Francis Crick, the discoverer of DNA, who had stated, "We can see how the brain takes the picture apart, but we do not yet see how it puts it together."[6] But, as Wolfgang Smith points out, "The brain itself cannot in fact 'put it together' at all."[7] Gibson, through sheer experimental methods, proved that visual perception cannot be explained solely by the functioning of the retina and the neurons in the affected cerebral regions. Smith remarked, "What to the neuro-scientist appears as a vast ensemble of neuronal activity constitutes in reality a single event, a single act of the living and sentient organism. The point is simple: if perception were merely a matter of neuronal firings, we would need a homunculus — a little man within the brain — to 'read' these events — which is of course absurd."[8]

The outcome is the sudden and shocking re-entry into the world of physics of a reality banished for centuries: the notion of the *soul* — the body-mind understood as a *unity*. In the worldview of Catholicism, the soul is the substantial form of the human body.[9] Unbounded by the limits of time, space, and matter, it is present integrally within every bodily organ and operation. The implications are stunning. Goodbye to the notion of ourselves as mere bodies with computer brains strapped on. Farewell to the notion that the human brain operates like a computer with algorithmic reasoning. There will never be any supercomputer with a human identity! This certainty helps us to recover our assurance of our human dignity, the grandeur of every human being, a magnificence that can bring strength amidst life's storms and energy for the defense of others' well-being.

As Michael Behe has stated:

> In the absence of any good answer ... the mind was assumed to be just another physical phenomenon, no different in kind than digestion. Frankly, that's crazy. I have no answer to the problem of how the mind affects the body or the reverse, but denying your mind because you can't solve a problem is like cutting off your head to cure a headache. Whatever difficulties dualism, hylomorphism, or some other proposed explanation may have, they pale in comparison to denying mind. When you make that move, no more arguments are left, because — to the extent you are consistent — there is no more mind to reason about them.[10]

With this discovery, Gibson assaulted the nonrelational, compartmentalizing modern mindset and culture with its splitting apart of mind/body, subjective/objective, perception/action, organism/environment. He reawakened us to the existence of our soul and therefore of what makes us different as humans: We are not mere conglomerations of atoms and energies, an outcome of a blind, ragingly chaotic Darwinian evolutionism, but a complex, integrated bodymind that is *essentially relational*. Due to the immaterial, spiritual nature of our thinking and free acting, we are partly in eternity and partly in time, for our thinking and loving are not confined by our bodies, environment, genetic code, and social conditioning. Instead, we live at the intersection of time and the timeless, of the immanent and the transcendent.

Gödel's Theorems

At the beginning of the twentieth century, some of the world's leading scientists, philosophers, and mathematicians such as Bertrand Russell had dreamed of being able to perfect the knowledge of math to the point that they could prove any fact, if it is really true, by giving a mathematical proof using the rules of logic and math. They hoped to show that, as Russell himself bluntly remarked, "Whatever knowledge is attainable, must be attained by scientific methods; and what science cannot discover, mankind cannot know."[11] A single, unifying mathematical "Theory of Everything"[12] was their dream. It would be a set of mathematical facts functioning as axioms that would be the basis for all mathematical conclusions and would prove itself by never resulting in contradictions.

Consequently, mathematics would reveal itself to be the master key to understanding reality. If something exists, math can prove it. If anything is provable, it is therefore true. Thus mathematicians and scientists would put the final nail in the coffin of metaphysics and Christianity.

In 1931, however, a twenty-five-year-old Austrian logician, Kurt Gödel, arrived on the scene and laughed at the notion. He rocked the world of mathematicians and theoretical physicists when he published a paper that showed beyond any possibility of doubt that a single "theory of everything" is impossible. He proved it by showing that you can present a statement that is necessarily true but which math is incapable of proving. There are unprovable statements. The claim "If it is true, math and science can prove it" had been reduced to rubble without any possibility of being rebuilt.

Gödel was a friend of Einstein, his colleague at the Institute for Advanced Studies in Princeton from 1940 to 1955. Indeed, their mutual colleague Oskar Morgenstern stated that when Einstein became discouraged in his research, he would go to Gödel's office "just to have the privilege of walking home with Kurt Gödel."[13] Another Princeton physicist, Freeman Dyson, remarked that Gödel was "the only one who walked and talked on equal terms with Einstein."[14] Some would even argue that "Gödel's intellect was in many ways much subtler than Einstein's, in philosophy and perhaps even in physics."[15]

Gödel's discovery, formulated as the "incompleteness theorems," was two theorems of mathematical logic that show the limits of provability in formal axiomatic theories.[16] It was a breakthrough more culture-changing than that of Einstein's theories of relativity. The Princeton professor's findings apply to all branches of science because all depend on math and on the logic of his theorems. Gödel proved that no matter which set of mathematical facts you place as the foundation for math, it will always be incomplete: There will always be mathematical facts that *are true but are unprovable* by these axioms. Nor can any set of mathematical axioms ever guarantee itself to be incapable of leading to contradiction. Writes scholar Douglas R. Hofstadter, "The paraphrase of Gödel's Theorem says that for any record player, there are records which it cannot play because they will cause its indirect self-destruction."[17] The father of modern computer science, Alan Turing, provided further proofs in favor of Gödel's thesis by showing that some problems (such as the Turing halting problem) are non-algorithmic and thus cannot be described by computer code.[18]

As a result of these discoveries, we are now recovering the sense of the mystery of mathematics held notably by our Catholic forefathers at the School of Chartres, by the Greeks, and indeed by all the ancient civilizations going back to ancient Sumeria. The mathematician Wigner has spoken of "the unreasonable effectiveness of mathematics"[19] for understanding the world around us. He remarked, "The miracle of the appropriateness of the language of mathematics for the formulation of the laws of physics is a wonderful gift which we neither understand nor deserve."[20] As another mathematician, Marston Morse, remarked: "Mathematics are the result of mysterious powers which no one understands, and which the unconscious recognition of beauty must play an important part. Out of an infinity of designs a mathematician chooses one pattern for beauty's sake and pulls it down to earth."[21]

Gödel's theorems also subversively imply the limits of the experimental sciences. Mathematical conclusions — and therefore all scientific conclusions due to the dependence of the experimental sciences on math — depend on the starting point of the mathematician and on the premises in his mind. As Werner Heisenberg had stated: "What we observe is not nature itself, but nature exposed to our method of questioning."[22] Thus Gödel's discovery supports the conclusions of Thomas S. Kuhn in his classic work, *The Structure of Scientific Revolutions*, which confirms the logical necessity of metaphysics for the experimental sciences.[23]

Gödel's discovery achieves in the area of mathematics what Heisenberg's uncertainty principle does in physics. The latter "restricts the applicability of pre-quantum physics to a macroscopic domain within which quantum effects can be neglected. And this is one way in which quantum theory can be seen as entailing a limit theorem."[24] Moreover, Heisenberg recognized that science is not the "objective" knowledge that modernity so naively made it out to be:

> Natural science does not simply describe and explain nature; it is part of the interplay between nature and ourselves; it describes nature as exposed to our method of questioning. This was a possibility of which Descartes could not have thought, but it makes the sharp separation between the world and the impossible. If one follows the great difficulty which even eminent scientists like Einstein had in understanding and accepting the Copenhagen interpretation of quantum theory, one can trace the roots of this difficulty to the Cartesian partition.[25]

The outcome is the recognition of the limits of science due to the mystery of the cosmos: "Only a few know how much one must know to know how little one knows." Neither mathematics nor the experimental sciences are sole lord of the mind. Each is merely one of the useful tools by which the human can understand reality, which is not mere quantities, but much, much more. As historian Modris Eksteins recognized, "Through the discoveries of Planck, Einstein, and Freud, rational man undermined his own world."[26] We had been playing on modernity's home ground. We had even accepted its definition of science as only experimental science, labeling all other branches and disciplines as second-level ways of connecting with reality.[27]

This is one of the reasons why the general population, no longer encouraged to treasure history, literature, the arts, philosophy, and theology, is uprooted from its identity. Scientism had carefully educated us moderns to develop a bloated left brain and to allow the right side of the brain to atrophy. We became excellent at analyzing and dissecting but less holistic, empathic, and synthetic. Yet ultramodern neurology and psychiatry have rebelled against this. They have seen how the left hemisphere perceives more our view of reality rather than the reality itself. As Iain

McGilchrist remarks, "The left hemisphere sees truth as internal coherence of the system, not correspondence with the reality we experience."[28]

This is why science is not enough for knowing reality. As McGilchrist states: "Man has to awaken to wonder — and so perhaps do peoples. Science is a way of sending him to sleep again."[29]

Physics, because its object is the mathematical dimension of realities and its method is the experimental, is incapable of reaching conclusions about anything's *identity* and *purpose*. For that, metaphysics is needed. Some of the world's leading cosmologists are convinced that what is *true* and of stable, permanent value is the *metaphysical* vision in the cosmology founded upon universal human experience and rationally developed by the criteria of the Platonic-Aristotelian-Thomistic synthesis of Aquinas. The ultramodern theoretical physicists and mathematicians, from Werner von Heisenberg to Edward Frenkel, know that in order to glimpse something of the *real world* through their findings in physics and pure mathematics, they need the key of the Platonic eternal ideals. These alone can explain the rational, changeless design "behind" the changing realities of the "real world." As mathematician Sylvain Cappell recognized: "All mathematicians live in two different worlds. They live in a crystalline world of perfect platonic forms. An ice palace. But they also live in the common world where things are transient, ambiguous, subject to vicissitudes. Mathematicians go backward and forward from one world to another. They're adults in the crystalline world, infants in the real one."[30]

The totalitarian dream of modernity's scientism to describe reality by math and experiment has come to an end — at least theoretically. Attempts to find "theories of everything" continue: string theory, multiverse, m-theory. How to explain this curious fact in the light of Gödel's theorem and the implications of quantum theory? As the physicist Stephen M. Barr stated:

> Why, simply the idea that all of reality is nothing but physics!
> So we come full circle: it is said that materialism is true because
> materialism is true, because it must be true. We saw the same
> circular reasoning applied to the origin of the human soul: human beings must be reducible to matter, it is said, because anything nonmaterial about human beings could not have arisen

by physical processes; and if it cannot have arisen physically, it cannot have arisen at all — certainly it cannot have been created by God. And this, finally, follows from the fact that only physical processes exist. In other words, materialism is true because materialism is true.[31]

Gödel's theorems by implication also provide a powerful basis for the uniqueness of the human mind: It is no mere glorified computer.[32] It infinitely surpasses the power of even the most complex computer or formal system. This is because, although we can express our understanding of things in mathematical formulas, symbols, and laws, our *understanding* of them can never be explained mathematically. The scientist's mind with its standards and premises has to be always outside its own calculations when it applies and judges them. Human knowing is therefore nonmathematical: It is mysteriously some other type of action outside of matter, space, and time. Wolfgang Smith thus argues: "The thing that formulates them, i.e. the human mind, cannot itself be formulated mathematically: its actions of reasoning and capacity for intuiting that the formulas represent or signify or give meaning is utterly and impossibly nonmathematical, non-'scientific.'"[33] This finding argues for the uniqueness of our humanity, a truth that must be taught to our youth in an era when mega corporations are working to produce cyborgs.[34]

John Lucas, a philosopher, and Roger Penrose, a physicist and mathematician, developed Gödel's argument. As Barr noted:

Both Gödel's Theorem, and the Lucas-Penrose argument that is based on it, are extremely subtle. But the gist of it can be summarized as follows. One consequence of Gödel's Theorem is that if one knew the program a computer uses, then one could in a certain precise sense outwit that program. If, therefore, human beings were computers, then we could in principle learn our own programs and thus be able to outwit ourselves; and this is not possible, at least not as we mean it here.[35]

Rediscovering the World as a Stained-Glass Window

Quantum physics, the complexity specific information theorem, Gödel's theorem, and Gibson's visual perception theory — along with countless discoveries from microbiology to astrophysics — have empowered us to think about the universe in a new way. We can now see it as a vast stained glass window through which we glimpse ever-so-faintly the Cosmic Artist. Moreover, as Judaism and Catholicism have always affirmed — a conviction we shall unfold in future chapters — just as light streams through stained glass windows, so can the supernatural light and energy filter into the universe through sheer matter, space, and time. This is what we call *the sacramental worldview*, which we will consider in depth in coming chapters.

By its overthrow of the materialist machine worldview that has been dehumanizing us since the seventeenth century, the new ultramodern horizon has taken away scientistic difficulties about the supernatural. Heisenberg expressed it bluntly: "Atomic science has turned science away from the materialistic trend it had during the nineteenth century."[36] Max Planck was convinced that the constants of nature, such as Planck's constant, had "a superhuman significance" that both "cut into the bedrock of physical reality" and pointed to the Mind at the origin of all material reality.[37] As philosopher Joshua M. Moritz remarked: "To understand the constants of nature was to disclose the beautiful thoughts of the Mind of God. According to Planck, the power of God's thoughts was expressed in the forces and energies that breathe vitality and form into material existence. ... Nature's laws and constants unified humanity into one brotherhood under the Creator of those laws."[38]

Leading quantum theoretical physicists, through their search for an explanation of the apparently nonlocal and instantless behavior at the subatomic level, have intuited that there is not only the experimentally verifiable horizontal cause and effect, but a "vertical causality." Heisenberg's recognition that the solution of the quantum enigma seems to lie in the configuration of subatomic *potentially* real particles and waves into *identifiable, real-world realities* implies the existence of another dimension of time: This is the "aeviternal" time as defined by Saint Thomas.[39] The aeviternal is where eternity overlaps with chronological, everyday time and configures the "real world." Within the universe there is what can only be called a *semi-eternal dimension of time*. Within it are what Plato defined as the "forms" — the designer-defined identities of cosmic things, from the humanness of humans and the "roseness" of the rose, to the mathematical laws encoded into the cosmos that become evident in the sciences from geometry to astrophysics and microbiology.

The biblical worldview unpacks the Platonic insight further. In the cosmos, the identity of everything that exists is due to the Creator's creative action, which is not an action in the past when he banged out the "big bang" but is ever occurring. This explanation of the quantum enigma recognizes that things from one-celled microbes to giant blue whales, from moonlit Alpine lakes to lapping ocean waves, are born when the raw quanta of each is united to the complex specific identity of each thing through the instantless, outside-of-Einsteinian-space creative act of the Creator. He is ever creating!

This mysterious glimpse of the frontiers of eternity within scientific labs and university halls — for those with eyes to see, of course — explains why more than a few theoretical physicists and mathematicians, such as Werner Heisenberg, Erwin Schrödinger, David Bohm, Paul Davies, and Wolfgang Smith have turned to mysticism in order to find answers to the great enigmas of reality. The most basic general questions asked by the great scientists and mystics are *how* things are and *why* things are: Why is there a cosmos rather than nothing? Why are things the way they are? We have the privilege of living in the era when ultramodern science is showing that the answer to the *how* question points to the answer to *why*. With the breakthroughs in ultramodern science previously outlined, we can clear our minds of modernity's view of the universe as a mechanistic cosmos which had its origin as a senseless big bang, and of its destiny as a dissolution into chaos due to the increasing dispersion of energy and disorder of macro and micro systems.

The bringing together of the *why* and *how* questions by ultramodern physics is mightily important for our everyday existence. As one of the famous psychologists of the twentieth century, the Jewish Viktor Frankl, who survived Auschwitz, stated: "One who has a why to live can bear with almost any how."[40] However, the why and how questions had been rigidly isolated from each other by modernity's worldview. It imprisoned the ultimate questions about God, eternity, and the meaning of earthly lifetime inside the intellectual basement of the nonrational, nonscientific, and the emotional. Thus it denied them any role in the public square. Now, ultramodern physics has unlocked the cellar's door. We can go upstairs and outdoors to search for even deeper explanations which, however, require supernatural disclosures from the Author of the cosmos. To these we will turn our attention in the upcoming chapters, suspecting even before we begin, in the light of nature's workings which, as the atheist Nagel recognized, are "biased toward the marvelous," that what we will discover will be even more awesome.[41]

Physicists and Mathematicians — and the Return of God

The astronomer, physicist, and mathematician Sir James Jeans once remarked, "The Great Architect seems to be a mathematician" and "opined that the universe seems more like a great thought than a great machine."[42] Gödel would have heartily agreed with him. He was convinced of the existence of a personal God — that "the world is rational" and "the order of the world reflects the order of the supreme mind governing it."[43] Indeed, he developed an ontological argument along the lines of that of St. Anselm of Canterbury but using the modal logic used in computer science. Gödel held that "Einstein's religion [was] more abstract, like that of Spinoza and Indian philosophy. ... Spinoza's god is less than a person; mine is more than a person; because God can play the role of a person."[44] After his death, Gödel's wife, Adele, said that he was religious and read the Bible every Sunday morning, although he did not belong to a church. It seems that — as Gödel wrote in a letter to his mother in 1961 — fear of ridicule from his peers led him not to express his convictions publicly. "Ninety percent of contemporary philosophers see their principal task to be that of beating religion out of men's heads," he noted.[45]

Agreed. But the ten percent includes the minds behind the revolution that has ushered in ultramodern physics. They have a different view. An anecdote confirming this, narrated by Heisenberg, occurred during the by-invitation-only 1927 Solvay Conference in Brussels, when the world's scientific elite gathered to discuss the newly formulated quantum theory:

One evening during the Solvay Conference, some of the younger members stayed behind in the lounge of the hotel. This group included Wolfgang Pauli and myself, and was soon afterward joined by Paul Dirac. One of us said: "Einstein keeps talking about God: what are we to make of that? It is extremely difficult to imagine that a scientist like Einstein should have such strong ties with a religious tradition."

"Not so much Einstein as Max Planck," someone objected. "From some of Planck's utterances it would seem that he sees no contradiction between religion and science, indeed that he believes the two are perfectly compatible."[46]

Einstein, even if his metaphysical explanations for his intuition were pantheistic, once remarked, "You will hardly find one among the profounder sort of scientific minds without a peculiar religious feeling of his own."[47] Heisenberg was of the same opinion: "In classical physics, science started from the belief — or should one say, from the illusion? — that we could describe the world, or least parts of the world, without any reference to ourselves."[48] Planck, the 1918 recipient of the Nobel Prize in physics, thundered the revolutionary message of the new physics: "Therefore, while both religion and natural science require a belief in God for their activities, to the former He is the starting point, to the latter the goal of every thought process. To the former He is the foundation, to the latter the crown of the edifice of every generalized world view."[49]

Elsewhere, Planck stated:

Our drive toward unity obliges us to identify the world order of science with the God of religion. There is, however, this difference: for the religious man, God stands at the beginning; for the scientist, at the end, of all thinking. We must believe to act ethically, and we must act; society could not survive if its members went about without proven moral precepts or waited until acquiring wisdom to decide how to behave. Therefore each individual must strive to develop both sides of his nature, the religious and the scientific, which complete and complement one another: It is the steady, ongoing, never-slackening fight against skepticism and dogmatism, against unbelief and superstition, which religion and science wage together! The directing watchword in this struggle runs from the remotest past to the distant future: "On to God!"[50]

The outcome is that ultramodern physics— after five hundred years of amnesia — has begun the journey to rediscover mystery and wonder. We will begin once more to convincingly repeat Hamlet's utterance: "There are more things in heaven and earth, Horatio, than are dreamt of in your philosophy."

Gödel, like the twelfth-century Catholic intellectuals of the School of Chartres, was a Platonist, viewing the universe as a place of shadows. Everything that we perceive around us is a silhouette, an echo of the perfect, unchanging, eternal dimension of reality: what Catholicism in its biblical language calls the "heavenly" and defines as the dimension of the aeviternal, where we come into contact with the ideal, the natural, the formal and final causes of realities.

This is why Gödel's discoveries about math can impact our way of thinking about everything. For it is when we look at mathematics through the realist Platonic premises underlying math that we awaken to the fact that numbers exist as really as stars and people, and that existence doesn't require physicality.[51] Moreover, because mathematical truths ever remain the same, they are necessarily universal.

This is revolutionary for every dimension of contemporary lifestyle because it leads us to suspect that every reality, from humans to society to human behavior, politics, economics, and the arts is encoded with universal patterns necessary for human flourishing. It is a massive assault on modern relativism with its conviction that we can twist human nature, the biosphere, and all else as we arbitrarily decide. It is a shout that absolutes, universals, constants, and patterns exist, such as human nature and the natural law. It is a roar: *Reality exists before we do, and we are meant to become "real" — our ideal selves — by discovering the universal patterns encoded by the Author in reality and inside the human psyche, in order to pattern ourselves by them.*

A New Understanding of Understanding

Quantum physics, in order to explain the connection between the quanta and the realities we see all around us, perplexes and thus provokes a search for an understanding of what type of universe is "underneath." This has led to a new understanding of reality because it has led to a new understanding of understanding.[52] As Heisenberg remarked, "Whenever we proceed from the known into the unknown we may hope to understand, but we may have to learn at the same time a new meaning of the word 'understanding.' … In this way modern physics has perhaps opened the door to a wider outlook on the relation between the human mind and reality."[53] It has led to the destruction of the Cartesian-Kantian-scientistic theory of how humans know reality.

A "wider outlook" is something of an understatement: It is a *revolution* that has overthrown modernity's characteristic way of thinking as inaugurated by Bacon and Descartes. The outcome is twofold. First, quantum physics, Gödel's theorems, and Gibson's theory of visual perception have destroyed the view that man does not know realities but only *his ideas about* them. Second, these breakthroughs have ended the presupposition that man only knows with certainty those parts of reality that can be verified experimentally: the measurable mathematical dimensions.

The scientistic worldview, with its conviction that all that can be known for certain are the mathematical, measurable dimensions used in the experimental sciences, is a total revolt against the realism characteristic of the human psyche. This realism was formulated philosophically by the great Platonic-Aristotelian tradition that reached its zenith in the Catholic ("universal") synthesis of Aquinas. In the modern view, all that enchants and beautifies existence is "subjective" and mere make-believe. As that fiery critic of modernity's scientism, the British mathematician Alfred North Whitehead, sarcastically remarked:

> Thus nature gets credit which should in truth be reserved for ourselves: the rose for its scent: the nightingale for his song: and the sun for his radiance. The poets are entirely mistaken. They should address their lyrics to themselves, and should turn them into odes of self-congratulation on the excellency of the human

mind. Nature is a dull affair, soundless, scentless, colorless; merely the hurrying of material, endlessly, meaninglessly.[54]

You might be thinking, "Even if this is true, ordinary people still value qualities such as beauty and goodness. We just don't think like that." You are partly right. Even scientists, for instance, on returning home in the evening relate to their spouse and children in a most unscientific way! However, as we shall explain further on, this split-mind attitude has deeply conditioned our patterns of thinking. It has numbed a fully human way of connecting with reality. To give one dramatic example: More than one historian of World War II has been bewildered by the discovery of the minutes of meetings of "ordinary," family-loving, non-Nazi German engineers calmly discussing how they could design more effective concentration camps to murder more Jews at a faster rhythm. Decades before, during World War I, as Winston Churchill noted, it was the most highly educated, rational, and scientific nations that committed the most inhuman atrocities. The materialistic mentality subtly desensitizes us in our relations with others because we no longer view our fellow humans as wholes, integrally, with qualities that are sublimely beyond the quantifiable.

Therefore, thrilling indeed is the era in which we live. These scientific and mathematical breakthroughs are giving unprecedented strength to the arguments for God's existence, human grandeur, and the importance of the natural. No wonder Einstein exclaimed, "The eternal mystery of the world is its comprehensibility ... the fact that it is comprehensible is a miracle."[55] As we shall examine in the upcoming chapters, when all of this is integrated with the divinely revealed certainties upheld by Catholicism, it empowers us to develop blueprints for building a new civilization which will empower human flourishing. When we unite the findings of ultramodern science to the worldview of Catholicism as shaped by the biblical texts and millennia of insights by some of history's greatest minds, we begin to inhabit the Catholic story of the world. Then we discover that its vision of the universe *re-enchants* our experience of the world and of life.

CHAPTER 9

WHICH STORY DO
I INHABIT?

When we read a story, we inhabit it. The covers of the book
are like a roof and four walls. What is to happen next will
take place within the four walls of the story. And this is
possible because the story's voice makes everything its own.

— _John Berger_, Keeping a Rendezvous

The story of the world that we are going to read in order to discover
our own story is the biblical narrative of world history. Indeed, we
intend not merely to read it, but to inhabit it. Its covers are "Beginnings"
(_Genesis_) and "Disclosure" (Revelation).[1] It is an ongoing story because
the Author is still speaking it; his voice is still bringing everything to
fulfillment. When we understand it in this way, it becomes for us the
story whose covers "are like a roof and four walls,"[2] inside which we find

the meaning for our life's time. This is possible because the voice that is telling the story is *the* Voice, the Second Person of the Trinity.

The voice speaking to us through Genesis 1–11 gives us more than a description of the beginnings of the universe. It tells us why the universe is and gives us the big picture in which to view world history. As the theologian Terence E. Fretheim has documented, it is a masterpiece of complex writing: Its "strategy is to catch the reader up into a universal frame of reference. Readers are invited to view a screen that is cosmic in scope and to engage in an act of the imagination that carries them beyond — way beyond — their little corner of the world."[3] These opening chapters are the prologue which unfolds the fundamental plotline of the Pentateuch (the first five books of the Bible). This prologue enables us to see the unity between the purpose for which the world was created and the divine strategy for bringing the project to fulfillment.[4] Stunningly, the inspired author of Genesis shows us God creating the cosmos, not with the detached attitude of an industrial manufacturer producing a machine, but with the personal involvement and creativity of a lover. This is because the Creator's goal is to build a "home" for himself and humanity — a home and not a house. He wants a permanent place for bonding, relationship, and intimacy.

"Forevering" Himself to the Cosmos and to You

The author of Genesis communicates this through the seven-day structure of the literary description. The Hebrew verb for giving your word or oath-swearing is *shaba*. It is derived from the Hebrew word for seven, *sheba*.[5] In other words, to swear is to "seven oneself, or bind oneself by seven things."[6] Through the seven days of activity which climax on the unique seventh day, God "forevers" himself to the universe. By swearing an oath of bondedness to it, he has promised to put his very self into ensuring its well-being and bringing about its fulfillment.

The cosmos is bonded to him forever! As the philosopher Donald W. Mitchell remarks: "Creation is an eventing of the relationship between God and what God has created. This means that God is not apart from creation, but 'fills all things in every way' (Eph 1:23)."[7] The Creator-Lover is close to this universe, involved in its events. This should radically alter our vision of the skyscape and the landscape. Through glittering stars and gliding eagles, zesty sea waves and whispering wheatfields, fiery-orange autumn leaves, birthstone-blue skies, and russet roses, the Lover murmurs, "I am continually with you" (Ps 73:23).[8] And we can rely on him never to walk out on his oath, for "the word of the Lord abides for ever" (1 Pt 1:25), and "God is faithful" (1 Cor 1:9). This is the chief disclosure from him who has revealed himself: "I am the Alpha and the Omega, the first and the last, the beginning and the end" (Rv 22:13).

What we call "salvation history" is the unfolding of the Creator-Lover's forever resolve. It shows in the covenants with Noah, Abraham, and Moses, culminating in "the new and eternal covenant" of Jesus.[9] These bonds were the strategy of a lover because in the Jewish mind a covenant is more like a marriage bond than a business contract. By these covenants, the Creator-Lover renewed, confirmed, and specified his bondedness to the world. They expressed the Lover's stubborn resolve in the face of human betrayal to bring "Operation Genesis" — the Creator's dream for the universe — to achievement in the bridal civilization of the final era of history, a fact confirmed by Revelation 22.

As the young Jesus climbed the Mount of Olives that night after he had initiated "the new covenant" (Lk 22:20) and before his passion began, the poignant refrain from the song he had just sung may well have been resounding in his mind: "His mercy endures forever" (Ps 136:1). Only days before, he had uttered words, as tears welled up in his eyes, alluding to this unbreakable bond. Upon his arrival to the outskirts of Jerusalem, he spoke from the heights of the same Mount of Olives as he looked down upon the city he so cherished: "O Jerusalem, Jerusalem, killing the prophets and stoning those who are sent to you! How often would I have gathered your children together as a hen gathers her brood under her wings, and you would not!" (Mt 23:37). These words are weighty with the pathos of the millennia during which the Creator had been reaching out, longing to keep his commitment to the cosmos.

Due to the creation of the cosmos in a love-bonded relationship with the Creator, we have grounds for optimism. No matter how horrendous the catastrophe, whether social, political, or ecological, we know that a restoration is possible because reliability characterizes the "God of Israel, the Savior" (Is 45:15). The biblical pages thunder that "the thoughts of his heart" endure through the millennia (Ps 33:11), and we see it even more so after the final shout Jesus gave on that Friday afternoon — "It is finished" (Jn 19:30) — and the piercing of his heart. Centuries later, in 1645, as modernity's revolution began, he would give the world a wakeup call at Paray le Monial when, in mystical visions to St. Margaret Mary Alacoque, he called upon Christians to gaze upon his heart in order to begin, once again, to understand that "God so loved the world" (Jn 3:16).

This understanding of God imbues us with deep serenity in the midst of life's challenges. It is the ultramodern Catholic vision of reality clashing with modernity's idea of the all-powerful but arbitrary god on whom we cannot rely — the "God" who has authored the universe but who may also annihilate it at any instant. By contrast, the biblical God who swore an oath to the cosmos made it clear that he intended to be so intimately present in the newly created universe that the only adequate way to express this was by stating that he intends to live in it. Yet we must distinguish two ways in which the Creator is active within the spacetime universe. First, because he is transcendent —that is, not limited by space, time, and matter but their ongoing Creator — he is also absolutely immanent to the cosmos and to each reality. That is why St. Augustine of Hippo could exclaim: "higher than my highest and more inward than my innermost self."[10] The Creator-Lover is intimately inside the depths of our "I" while at the same time he is above and beyond all that we experience in the visible spacetime universe.

It is his power that keeps the hard drive and operating system of the universe functioning. The inbuilt mechanisms he created in the universe — the causes that physics recognizes — are secondary causes. That is why, although we acknowledge the operation of secondary causes such as gravitation and the speed of light, we know that these operate through the ongoing involvement of the Creator. The Creator did not merely institute them and leave them functioning independently of himself: They function in every instant only because of his power. This is what modernity will not accept. Because if it did, it would have to accept that just as his power preserves the universe, so likewise does it conserve humans. Consequently, humans should acknowledge his power publicly as well as privately and should design a lifestyle according to the Designer's blue-prints encoded into human nature.

The Creator is also present within the universe in another, very different way. When Genesis and the entire Bible presents the resolve of God to live in his universe, it is not referring to an impersonal way of being present by means of his ever-active power and all-pervasive knowing. Instead, the inspired biblical texts refer to another type of divine presence. The only way to describe it is to say that it is personal and personable. It is the presence of God, which we can visualize through the metaphors of tent and Temple. These two metaphors would have sprung spontaneously to the mind of the ancient Jews, a nomadic people who imagined the universe as a tent (Tabernacle — Ps 104; Jb 9:8; Is 40:22) or as a house in the architectural shape of a temple whose architect is Yahweh (Jb 26:11; Gn 7:11; Ps 78:23). In the Ancient Near Eastern civilizations, a temple existed for only one purpose: to be the home of a deity. This is an apt metaphor because it indicates a permanent building as well as one wholly given over to the deity for his purposes — truly his home.[11]

The Pentateuch describes the universe as the temple of Yahweh by presenting us with the parallelisms between the authoring of the cosmos and the building of the Tabernacle during the Exodus journey and later of the Jerusalem Temple. Moreover, in the architecture, interior furnishings, and rituals of both the Tabernacle and the Temple, we see that they were made to function as a symbolic microcosmos,[12] a scale model of the universe. This becomes clear in Yahweh's detailed instructions to Moses about the building of the tent of meeting (Ex 25–31). These instructions, which occur in seven distinct speeches, mirror the rhythm of Yahweh's seven-day creation of the cosmos. The phrase that is repeated with each command in Exodus about how the building is to be designed — "the LORD said" — echoes the Genesis refrain repeated in the description of the creation of each day: "And God said" (Ex 25:1; 30:11, 17, 22, 34; 31:1, 12; Gn 1:3, 6, 9, 14, 20, 24, 26).

Earth and Heaven

Although the Egyptians and others had similar cosmologies to that of Genesis, the Jewish one differed radically because it identified Yahweh as the sole source of the cosmos. From this axiom, the Chosen People drew out the implication: Every cosmic reality and every living being has meaning and purpose through its relationship with him.

The chief characteristic symbolized architectonically by the Tabernacle and Temple is that of a universe which is bipartite, meaning it has two dimensions: Earth and Heaven. Earth in the biblical worldview refers to the world around us as we know it, including space, time, and matter. It is incomplete: a work in progress that has been entrusted to humans. Human beings are subcreators, divine vice-regents with the mission to "be fruitful and multiply ... fill the earth and subdue it" (Gn 1:28). The verb *subdue* does not mean "exploit" but refers to the conquest of the anti-ecological forces that impede the flourishing of the biosphere.[13] These chaos-directed energies, along with human misuse of freedom, are what make the world a fragile, tumultuous environment.

Heaven is the counterpart to what the Bible calls *Earth* or *World*. Heaven is the dimension of reality where God is intensely present and active, where he is totally in control, and where everything functions according to his designs: "The heavens are the LORD's heavens, / but the earth he has given to the sons of men" (Ps 115:16). But Heaven as envisioned by Genesis is part of the created universe. It is not outside but inside it. As biblical theologian Terence E. Fretheim notes: "The Old Testament most sharply witnesses to what might be called a single-world image."[14] Therefore, "The heavens (or semantic equivalents) thus become a shorthand way of referring to the abode of God within the world."[15]

Heaven has its own "space" and "time," not limited by our earthly space and time. Rather, Heaven's "space" and "time" enclose cosmic space-time. To put it more technically, Heaven is transcendent: It is the dimension of reality that surpasses all that we experience while encompassing and empowering it both to be and to be what it is. In this sense, "transcendent" does not mean "disconnected." In every divine disclosure that we encounter in Scripture, God murmurs — and sometimes thunders — through persons, events, and institutions that Heaven is connected, connected, connected to Earth!

The New Testament scholar N. T. Wright explains:

> Basically, heaven and earth in biblical cosmology … are two different dimensions of God's good creation. … When the Bible speaks of heaven and earth it is not talking about two localities related to each other within the same space-time continuum or about a nonphysical world contrasted with a physical one but about two different kinds of what we call space, two different kinds of what we call matter, and also quite possibly (though this does not necessarily follow from the other two) two different kinds of what we call time.[16]

It is crucial that we become convinced that Earth and Heaven are close to each other and interactive. Heaven, as Wright states, is "the 'control-room'" for Earth.[17] "Heaven, God's space, is the sphere from which the whole world is run" although, as we shall see, the Creator-Lover makes this contingent to a large extent on human freedom. It is where the blueprints are located for how Earth should operate and achieve its destiny to be the dwelling place of the Creator with humans. These include the natural law, the laws of space, time, and matter, and the identity of every reality. But the heavenly dimension of the universe is also the source of what Catholicism terms the "supernatural."[18] It is through its transforming powers of vision and energies ("sanctifying grace" and "actual grace") that the Creator intends Heaven and Earth to function harmoniously.

These powers are absolutely necessary for us humans because of the fallout from the original catastrophe of "the Fall," in which the first humans degraded themselves from the sublime status of persons participating in the divine life (see CCC 375). Consequently, as with radioactive fallout, we have toxins that have damaged our psyche and every dimension of society. As the *Catechism of the Catholic Church* states, "Human nature has not been totally corrupted: it is wounded in the natural powers proper to it, subject to ignorance, suffering, and the dominion of death; and inclined to sin" (405). However, by comparison to our ideal humanness, we are "subhumans" who with every choice of sin "dehumanize" ourselves further. Therefore, the supernatural is vital! As G. K. Chesterton remarked, "Take away the supernatural, and what remains is the unnatural."[19]

Astoundingly for the modern mind, there are concrete institutions on Planet Earth where the Creator has established bases of operations for energies supernaturalizing humans. Historically, these have been the Temple of Jerusalem, its predecessor the Tabernacle, and its successor, the Mystical Temple of the God-Man, the Church.[20] The Temple is where Heaven interacts with Earth because it is where the Creator-Lover-Rescuer who desires to be close to humans provides, through the activities characteristic of the Temple (the liturgy), the supernatural powers whereby humans become capable of this closeness. We will unpack this further on. First, let us look at why the Tabernacle and the Temple of Jerusalem, through their architecture and furnishings, disclose this Heaven-Earth structure of the cosmos and the purpose of the Church.

Architectural Scale Models of the Heaven-Earth Universe

Thanks to the Jewish historian Josephus (AD 37–c. 100), who had served as a priest in the Temple, we have descriptions of the sacred building as it existed during the earthly lifetime of Jesus. Constructed as a symbolic microcosm, its contents were intended "to recall and represent the universe."[21] One entered the Temple by the eastern gateway, symbolizing the eastern entrance to the primeval Paradise, through which the first humans had gone into exile after the Fall. As we read in Genesis, Yahweh "placed the cherubim, and a flaming sword which turned every way, to guard the way to the tree of life" (3:24). Subsequently, Yahweh had communicated through his prophets that only by the one who could aptly be described as the "Promised One," the Messiah, would the gateway be reopened so that humans might re-enter Eden. One such revelation occurs in the vision given to Ezekiel:

> Then he brought me back to the outer gate of the sanctuary, which faces east; and it was shut. And he said to me, "This gate shall remain shut; it shall not be opened, and no one shall enter by it; for the LORD, the God of Israel, has entered by it; therefore it shall remain shut. Only the prince may sit in it to eat bread before the LORD; he shall enter by way of the vestibule of the gate, and shall go out by the same way." (Ez 44:1–3)

Thus, as you made your way into the sanctuary, you were symbolically journeying homeward toward the integral "Godworld," the future Paradise in the final era of history, thereby reversing the journey into exile of the first humans.

The outer courtyard symbolized Earth. To enter the inner courtyard of the sanctuary, the holy place, you had to walk through a gate flanked by two pillars, which symbolized the Temple as the bridge between Earth and Heaven. Stylized as trees, these pillars called to mind the trees at the center of Eden: "The tree of life also in the midst of the garden, and the tree of the knowledge of good and evil" (Gn 2:9). This meant that here was the point of access to wisdom and to complete, forever vitality. It was the place where the Creator could fulfill his dream about humans. That is why the final scene in the great drama at the end of history, as mystically seen by John on the island of Patmos, is a renewed Planet Earth — an ecological civilization with the Triune Creator-Lover present at its center, and a new tree of life (see Rv 21:22 and 22:1–2).

As one entered the inner holy place from the outer courtyard, one passed through a magnificent, embroidered curtain (Ex 26:33). Josephus describes its needlework as depicting a panoramic view of the visible stars and planets, with "colors seeming so exactly to resemble those that meet the eye in the heavens."[22] Elsewhere, he remarks that it "typified the universe."[23] "Across this colored veil of blue, purple, and scarlet drifted a cloud of sweet-smelling incense," a symbol of the prayers of the worshipers ascending heavenward.

The inner sanctuary, the holy of holies, was located in the westernmost part of the Temple. It was a perfect cube: twenty cubits by twenty cubits by twenty cubits. Inside this completely dark place resided the Ark of the Covenant until it disappeared around 597–586 BC, when the Babylonians captured Jerusalem and deported most of the Jewish population. Gilded inside and out, the Ark contained the tablets of the covenant, Aaron's rod, and a pot of manna. The cover of the Ark was a lid of pure gold, the "mercy seat" (Ex 37:6), over which were extended the gold wings of the cherubim, also made out of gold, symbolizing the Divine Presence (Ex 25:22).

This innermost space represented the Garden of Eden (Paradise), the place where Heaven and Earth intersected. Genesis describes Yahweh at the beginning of history as dwelling not in the entire cosmos but in a part of the world named Eden (Paradise).[24] Because Genesis presents Eden as an ideal ecological environment, palmettes and depictions of flora and fauna adorned the Temple. The utter holiness, grandeur, and goodness of Yahweh were symbolized by the fact that the holy of holies was off-limits to almost everyone. Only one man, the High Priest, was allowed to enter it once a year to sprinkle the blood of a sacrificial bull onto the mercy seat as an atonement for sins. But even he was prevented from fully seeing the interior because of the cloud of smoke from the incense. The sovereign divine rights over Earth were symbolized by the Ark, which King David described as "the footstool of our God" (1 Chr 28:2). In this way, the Jews imagined Yahweh as seated above it upon his royal throne. Thus the Ark expressed the relationship between the two parts of the universe: "Heaven is my throne and the earth is my footstool" (Is 66:1). Yahweh can rest his feet on Earth in this sacred spot because here Heaven's blueprints for the planet have been implemented, and harmonious order reigns. The sculptures in olive wood of the two seraphim on either side of the throne reminded the Jews that these were the powers who, after the Fall of the first humans, had replaced humans as *shamars*, guardians of the entrance to the heavenly dimension.

In the lobby of the holy of holies was the Menorah, a lampstand with seven lights. These symbolized the seven "moving stars" (as viewed by the naked eye) — the sun, moon, and the five planets closest to Planet Earth. The Menorah's light fell upon the acacia table overlaid with pure gold, holding the twelve loaves of the bread of the Presence placed on plates of pure gold as Yahweh had commanded: "And you shall set the bread of the Presence on the table before me always" (Ex 25:30). The Menorah was a symbol calling on the Jewish people to gaze on the Zodiac, which showed the transit of the moon and the sun through its stars and planets, indicating the liturgical timing of the cosmic year. After the exodus from Egypt, the Passover event became the central event of the Jewish calendar and, because the Good Friday–Easter Sunday event coincided with it, it has become the axis going through the center of world history. Thus, as Moyshe Shtarkman, a Hebrew writer, remarked, "Jewish history is a ring that encircles the history of all humanity."[25]

The altar of incense with its thirteen spices from throughout the Mediterranean and Middle East symbolized through the ascending of its smoke the bonding of humans with Yahweh through prayer: "Let my prayer be counted as incense before you" (Ps 141:2). For prayer, the uniting of the powers of one's complete bodymind to the Creator, is the necessary route by which humans can enter into the heavenly dimension of reality.

All this symbolism meant, as Josephus remarked, that "all things are of God and for God" — the universe in its entirety.[26] Even the outer robe of Aaron, the first high priest, according to the Wisdom of Solomon (see 18:24), depicted "the whole world."[27] This cosmology was no abstract theory. Because the holy of holies was where Heaven interacted with Earth, it was regarded as the source of Earth's order, vitality, and stability. For the highly practical, earthly Jewish mind, it was a working model, a scaled version that displayed why the universe existed, what its purpose was, and how society should function.[28] The Temple was, as Charles Taylor expresses it, a "social imaginary,"[29] a design in stone and fabric to permanently alert the Jewish people to the order of the world — and to their mission to restore that world order in its integrity as it had once existed in Eden. The Tabernacle and later the Temple were meant to function as the space where Heaven interacts with Earth in order to bring Operation Genesis to completion — a most practical, down-to-Earth, and (implicitly and even shockingly) political purpose.

But the Temple was not merely a picture in stone, a representation of what the relationship between Earth and Heaven should be; it was a source of supernatural energy for accomplishing that mission. This is what we Catholics call a *sacramental*.[30] The *Catechism* gives this definition: "Holy Mother Church has, moreover, instituted sacramentals. These are sacred signs which bear a resemblance to the sacraments. They signify effects, particularly of a spiritual nature, which are obtained through the intercession of the Church. By them men are disposed to receive the chief effect of the sacraments, and various occasions in life are rendered holy" (1667).

Because the Jewish people were the nation chosen by the Creator to prepare the world for the arrival of the Messiah, he equipped them with the supernatural vision and energies necessary for fulfilling this mission through the Temple and its rituals. The Jewish priesthood, sacrifices, liturgical feasts such as Passover, symbols such as circumcision, the Menorah, and blessings functioned as the means by which those who *consciously and willingly* participated in them became ardent lovers of Yahweh, longing for and preparing the way for the Messiah. These were men and women such as Moses, Jeremiah, Isaiah, Daniel, Ezekiel, John the Baptist, Simeon, Anna, Joseph and above all, the most sublime woman of Jewish and world history, Mary.

A Place Where the Creator Is Intensely Active

Therefore, the Temple building, furnishings, and rituals were not only windows but gateways through which one entered the heavenly dimension of reality and participated therein.

The Temple could achieve this because it was where Yahweh was present and active in this epoch of history, inaugurating what will become his all-pervasive Presence in the final era of history on the heavenized Earth. Let me unpack this. God is everywhere present but not always in the same way or with the same intensity and intensive level of activity. Everywhere he is present through his power. Everywhere he is present through his omniscience. But not everywhere is he present personably as the Triune Creator-Lover-Rescuer acting in relationship-building with humans and angels.

In the Tabernacle and later in the Temple, God was most personably present. This was where "the living God" (Jer 10:10; Ps 7:12), the most lively and active Creator, was intensively acting on Earth. The parallels between Genesis and Exodus confirm this. They do so by showing how the "Spirit of God" (Gn 1:2; Ex 31:3), is involved in both the creation of the cosmos and the construction of the Tabernacle. In Genesis, "The Spirit of God was moving over the face of the waters" (1:2), implying that the newly constructed universe would be filled with the divine presence. Then, in Exodus: "The cloud covered the tent of meeting, and the glory of the LORD filled the tabernacle. And Moses was not able to enter the tent of meeting, because the cloud abode upon it, and the glory of the

LORD filled the tabernacle" (Ex 40:34).

The biblical authors also parallel Yahweh's Presence in Paradise, the original divine temple, and in the Jewish Tabernacle and later Temple. Genesis shows us God actively present in the created world. He "walks" in the Garden of Eden with the first humans. The same Hebrew verb used for this "walking" (Gn 3:8) is also used to describe the Divine Presence in the Tabernacle (see Lv 26:12; Dt 23:14; 2 Sm 7:6–7). Likewise, when David plans to build a temple in 2 Samuel 7, the Lord reminds him that "I have been moving about in a tent [Tabernacle] for my dwelling" (2 Sm 7:6). The Creator has been dynamically active in the Tabernacle as he had been in Eden.

The Creator is passionately present in his universe, as he constantly repeats through his prophets. "Thus says the LORD: 'Heaven is my throne and the earth is my footstool'" (Is 66:1). Thus, "The whole earth is full of his glory" (Is 6:3), and "The earth is full of the mercy of the LORD" (Ps 33:5). Psalm 139 shows how intensely the Jewish mind experienced God's closeness during prayer:

> O LORD, you have searched me and known me!
> You know when I sit down and when I rise up;
>   you discern my thoughts from afar.

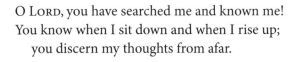

> Where shall I go from your Spirit?
>   Or where shall I flee from your presence?
> If I ascend to heaven, you are there!
>   If I make my bed in Sheol, you are there! (1–2, 7–8)

Yahweh constantly reminds his Chosen People that he is close to his world: "Do I not fill heaven and earth?" (Jer 23:24). Even when the evil deeds of humans "force" him to abandon the Temple, he does so in a way that shows how intensely he regrets it. Ezekiel in his vision of this departure saw the Shekinah (the cloud symbolizing the Presence of Yahweh) halt above the Mountain of Olives: "And the glory of the LORD went up from the midst of the city, and stood upon the mountain which is on the east side of the city" (Ez 11:23). As Fretheim recognizes: "The language of God's forsaking and abandoning (for example, Jeremiah 12:7–13) is not a move from presence to absence, but a move to distance, to a less intense presence, with the effect that the forces that make for death and destruction will often have their way."[31]

The Creator-Lover-Rescuer's intense level of presence in the Temple first in Jerusalem and then in the Mystical Temple of the Church is at the center of the dramatic saga of his efforts through the millennia to bring Operation Genesis to fulfillment. Stunningly, it reveals that he has resolved to be the God who intends to work for cosmic and human fulfillment through the human-divine synthesis and synergy of these earthy institutions. To this we will now turn our attention.

CHAPTER 10

BREAKING THE CODE TO UNDERSTAND THE DIVINE STRATEGY

If every event which occurred could be given a name, there would be no need for stories. As things are here, life outstrips our vocabulary. A word is missing and so the story has to be told.

— *John Berger*, Once in Europa

"It is finished" (Jn 19:30). *Tetelestai!* This Greek word in John's text comes from the Greek root word *teleo*, which means "to bring to completion." In the ancient Mediterranean world, when a debt was collected, the person received a receipt stamped with the word *tetelestai*, meaning the debt had been paid in full.

We have forgotten what Jesus meant by the "it" of his great shout, heard moments before he died on that Friday afternoon. "It" refers to nothing less than the completion of Operation Genesis: the creation of the cosmos and, in a special way, the creation of humans. "It is finished" echoes the words: "And on the seventh day God finished his work which he had done" (Gn 2:2). He, the embodied second self of the Eternal Father of whom we read, "All things were made through him, and without him was not anything made that was made" (Jn 1:3), had initiated the creating of the universe "in the beginning" (Gn 1:1). It was only the beginning of the project of making a universe with the aid of men and women acting as cocreators. As Chesterton explained:

> The principle of progress in which all sane men believe is mainly this: that we are engaged and ought to be engaged in a persistent effort to change the external world into the image of something that is within ourselves; to turn what is, as far as we are concerned, a chaos into what shall be, as far as we are concerned, a cosmos.
>
> God did not give us a universe, but rather the materials of a universe. The world is not a picture, it is a palette. ... Heaven gave us this splendid chaos of colors and materials. Heaven gave us a few instinctive rules of practice and caution corresponding to "do not put the brush in the mouth."
>
> And Heaven gave us a vision. ... It may be that we shall never reach perfection, but we may continue to approach it. But even if we only approach it, we must believe that it exists, we must believe that there is some comprehensible statement of what it is and where it is.[1]

The vision in the final biblical text of the climax of world history confirms what Genesis had asserted: The divine project for Planet Earth was to make it to be nothing less than the place where God would dwell with humans.

However, perplexingly, it is through his passion that he brings the cosmos and humans to their fulfillment. To understand this, we must first ask: Why did God author the universe? In a sense, one could say with Saint Irenaeus that he created it to save it:

> He recapitulates in himself all the nations dispersed since Adam, and all the languages and generations of men, including Adam himself. This is why St. Paul calls Adam the "type of the One who was to come" (cf Rom 5:14), because the Word, the maker of all things, did a preliminary sketch in Adam of what, in God's plan, was to come to the human race through the Son of God. God arranged it so that the first man was animal in nature and saved by the spiritual Man [i.e., Jesus]. Since the Savior existed already, the one to be saved had to be brought into existence, so that the Savior should not be in vain.[2]

From the depths of eternity, the Creator knew what he was doing. He saw the problem — and the solution. The passion brought to completion the creation of the cosmos that was begun in Genesis, but which was then endangered by that catastrophic event we call "the Fall" or "original sin."[3] The Creator, who gave humans the mission to be his agents for world transformation, foresaw the original catastrophe and its fallout. For in God there is no "before" and "after" in his seeing, knowing, and deciding. He sees all of history synchronically, not diachronically: He views all events as occurring together, all at once, at the same time — not in succession. Therefore, the creation of humans, the Adamic catastrophe, and the rescue of humanity are a single big picture and complex strategic plan in the Divine Mind. As C. S. Lewis wrote:

> He creates the universe, already foreseeing — or should we say "seeing"? there are no tenses in God — the buzzing cloud of flies about the cross, the flayed back pressed against the uneven stake, the nails driven through the mesial nerves, the repeated torture of back and arms as it is time after time, for breath's sake, hitched up. If I may dare the biological image, God is a "host" who deliberately creates His own parasites; causes us to be that we may exploit and "take advantage of" Him. Herein is love. This is the diagram of Love himself, the inventor of all loves.[4]

We could say that in one "moment," the Trinity saw the universal problem and willed the universal solution.[5] And, most mysteriously, the Second Person entered history and brought the resolution of this challenge to a climax in a most humanly unexpected way during the hours of a certain Friday afternoon.

Yet to our modern minds, both the universal problem and its solution sound strange to us. This is because of our big picture. Through the glasses given us by modernity, we see history as a series of haphazard events, beginning with the big bang, that brought into existence a universe in which we live but with which we feel no organic relation. We sense the universe as a reality "outside" us. The environment is something we need to manipulate to survive. Time is a series of disconnected moments — past, present, and future are merely psychological with no real connection between them. In this worldview, Good Friday is merely one event among many. It is a "religious" occurrence that no longer affects anyone except those who opt to remember it for the sake of their "spirituality." But it has no real effect on the world.

To begin to understand the *why* of Good Friday, we need to reject modernity's split mind between "reality" (the spacetime universe) and God; between the day before the days began and Christmas; and between the events of Jesus' lifetime and ours. In the biblical worldview, history is a single story about Operation Genesis being brought to fulfillment in "a new heaven and a new earth" (Rv 21:1) through Jesus' shout, "It is finished!" What we call *salvation* is not a subplot of the great story of the universe, but its purpose. Humans were created in order to become Christlike by participating in the perfected humanness that resulted from Jesus' passion. As the Greek mystic Nicholas Kabasilas (c. 1323–92) magnificently expressed it:

> It was for the new human being that human nature was created at the beginning, and for him mind and desire were prepared. ... It was not the old Adam who was the model for the new, but the new Adam for the old. ... Because of its nature, the old Adam might be considered the archetype to those who see him first, but for him who has everything before his eyes, the older is the

imitation of the second. … To sum it up: the Savior first and alone showed to us the true human being, who is perfect on account of both character and life and in all other respects.[6]

In Genesis, "Adam," the first human, refers to three realities: first, to a historical person; second, to the whole human race, because he is also an archetype; third, to each individual — including me and you. As the Lexham Bible Dictionary explains:

> Adam means "man" or "mankind/humankind" and is a wordplay on the Hebrew term meaning, "ground." This wordplay demonstrates the intimate relationship between humankind and the dust of the earth (Gen 2:7) from which the first man was fashioned. "Adam" is used both as a name and a title in Scripture, referring to his identity as the first human and his status as the representative of humanity before God.[7]

Adam represents every human because in him are the patterns of behavior characteristic of us all. Through knowing Adam, we learn much about ourselves. The description of the Adamic sin is a description of every sin with its effects, rippling or roaring across history, leading to sin-infected cultures and civilizations. In him we see ourselves as in a cracked mirror. In Jesus, we view ourselves as the Creator-Lover intends us to become: the complete human. "Thus it is written, 'The first man Adam became a living soul; the last Adam became a life-giving spirit'" (1 Cor 15:45).

God reckoned Adam's cataclysmic action into his decision to author the universe and humans. The Triune Author knew perfectly well what he was doing. And yet he went ahead. He factored the first sin and every sin into the risk of birthing the cosmos and humanity into existence. But he never intended to let the Fall have the last word. Nor does he want our falls to have the last word. He made this clear in the immediate aftermath of the Fall, when he promised that the Enemy of humankind would not destroy his project: "I will put enmity between you and the woman, and between your seed and her seed; he shall bruise your head, and you shall bruise your heel" (Gn 3:15). This most mysterious oath inaugurates the great and dramatic saga of world history because it predicts ongoing warfare between the Deceiver and the humans who unite themselves with their Creator, until the latter eventually triumph.

The most stunning implication of all this is that, as C. S. Lewis expressed it, "God, who needs nothing, loves into existence wholly superfluous creatures in order that he may love and perfect them."[8] The universe, humanity, and each individual human were known and cherished by the Author of all things from before the big bang. He has known each one of us since "before I formed you in the womb" (Jer 1:5). All of creation is a work in progress, a project to be brought to completion. And it is a task in which the Author has always intended to get personally involved — indeed, passionately so. He knew it was going to be messy from the beginning; he "foresaw" that he was going to get his own hands bloody.

Throughout all of history, with the relentless — one may even say stubborn — resolve of a passionate lover, the Creator has pursued the solution, using a lover's noncoercive methods. The Triune God insists on his world order being brought about through freedom driven by love. Operation Genesis is achieved in a particular way through the embodied Divine Person of the Son, for God wants to bring about the fulfillment of his creation and the necessary rescue operation involved by keeping to the same strategy he put into effect when humans were created. God made human beings cocreators with him of Planet Earth, and for this he gave them freedom, resolving to be forever the God who works through humans. Notwithstanding the Adamic disaster, the Creator-Lover refused to abandon the strategy. The world is to become his homeland with humans through the cooperation of free humans. There must be no coercion — hence the dramatic saga.

Listening In on the Most Revealing Conversation in History

In my study, there is a painting by Swiss artist Robert Zünd depicting the scene of Jesus with the two disciples traveling toward Emmaus. This event occurred after the Resurrection, when the God-Man appeared incognito to Cleopas and his companion as they left Jerusalem and traveled to a village about seven miles distant (Lk 24:13–35). In the painting, Jesus walks between the two men, his right arm raised, pointing heavenward. The facial expressions are lively, pointing to an animated back-and-forth conversation.

The picture in my study is actually a modified version of Zünd's original, with the scene being viewed through a window whose two panes have been opened outward. We sense that we are being invited to listen in, because the discussion is of importance to us. In fact, this conversation is the most revealing conversation in all of history because in it is disclosed the road to achieving one's personal destiny, but — mark well — within the context of the world's destiny.

Jesus' purpose in speaking to the two men on the road to Emmaus was to provide them and us with the key to understanding the ultimate *why* of the universe, history, the human race, and each individual. With this most mysterious key, we are to unlock the meaning of his passion and death, seeing it as the fulfillment of Jewish history and therefore of world history. By reading that history backward from Good Friday, Jesus shows us the organic unity of the events stretching through the millennia narrated in the biblical texts from Genesis to Malachi. Thus, Luke tells us, "And beginning with Moses and all the prophets, he interpreted to them in all the Scriptures the things concerning himself" (Lk 24:27).

Cleopas bluntly expressed the reaction of his contemporaries to what had happened on Good Friday: "But we had hoped that he was the one to redeem Israel" (Lk 24:21). The Messiah was not supposed to end his life as Jesus had. Moreover, the reports about Jesus' dead body no longer being in the tomb and of his appearing alive to many of his disciples on the day after the Sabbath hadn't changed their perspective. Some Jews at that time believed that the resurrection was an event that would happen at the culmination of history in the Messianic age. Other Jews did not believe in resurrection at all. As for the rest of the Mediterranean world, well, the very idea of a resurrection was sheer nonsense, as Saint Paul would discover on Mars Hill in Athens (Acts 17:15–34). Jesus' tone as he explained salvation history to the two men on the road to Emmaus was marked by a certain tone of impatience. He seems to be asking, "Come on, men! Why are you being so foolish? Why are your hearts so sluggish when it comes to believing what the prophets have been saying all along? Didn't it have to be this way? Didn't the Anointed One have to experience these sufferings in order to come into his glory?" (see Lk 24:25–26.) It is a tone of voice that we hear at other moments in his lifetime, notably with Nicodemus ("Are you a teacher of Israel, and yet you do not understand this?" Jn 3:10), and with the apostles ("Do you not yet understand?" Mk 8:21).

The majority of Jesus' countrymen had a dulled sense of their mission and destiny. Jesus, by contrast, viewed the history of his people not as a haphazard succession of events without purpose, but as a story in search of a conclusion. Israel's past, personalities, and institutions of Temple, Sabbath, and kingship had been divinely instituted to empower the Jewish people to be the divine agents of world renewal. And then, to the amazement of Cleopas and his companion, Jesus showed that the conclusion had been reached on that bloody Friday afternoon.

Where did Jesus get the notion of his Passion as "necessary" (see Lk 24:26)? St. Thomas Aquinas states that in the created bodymind of Jesus there were, most mysteriously, three modes of knowing reality: First, because he is a Divine Person, he experienced the immediate beatific vision.[9] Second, his knowing was infused with supernatural data and power. Third, because he was fully human, he learned about reality in the normal way every human does. In his case, as is evident from his remarkable abilities to communicate through parables to the masses and his astonishing resolution of knotty problems that puzzled the intellectual elites of Jerusalem, it is clear he had — to put it mildly — a rather high IQ.

Within this human knowledge, he had a conviction of his own vocation. As a twelve-year-old boy, he had remarked to his parents, after they found him in the Temple, "Did you not know that I must be in my Father's house?" (Lk 2:49), expressing what he would state on the eve of his death: "Now is my soul troubled. And what shall I say? 'Father, save me from this hour'? No, for this purpose I have come to this hour" (Jn 12:27). In other words, "This is what I am here for, this is what I am meant to achieve in my life's time." So, how did he come to understand this personal mission? In a special way, by reading the texts narrating the history of his people from Genesis to Malachi *as a unified story*. From the first time that he attended the Nazareth synagogue, probably at five or six years of age, and heard the prophecies of Isaiah and Jeremiah and the narratives of liberation in the Book of Exodus, his extraordinary intellect began connecting the dots.[10] And, at some point, he recognized that the entire history of Israel was passion-bound.

This was nothing less than a revolutionary interpretation of the Jewish past. Yes, certainly, Jesus did not alter the positions and roles of the chief actors in the millennial epic, nor the content of what they had said. But he did interpret the entire history in a new way — indeed, in such a radical way that no group among the first-century Jews, whether Pharisees, Sadducees, or Essenes, was expecting it. He recognized that Jewish history was centripetal: It was rushing toward a center — and that center was himself! And at the center of this center, Jesus saw not his birth, not his three years of teaching and miracle-working, not even his resurrection, but his passion. Decades later, the author of the Letter to the Hebrews would write:

> Now in putting everything in subjection to him, he left nothing outside his control. As it is, we do not yet see everything in subjection to him. But we see Jesus, who for a little while was made lower than the angels, crowned with glory and honor because of the suffering of death, so that by the grace of God he might taste death for every one. For it was fitting that he, for whom and by whom all things exist, in bringing many sons to glory, should make the pioneer of their salvation perfect through suffering. (2:8–10)

(The phrase "perfect through suffering" needs to be understood in light of the fact that any action of any one of the three Divine Persons in the created universe is an action of the Trinity in unity. The passion was the love-drenched decision of the three Divine Persons.)

Jesus told the two men on the road to Emmaus that the only explanation for his triumph as resurrected God-Man was the historical event that had occurred only days before. Victory had been achieved during those blood-saturated hours on the hill outside Jerusalem — an event that, as Cleopas insinuated, everyone in Jerusalem knew about. Moreover, because "glory" in the sacred Jewish texts referred to the manifestation of the divine power in time and space, these words of Jesus imply that he, through his passion and death, was mysteriously now manifesting the inner reality of Yahweh. His triumph and new status were not in spite of his passion and death but were directly and intrinsically caused by them.

The Decisive Event of World History

This is just too much for our modern minds, as indeed it was initially for Jesus' own inner circle. This is because we tend to think of time as "just one damned thing after another,"[11] as wave follows wave, meaninglessly, pointlessly, destructively. We see history merely as a haphazard collection of events. In sharp contrast, the Bible reveals cosmic history to be a *story*. In its unified, structured narrative, notwithstanding the composition of its contents across various time periods, it tells one overarching story that reaches its climax on Good Friday and Easter Sunday through the action of the central personality of history, Jesus Christ. Reading the Bible in this light we discover world history — and our own personal history — to have a detectable pattern: like a drama with a plot, a symphony with a rhythm, a design with a predetermined pattern.

Even weeks after the first of the Resurrection appearances, at his ascension, some of Jesus' friends still doubted (see Mt 28:16–17; Acts 1:11). Reading the accounts of the appearances of the Risen Jesus, one gets the impression that their authors were writing in a state of bewilderment. After they had dipped their reed brushes in ink, they wrote of "that which was from the beginning, which we have heard, which we have seen with our eyes, which we have looked upon and touched with our hands, concerning the word of life" (1 Jn 1:1). But they seem to have been highly conscious that they had no adequate language with which to express their experiences. Indeed, even these accounts were written down only after Pentecost when the mighty wind of the Spirit breathed into their minds the understanding required for the synthesis to emerge. It was then that they understood the often-repeated, enigmatic "must" of Jesus, as when he had said, "The Son of man must suffer many things" (Lk 9:22). He had repeatedly affirmed this when he resolutely began the journey to Jerusalem for that final Passover (see Lk 9:51).

Therefore, for Jesus, it was all about living his life's time according to the Scriptures. Even from before his passion, he had been offering his followers this key. That is why the evangelists repeat it like a chorus throughout their accounts. Jesus, throughout his brief years in the public square, had bluntly stated that this dramatic event was the *raison d'être* for his existence, often referring to it as "the hour" or "his hour" ("My hour has not yet come," Jn 2:4). Indeed, he gave the impression that he saw his entire career as a journey of ascent to Jerusalem where the event would take place. As he chillingly remarked to his disciples, "Behold, we are going up to Jerusalem; and the Son of man will be delivered to the chief priests and scribes, and they will condemn him to death" (Mt 20:18). To the astonishment of his inner circle, he ardently wanted this hour to come: "I have a baptism to be baptized with; and how I am constrained until it is accomplished!" (Lk 12:50). For him, it was necessary within the web of events in which God's designs sought to work with and through humans' freedom. Good Friday was the outcome not of an absolute necessity, but of the relative necessity caused by divine love wanting to rescue humans through the passionate love with which Jesus embraced the cross.[12]

Thus, he said to the disciples on the road to Emmaus, "O foolish men, and slow of heart to believe all that the prophets have spoken! Was it not necessary that the Christ should suffer these things and enter into his glory?" (Lk 24:25–26). Indeed, it was so necessary that when the leader of his inner circle (Peter) had tried to dissuade him, he had called him "Satan" (Mt 16:23).

Jesus himself certainly seemed to acknowledge his years of public activity as a journeying to Jerusalem (see Mt 23:37). The inspired writers of the New Testament recognized this. Luke organized his Gospel around the final journey to Jerusalem, writing, "The time approached for Him to be taken back up *to the Father*; so strong with resolve, Jesus made Jerusalem His destination" (Lk 9:51, VOICE). From that point, Luke intersperses his account with reminders that Jesus was "on the way" (Lk 10:38; 13:22; 17:11). Matthew also writes about this: "From that time Jesus began to show his disciples that he must go to Jerusalem and suffer many things from the elders and chief priests and scribes, and be killed, and on the third day be raised" (Mt 16:21). Although why this had to be so perplexed his inner circle, there was no doubt about the danger latent in his decision for the entire group. As Thomas remarked, "Let us also go, that we may die with him" (Jn 11:16).

It is clear that Jesus saw everything in his life as connected to his passion. Pacino di Buonaguida's complex masterpiece *The Tree of Life* communicates this. At the center of the tree-shaped crucifix is Christ Crucified, surrounded by twelve branches and forty-eight medallions represented as fruits, which show the events of the God-Man's life. The tree rises to Heaven where angels, prophets, and saints are active. But it is rooted in Planet Earth and, stunningly, in the human archetype, Adam.

When did Jesus became conscious of his Jerusalem destiny? Even when he was only twelve years old, his response to his worried mother and foster father points to a preteen boy with a clear knowledge of his vocation.

Indeed, Jesus hurried the arrival of his passion by provoking the hostility of both the Jewish and Roman elites during his final journey to Jerusalem. He performed symbolic gestures that threatened the status quo, such as his entry into the city riding on a foal. This was how David had entered for his royal coronation a millennium before. So likewise had the liberator of the city, Judas Maccabeus, in 164 BC. As the God-Man entered the city on Palm Sunday, the population acclaimed the conquering liberator "with praise and palm branches" (1 Mc 13:51). But then, to the amazement of everyone, he proceeded to aggressively cleanse the Temple. His action of overthrowing the tables of the money changers brought the liturgical activity in the Temple to a temporary halt, thus implicitly declaring him to have divine authority. It was a public manifesto disclosing his intention to bring the mission of the Temple to an end. Because the Temple symbolized the world, for the Jews, these gestures of Yeshua dramatically represented the overthrowing of the existing sociopolitical order and the inauguration of a new kingship. As N. T. Wright remarks: "More particularly, what Jesus did in the Temple, interpreted (as seems most likely) as a Jeremiah-like symbolic prediction of its forthcoming destruction, must have had to do in some way with his aim of declaring that Israel's God, returning to his people at last, had found the Temple sadly wanting and was establishing something different instead."[13]

Therefore, with this gesture, Jesus implied the end of the Jerusalem Temple as the place of the intensively active presence of the Creator on Planet Earth. He was mysteriously inaugurating a new Temple in and through himself. He hinted at this when he told the Jews, "Destroy this temple, and in three days I will raise it up" (Jn 2:19). Because the Temple in the Jewish mind was nothing less than the scaled model of the cosmos as a sociopolitical reality, Jesus hereby implied the inauguration of a new world order configured around himself.

In hindsight, his first followers realized that this fulfilled the ancient prophecies that Yahweh himself would return to Israel to fix her situation — and therefore humanity's. Malachi had prophesied that Yahweh would enter his Temple: "Behold, I send my messenger to prepare the way before me, and the Lord whom you seek will suddenly come to his temple; the messenger of the covenant in whom you delight, behold, he is coming, says the LORD of hosts" (Mal 3:1). This is because, as N. T. Wright points out, the cleansing of the Temple points not only to the purpose of the Temple but also to the liberation event of the exodus journey from Egypt to the promised land.[14] As Moses had made clear to Pharaoh, he wanted the dictator to allow the Israelites to leave Egypt for the purpose of liturgy: to worship Yahweh. This worship would happen first in the Tabernacle and later in the Temple through liturgical rituals of sacrifice.[15]

These had two purposes which were as inseverable as the two sides of a coin. First, they ritualized the meaning of the exodus journey, empowering the participants to experience *liberation* from the sinister, behind-the-scenes, ultimate source of the deepest enslavement: Satan, who is "the god of this world" (2 Cor 4:4). It is he who "has blinded the minds of the unbelievers" (2 Cor 4:4). The ruler of mental and social darkness is "the spirit that is now at work in the sons of disobedience" (Eph 2:2), and people are "being captured by him to do his will" (2 Tm 2:26). Consequently, we are in psychic captivity and, therefore, as the *Catechism* states, humanity is "weakened in its powers, subject to ignorance, suffering, and the domination of death; and inclined to sin" (418). Second, through experiencing the liberation achieved by full participation of heart and mind in these sacrifices, eschatological Sabbath time — time as it will be in the final era on the heavenized Planet Earth — was mysteriously inaugurated in the minds of the participants, empowering them to experience *shalom*, a deep order between their intelligence, willpower, and passions, and to become builders of a new world order in which Yahweh would be at the center.

However, as Jesus clearly recognized, the Temple rituals were no longer fulfilling their divine purpose. The Temple had become in the minds of many of his countrymen more a political rather than a religious reality, a narrowly nationalistic symbol rather than the inspiration for the mission of the Jewish people to be a world-changing movement. They viewed the occupying Roman legions as the only anti-Yahweh forces. Jesus, on the other hand, clearly saw the sinister forces of darkness behind Rome and all the world's political powers and perceived that they had even penetrated inside the institution of the extraordinary Divine Presence on Earth. With clarity he recognized the satanic "ruler of this world" (Jn 12:31) behind all of the cosmic injustice and violence and human "hardness of heart" (Mt 19:8). He intended by means of his own exodus journey through his passion and death into resurrection "to deliver us from the present evil age, according to the will of our God and Father" (Gal 1:4). We will now turn our attention to this new exodus on which he journeyed, so that we also may journey on it "through him, with him, and in him."[16]

CHAPTER 11

DEEPER MAGIC

"But what does it all mean?" asked Susan
when they were somewhat calmer.

"It means," said Aslan, "that though the Witch knew the
Deep Magic, there is a magic deeper still which she did not
know. Her knowledge goes back only to the dawn of time."

— C. S. *Lewis*, The Lion, The Witch and the Wardrobe

If only Luke would have provided us with Jesus' entire dialogue with his disciples on the way to Emmaus! While we do not have those details, Scripture does provide us with a detailed narrative of another event in which symbols and words dramatically show us the meaning of Jewish and world history in light of Good Friday.

On the night before his passion, Jesus disclosed the significance of the events that would take place the following day. He did this, not by a speech, but by an action: the mysterious ritual meal of the ancient Passover. His choice of Passover instead of Yom Kippur or any other Jewish festival is the key to understanding why his passion is the centripetal event of Jewish history and therefore the centrifugal event of world history. Passover was where all the major themes of Jewish history converged. On that day, the millennial history of the Jewish people came into focus, because Passover was the freedom festival. N. T. Wright explains:

> We have every reason to suppose that when the Jewish people celebrated Passover year after year they thought of it as the freedom festival that not only looked back to the original act of liberation, but ahead to another great act of liberation, especially when the people once more felt themselves enslaved or oppressed. And the point for our purposes is this: Jesus himself chose Passover as the moment to do what he had to do, and the first Christians looked back to Passover as one of the main interpretative lenses for understanding his death.[1]

Passover commemorated the great act of Yahweh's liberation of the Jewish people from slavery in Egypt. Wright continues, "The entire Passover context made sense of the entire event that Jesus envisaged as he went up to Jerusalem for that final visit. Passover said, 'Freedom — now!'"[2] "Now" because the Jews thronging the streets of Jerusalem as Jesus and his inner circle headed to the Upper Room for the meal were keenly aware that they had lost their national sovereignty and were in the firm grip of imperial Rome. In their minds, freedom would be restored by liberating the Jewish people from their dominators who prevented them from living under the reign of Yahweh. The Jewish prophets recognized Yahweh alone as ruler of Israel — even their own Jewish kings were held to be merely his viceroys. Therefore, Passover as freedom festival also shouted "Kingdom — now!"[3] It was a call for the restoration of a politically independent kingdom of Israel. This meant the recovery of the status of the nation prior to around 975 BC when, after the death of Solomon, the twelve tribes split into a northern and southern kingdom. And it meant the expulsion of the Roman armies.

Passover was not what we moderns call a "religious" event. The Jews did not compartmentalize politics and religion as we do. Their calendar was filled with feast days involving rituals and prayer for the changing of this world in order to align it with the Creator's plan. Jesus' enactment of the Passover meal "on the night when he was betrayed" (1 Cor 11:23) shows that he saw his passion and death as the long-awaited act of liberation that would destroy alien control of the Jewish people. Good Friday would be a revolutionary event inaugurating a new freedom. Wright explains:

> All the Jewish festivals are packed full of meaning, and Passover is the most meaningful of all. The festival involves a dramatic retelling of the exodus story, reminding everybody of the time when the pagan tyrant was overthrown, when Israel was set free, when God acted powerfully to save his people. Celebrating Passover always carries, to this day, the hope that God will do so again. Jesus' fresh understanding of Passover, given in interpreted action rather than abstract theory, spoke of that future arriving immediately in the present. God was about to act to bring in the kingdom, but in a way that none of Jesus's followers (despite his attempts to tell them) had anticipated. He would fight the messianic battle — by losing it. The real enemy, after all, was not Rome, but the powers of evil that stood behind human arrogance and violence, powers of evil with which Israel's leaders had fatally colluded. It was time for the evil which had dogged Jesus's footsteps throughout his career — the shrieking maniacs, the conspiring Herodians, the carping Pharisees, the plotting chief priests, the betrayer among his own disciples … to gather into one great tidal wave of evil that would crash with full force over his head.[4]

However, the contemporaries of Jesus no longer had a clear big picture by which they could understand the meaning of Kingdom, liberation, and who their real enemies were. Thus they were no longer capable of discovering the solutions to their plight under Roman occupation. This was chiefly because they had lost a strong sense of their God-assigned mission to be agents of world transformation. Nevertheless, even if they had retained this understanding, they would only have arrived at an understanding of Jesus' notion of Kingdom and liberation by the same way as the disciples of Emmaus: by reading Israel's history backwards in the light of his passion.

What Jesus communicated through the ritual meal of Passover he had also expressed in the actions of his public life. All his words and symbolic actions were liberating events,[5] especially his healings — not only of physical diseases but particularly of the mysterious inner corruption bound up with the presence of demonic forces. He himself had initiated conflict with these in the desert at the beginning of his public life. Evidently, he regarded this combat as essential for the sake of liberating individuals and the entire nation so that it could become the Kingdom of God. When John the Baptist from his dungeon sent his followers to ask Jesus if he was really the long-awaited, royal, liberating personality (the Messiah), Jesus gave an answer that is cryptic to us moderns but was crystal clear to his Jewish contemporaries. He pointed to his fulfilling of the Messianic prophecies through his actions of healing and exorcism and therefore to his inauguration of the reign of Yahweh. Then, enigmatically, he added, "And blessed is he who takes no offense at me" (Mt 11:6). He knew well that his passion and death as the liberating event was not what even John the Baptist expected.

The Renaissance Man: "In Him Love Was Sheer Action"[6]

Jesus accomplished the human vocation and mission during the hours of that Friday afternoon. Astoundingly, in the passion of the passionate Jesus, we see, finally, what all of history had been yearning to see: a fully human human — a perfect man. In him we see the Creator-Lover's project finally achieved: "So God created man in his own image, in the image of God he created him" (Gn 1:27). What Adam — who represents all of us — and later God's Chosen People, the Jews, failed to accomplish, Jesus Crucified achieved. Throughout his entire lifetime, in every thought, desire, and action, his goal was to be, in his humanness, the perfect image of his Eternal Father. And he achieved it: "He who has seen me has seen the Father" (Jn 14:9). As Søren Kierkegaard, the father of existentialism, wrote:

> Yes, he was Love ... everything in him was truth. ... In him love was sheer action; there was no moment, not a single one in his life, when love in him was merely the inactivity of a feeling that hunts for words while it lets time slip by, or a mood that is its own gratification, dwells on itself while there is no task — no, his love was sheer action. ... His love was totally present in the least things as in the greatest; it did not concentrate more intensely in single great moments, as if the hours of daily life were outside. ... It was equally present in every moment, not greater when he expired upon the cross than when he let himself be born. ... In his love there was no demand upon any other person, upon any other person's time, energy, assistance, service, or reciprocal love. What Christ required of him was solely the other person's bene-fit, and he required it solely for the sake of the other person; no one lived with him who loved himself as deeply as Christ loved him.[7]

His ambition was to embody the vocation of Israel to be the spearhead-ing movement of world transformation. Gradually, from the time he was a bright-eyed child in the synagogue of Nazareth hearing the texts about Jewish and world history being read aloud, their meaning began rushing together in his mind. Operation Genesis would be accomplished as in-tended by the divine strategy of his Eternal Father: by working through free humans. Yet this project would be achieved through one human — himself — cooperating through maximal self-sacrificing love with the Eternal Father's designs, in the power of the Creator-Spirit acting in his humanness.

But how to accomplish world transformation? By recapitulating — literally, by "re-heading" — the human race, Jesus as the God-Man replayed over again the history of humanity and the history of each human. Why? In order to make all humans into what they should have become. In order to reverse all the deadly, dehumanizing, destructive forces that had taken control of the world at the Fall. In order to re-begin history and humanity through himself. As the German theologian Albert Schweitzer (1875–1965) remarked, the God-Man threw himself "on the wheel of world history, so that, even though it crushed him, it might start to turn in the opposite direction."[8]

He would be Adam — the "last Adam" (1 Cor 15:45) — in the sense that he would become what the first Adam was meant to become: the fully human human because "in him there is no sin" (1 Jn 3:5). He would not "miss the mark" in his lifestyle.[9] "Miss the mark" is the literal meaning of the Greek term most frequently used for sin in the New Testament, *hamartia*. He would live a fully human existence because, as a transparent image of his Eternal Father on Planet Earth, he would live a fully relational lifestyle. Relationality is the meaning of the term *righteousness* so often used to describe the Creator and the greatest men and women in the Bible. To be righteous is to relate rightly to all dimensions of reality. Jesus connected sublimely with his beloved Father, "Abba" (Mk 14:36), with his awe-inspiringly beautiful mother, she who was "full of grace" (Lk 1:28), with his foster-father, the noble Joseph, and with all the women, men, and children he encountered in his journey through life. He was fully relational because his heart beat to the rhythm of self-sacrificing love, reflecting perfectly the love ceaselessly flowing between the three Persons of the Blessed Trinity.

He would be Abraham because, through his Mystical Body, the Church, his Eternal Father's promise to the patriarch (that his descendants would be as many as the stars in the sky; Gn 26:4) would be fulfilled. He would be Moses, liberating his people from the demonic forces behind the empires of this world.

In order to achieve this, he knew that he had to fulfill the human vocation in his own bodymind through the seasons of his life. He had to pass through all the stages of human existence from embryo to baby, child, teenager, and mature man. He had to take into his own bodymind all the human experiences meant to humanize us — from wonder to perplexity, joy to pain, fatigue to ecstasy — in order to raise them qualitatively to the maximal human level, the superhuman.

Just as he would be Adam, Abraham, and Moses, he would also be you, in order to raise your life to maximal humanness. He intended to recapitulate not only human history but your entire life — all the stages of your existence and all your longings, failures, successes, hopes, and actions — bringing everything to fulfillment. His final shout, "It is finished" (Jn 19:30), will be true in your own life, bringing about your true human greatness, if you unite your "yes" to his "Into your hands I commit my spirit" (Lk 23:46). Through him, with him, and in him, all that is summed up by the biblical notion of death — failures, heartaches, betrayals, pain, physical death — will be taken up by him through his passion into a new reconfiguring of all that constitutes your life. Failures, tragedies, pain, and even death will become gateways for triumph. Then, in the final era on the heavenized Planet Earth, the victory will spread through your complete bodymind. Therefore, nothing of value in your life will be lost. He will rescue all: "Behold, I make all things new" (Rv 21:5)!

The new human-divine synthesis, however, did not occur peaceably but through a violent, dramatic conflict that would reach its peak of fury on that Friday. Then and there, all the drama of world history rushed together, from, as Joseph de Maistre described it, "the day the days were born" to the final day.[10] On Golgotha, "the place of the skull" (Mt 27:33), Jesus resolved to empower each individual who would rely on him to bring to fulfillment the story of his life. It is understandable therefore that the Great Deceiver ("Satan, the deceiver of the whole world," Rv 12:9) and his pawns should unleash all their strength during this event. He who had whispered dehumanizing urges to the first humans by tempting them to distrust the Creator's goodness now appeared in Gethsemane, the Roman law court, and on Calvary. But this time it was with the accumulated power he had amassed through the millennia by means of humans giving him influence through idolatry. Through his puppets of Roman politicians and Judaean aristocrats and priests, he was able to inflict death on this mysterious individual threatening his dominion as the "ruler of this world" (Jn 12:31). Death — his ultimate weapon for controlling people. Death in the biblical worldview is not only physical decomposition but the symbol of all the demonic, dehumanizing, disintegrating forces in the cosmos. It has ever been the favorite weapon of tyrants seeking to create anti-God societies because, for those humans who are not "in Christ" (2 Cor 5:17), death seems to be the final end.

Yet the demonic strategy failed that Friday afternoon. The man hanging on that gibbet was not doing so passively but passionately. As the ever-so-stretched moments succeeded each other beneath the burning sun, he was actively taking all the chaotic, deadly power of all of history into his every thought and desire. Within his psyche, all the dehumanizing deadliness, chaos, and destruction from "the world rulers of this present darkness" (Eph 6:12) that ever had been or ever would be were transfigured by an unprecedented, unimaginable, passionately self-sacrificing love. By completely opening his humanness to the vitality pulsating within the Trinity, his humanness was deified, "in-godded."[11] The outcome was the maximal transformation of humanness. In it all the fallout from the Fall could no longer find a place. A new type of vitality that the world had never before experienced had birthed a radically new type of human. The "New Man" (Eph 2:15; 4:24), God's dream for every human, had finally appeared on Earth.

What began in his psyche on that Friday afternoon would become visible in his body three days later. His new bodymind was still human, but it was superhuman, indestructible, light-filled, energized beyond our imagination, beautified beyond our expectations. It was a mind in which all the powers of the left brain and right brain became fully activated for creativity because now all the connections are seen and lived: between Heaven and Earth, nature and nature's Author, self and others, 24/7 time and eternity's "time." What was occurring silently, invisibly in the underground of history that Friday afternoon became public news, visible, tangible, and explosive, two days later. And its explosive, bodymind-transfiguring power has been resounding through the millennia in all those who have bonded themselves to him through his Mystical Body, the Church.

Jesus could bring about the synthesis of the human-divine by summing up in himself the entire sweep of world history because, as one of his greatest followers wrote under the inspiration of the Spirit:

He is the image of the invisible God, the first-born of all creation; for in him all things were created, in heaven and on earth, visible and invisible, whether thrones or dominions or princi-palities or authorities — all things were created through him and for him. He is before all things, and in him all things hold together. He is the head of the body, the Church; he is the begin-ning, the first-born from the dead, that in everything he might be pre-eminent. For in him all the fullness of God was pleased to dwell, and through him to reconcile to himself all things, wheth-er on earth or in heaven, making peace by the blood of his cross. (Colossians 1:15–20)

This colossal truth impacts us more powerfully when we experience it through the reactions of characters amid the intuitive and emotional landscape of a story. There is a scene in C. S. Lewis's *The Lion, the Witch, and the Wardrobe* where Susan and Lucy are "walking aimlessly" after wit-nessing the horrendous execution of the Christ-figure, Aslan:[12]

The Stone Table was broken into two pieces by a great crack that ran down it from end to end; and there was no Aslan.

"Who's done it?" cried Susan. "What does it mean? Is it more magic?"

"Yes!" said a great voice from behind their backs. "It is more magic." They looked round. There, shining in the sunrise, larger than they had seen him before … stood Aslan himself. …

"But what does it all mean?" asked Susan when they were somewhat calmer.

"It means," said Aslan, "that though the Witch knew the Deep Magic, there is a magic deeper still which she did not know. Her knowledge goes back only to the dawn of time. But if she could have looked a little further back, into the stillness and the dark-ness before Time dawned, she would have read there a different incantation. She would have known that when a willing victim who had committed no treachery was killed in a traitor's stead, the Table would crack and Death itself would start working backward."[13]

V for Victory

That Friday afternoon, Operation Genesis was brought to fulfillment, even if in a most shocking way. It even strikes the modern mind as weird, because it does not fit with modernity's "god": the all-powerful, distant, disinterested, loner deity. But it is not weird for those who know the True God, the Living God, the Creator-Lover-Rescuer who is Trinity and therefore quintessentially Love. When we consider the passion and death of the Incarnate Son of God in its biblical context, the cataracts of modernity's fracturing, rupturing, disintegrating worldview begin to fall from our eyes. As we listen in on the conversation on the road to Emmaus, our hearts too begin to burn (see Lk 24:32) because a revolution is occurring in our minds. Listening to this dialogue will change us, if we let it. It will change our mental home, pulling us out of the walls built by the story of the world of modernity and placing us within the story of Jesus, whose beginnings are from before the day the days began unto the endless day of the new world that he will establish after the world's last night.

As we listen to Jesus walking with the two men amid the cool of the evening, we sense Yahweh walking again among humans as in Eden. Through the deep meaning of that conversation, we hear him say to us that he is the first and the last, the beginning and the end; that all times are his; that he is the designer of the cosmos who keeps it functioning; that he is its ultimate goal; that in him the history of the world has reached the conclusion it had been searching for.

The final book of the Bible, Revelation, confirms through its report of the visions of John on the Mediterranean island of Patmos that the Messianic expectations had been fulfilled in Jesus. Jesus (Yeshua or "Rescuer") was the *Mashiach* (Messiah), the anointed, freedom-fighting, Davidic, royal personage who had emerged victorious from the struggle with the demonic forces on that bloody Friday. By his passionate struggle, he had inaugurated the new and definitive exodus liberation journey from enemy-occupied territory. He had constituted "a chosen race, a royal priesthood, a holy nation, God's own people" (1 Pt 2:9) around himself. He was leading the way as the new pillar of fire (see Ex 13:21) to the definitive promised land of which the land of Israel was the advance signpost: the heavenized Planet Earth. On Patmos, John glimpsed this promised land with its Sabbath time and its atmosphere of utter freedom in which all the deadly, dehumanizing forces will be noticeable by their absence. In Revelation 22 we see the bookend matching the other bookend of Genesis 1. The Creator-Lover's project of a world transformed into a homeland by humans acting as divine image-bearers has been accomplished by the perfect human and all those who have bonded themselves to him in his Mystical Body.

How can you and I experience the passionate certainty that all our restless searching for meaning and joy can find its answer in this knowledge? The proposal of C. S. Lewis is helpful:

> Supposing you had before you a manuscript of some great work, either a symphony or a novel. There then comes to you a person, saying, "Here is a new bit of the manuscript that I found; it is the central passage of that symphony, or the central chapter of that novel. The text is incomplete without it. I have got the missing passage which is really the center of the whole work." The only thing you could do would be to put this new piece of the manuscript in that central position, and then see how it reacted on the whole of the rest of the work. If it constantly brought out new meanings from the whole of the rest of the work, if it made you notice things in the rest of the work which you had not noticed before, then I think you would decide that it was authentic. On the other hand, if it failed to do that, then, however attractive it was in itself, you would reject it. Now, what is the missing chapter in this case, the chapter which Christians are offering? The story of the Incarnation. … If I accept this supposed missing chapter, the Incarnation, I find it begins to illuminate the whole of the rest of the manuscript.[14]

We cannot forget that Jesus utters the mysterious words, "Behold, I make all things new" (Rv 21:5). All things! Operation Genesis is world transformation. It is not a matter of only rescuing individual humans for an otherworldly "Heaven" but of inaugurating a heavenized Earth. That is now possible because the Rescuer of the planet is the One who "is before all things, and in him all things hold together" (Col 1:17). Thus all the ruptures in relationships, so evident in modernity, can be restored through him, with him, and in him. For he is the One through whom all things came to be, who makes the cosmos a *uni*verse, a unified reality. Thus we too can make our own the exultant shout of Saint Paul: "Indeed I count everything as loss because of the surpassing worth of knowing Christ Jesus my Lord. For his sake I have suffered the loss of all things, and count them as refuse, in order that I may gain Christ" (Phil 3:8). And "far be it from me to glory except in the cross of our Lord Jesus Christ" (Gal 6:14).

CHAPTER 12

YOU ARE A SHADOW OF YOUR FUTURE SELF

I do not want to die — no; I neither want to die nor do I want to want to die; I want to live for ever and ever and ever. I want this "I" to live — this poor "I" that I am and that I feel myself to be here and now, and therefore the problem of the duration of my soul, of my own soul, tortures me.

— *Miguel de Unamuno*, The Tragic Sense of Life

The Resurrection was about *body*!

At the resurrection of the dead, what will you experience in those first moments when you discover that you have a resurrected body? What will you feel? What will you think when you become stunningly aware that once again you are not merely a soul but have an intact body? And that with this body your Creator-Lover-Rescuer wants you to live *forever*?

This forever existence, "eternal life," refers only secondarily to quantity of time. Its primary meaning is quality of life. As a participation in the vitality of the Creator who authored everything that is alive and beautiful, this "eternal life" will be experienced as a thrilling explosion of vitality, empowering a crescendo of joy, creativity, and ever-intensifying fulfillment. During this mortal existence, you begin to faintly experience eternal life in rare and brief moments of ecstasy (from the Greek *ékstasis*, "outside of oneself"), provoked by the total involvement of your entire psyche in a reality that so fulfills your deepest longings that you lose consciousness of everything else. This can occur in a romantic relationship, amid a scenic landscape, under a starry sky, and, most sublimely and deeply, in prayer. This quality of life is why Jesus lived, died, and rose: "I came that they may have life, and have it abundantly" (Jn 10:10). He stated its cause: "And this is eternal life, that they know you the only true God, and Jesus Christ whom you have sent" (Jn 17:3). It is about the whole you — and that includes your body!

There is a text in the Gospel of John with an apparently insignificant detail that gives us an insight into this experience. The author describes his arrival with Peter to the tomb of Jesus: "They both ran, but the other disciple outran Peter and reached the tomb first; and stooping to look in, he saw the linen cloths lying there, but he did not go in. Then Simon Peter came, following him, and went into the tomb; he saw the linen cloths lying, and the napkin, which had been on his head, not lying with the linen cloths but rolled up in a place by itself" (Jn 20:4–7).

The mention of the rolled-up cloth that had been around his head is a curious detail to include when describing the most important event that ever occurred in world history. Why bother referring to a cloth and even add the detail that it was folded "in a place by itself" (Jn 20:7)? If we allow ourselves to ponder these words which, after all, are divinely inspired, we can come to the awareness that what at first glance seems trifling is most revealing. It becomes a window through which we understand the gritty, earthy humanness of the resurrected God-Man.

He folded the cloths.

Read that again: He. Folded. The. Cloths.

Let us try to imagine the scene.

We picture him lying lifeless in the tomb after the agonizing tortures he had experienced on the previous Friday afternoon. And then, at some point, we are startled as we see his body responding to a completely new vitality surging from within the depths of his being, indeed, from the source of all life: the Eternal Triune Creator.

He stirs; he takes a breath; his heart begins to beat; his eyes open. Color and suppleness return to his flesh. His hands touch his limbs. His large and beautiful eyes, so noticed by his contemporaries and so evident on the Shroud of Turin, flicker. He feels himself breathing. With one of his hands, he pulls off the cloth covering his face. He raises his head. Then his upper body. He removes the linen cloths covering the rest of his body. He stands.

But what was the first action of this resurrected body? It was — most perplexingly — to fold the linen cloth that had covered his head and to place it apart inside the cave that had been his tomb.

Think how absurdly out of place this is. At this dramatic moment, when death and all the deadly forces in the universe have been conquered, what does the conqueror decide to do? How did he mark the moment in which the history of the human race stopped — abruptly — and headed in the opposite direction?

He folded cloths! The simplest and plainest thing imaginable. Those hands of his, still in some mysterious way displaying scars from the previous Friday, were first employed in a simple household task: folding a kerchief. Probably something he had learned as a young kid from that sublime mother of his. If we ponder this fact, we will see how utterly, totally, radically, integrally human the resurrected Jesus was — and is.

He did not leave behind his humanness at the Resurrection. Rather, it is in the Resurrection that everything that makes him human is now harmoniously united to his divinity and to the eternal Trinity, for endless ages. This includes every experience of his thirty-three years of earthly existence: his relationships, the imprints of each moment of his existence, and the DNA received from his mother in which is found also that of her Jewish forefathers through the royal bloodline of King David. Everything that connects him with us mortals — the power to laugh, rejoice, weep, agonize, empathize, feel wonder, and exercise compassion — is mysteriously preserved *forever*.

Waking Up in a Resurrected Bodymind

Now let us imagine another scene: your resurrection.

What will you feel that first moment as you become aware that your body — with all its joints and arteries, with its skin, hair, muscles, legs, hands, feet, eyes — is all yours once again? What will it feel like to rub your eyes and rediscover yourself as not merely a soul, a ghostlike reality, but a complete body?

You feel your bones and muscles; you touch the skin on your face; you experience your body pulsating with life. Stunned, you detect an energy and dynamism throbbing inside you that you never experienced during your mortal life — not even in the rollicking days of your teens and twenties. What will it be like to become aware of having an intelligence vibrating with intensity, intuitiveness, and speed of reasoning? Of having a startling energy for action? And then to be struck with the awareness that you are going to live for unending years in a crescendo of vitality?

But wait! This is not just about you. For you are going to rediscover others like you all around. Real people full of vim, with vivacious smiles and eyes aglow. Among them, others whom you knew and loved in your previous life, each of them with their quirky traits that made them unique, whether a sure-footed walk, a leonine poise, a craggy jaw, a falcon's nose, raven-black hair, come-hither eyes, or a nightingale's voice.

And as you gaze around, dazzled by the wonder of it all and afire with passion to discover, you find a transformed landscape, seascape, and skyscape. You feel your skin tingle with cool summer breezes wafting in from the ocean. You are mesmerized by the light from the claret-red sun that bathes the meadows where the cows are calmly masticating. You gaze on the foals nuzzling. You hear grown horses neighing and, a moment later, hear the intoning of the bumblebees. The soul-lulling smell of the sweet honeysuckle surrounds you. Far above you, an eagle soars in majestic arcs. In the evening, a wondrous sunset. The night brings shafts of moonlight poured onto a mountain lake. In the distance you hear the purring call of the barn owl, and beneath your bare feet feel the velvety touch of the jasper-green grass.

You recognize everything. It's like what you knew in your embryonic life in the embryonic universe. However, it is also different, for it is sublimely more splendid, radiant, and — how can I express it? — beautiful beyond beauty.

There is another question you can ask at this point: "What will I do on this heavenized Planet Earth?" Perhaps — in order to get a more incisive answer — you might ask, "What will I do after my first million years?" But to find an answer, you should first move around the new Heaven and new Earth (see Rv 21:1), which is now your home. As you do so, you begin to discover the answer. This will be the great, unending adventure, going from wonder to wonder, beauty to beauty, love to love, in a forever crescendo of thrilling excitement, joy, and fulfillment.

If you will let him have his way, this is what the Creator-Lover-Rescuer intends. As C. S. Lewis remarked: "All your life an unattainable ecstasy has hovered just beyond the grasp of your consciousness. The day is coming when you will wake to find, beyond all hope, that you have attained it, or else, that it was within your reach and you have lost it forever."[1]

Seeing the Big Picture

The God-Man has disclosed the nature of our future life so that we might inaugurate that future existence here and now. Indeed, as we shall see, the description of life given to John on the island of Patmos as narrated in chapters 21 and 22 of the Book of Revelation is not only about the future but about the present invaded by the future. It is a divine disclosure given for the sake of making us think and live futuristically. This is because the term *life* in both the Book of Revelation and John's Gospel refers to the radically new quality of life as already present in the psyche of those who have bonded themselves to Jesus. We can already experience the beginnings of the divine vitality that will thrill us to our depths in the forever-future.

John, exiled to the island of Patmos around the year AD 95 by the Roman emperor Domitian, describes the beginning of his momentous vision of the final outcome of world history as follows: "I was in the Spirit on the Lord's day, and I heard behind me a loud voice like a trumpet saying, 'Write what you see in a book'" (Rv 1:10–11). Turning to find the source of the voice, he is brought into the presence of Jesus whom he had once seen pain-filled on a cross but now sees in the grandeur of his cosmic power:

> One like a Son of man, clothed with a long robe and with a golden sash across his chest; his head and his hair were white as white wool, white as snow; his eyes were like a flame of fire, his feet were like burnished bronze, refined as in a furnace, and his voice was like the sound of many waters; in his right hand he held seven stars, from his mouth issued a sharp two-edged sword, and his face was like the sun shining in full strength. (Revelation 1:13–16)

When Jesus addresses John, it is as the Lord of History: "I am the first and the last, and the living one; I died, and behold I am alive for evermore, and I have the keys of Death and Hades" (Rv 1:17–18). His reason for appearing to John is to disclose the deep meaning of time and, within it, of each individual's lifetime. In a subsequent vision, the Triune God confirms that the purpose of the revelations is to glimpse the big picture of history through the mind of the Lord of History: "I am the Alpha and the Omega, the beginning and the end" (Rv. 21:6). As the biblical scholar G. K. Beale notes: "Use of the first and last letters of the alphabet was an ancient figure of speech for the totality of everything in between."[2] Jesus, through whom time had been cocreated with the universe, is he who through his passion will bring the universe to its fulfillment. But now, as Peter J. Leithart, a leading contemporary theologian, states, he discloses his identity within the Trinity:

> The singular name is elaborated as the triple name of the Triune God. As Father, God is [the "I am who am"] *ego eimi*; as Word, God is the first and last letter of creation's alphabet; as Spirit, God is the creative source of the beginning and all beginnings,

the headsprings from which everything flows, the end toward
which everything moves, the power that ensures that all that is
flows from source to destination.[3]

John is seeing the final outcome of history and of Planet Earth because
of the lifetime's work of the Incarnate Second Person of the Trinity. This
is made clear by the God-Man's words to him: "And he said to me, 'It is
done!'" (Rv 21:6). The shout at the end of history is the same shout, "It
is finished" (Jn 19:30), at the climax of history, at three o'clock in the
afternoon on that Friday. This, in turn, echoes the Creator's inaugural
completion of the universe at the beginning of history (see Gn 2:1–3).
Stunningly, the making new of all things has come about through Jesus'
passionately lived passion. Through his wounds, the universe has been
healed; his pains were the birth pangs of a new world order. The visions
make this clear to John, as he repeatedly sees Jesus, "the Lamb" — the
self-sacrificing victim. The cosmic rescue operation originates "from the
throne of God and of the Lamb" (Rv 22:1).

The climax of the vision is narrated in chapters 21 and 22: "Then I
saw a new heaven and a new earth; for the first heaven and the first earth
had passed away, and the sea was no more. And I saw the holy city, new
Jerusalem, coming down out of heaven from God, prepared as a bride
adorned for her husband" (Rv 21:1–2). If John had been perplexed as to
the purpose of this city from Heaven coming to Planet Earth, he soon
received the explanation:

> I heard a great voice from the throne saying, "Behold, the dwell-
> ing of God is with men. He will dwell with them, and they shall
> be his people, and God himself will be with them; he will wipe
> away every tear from their eyes, and death shall be no more, nei-
> ther shall there be mourning nor crying nor pain any more, for
> the former things have passed away."
>
> And he who sat upon the throne said, "Behold, I make all
> things new." Also he said, "Write this, for these words are trust-
> worthy and true." And he said to me, "It is done! I am the Alpha
> and the Omega, the beginning and the end. To the thirsty I will

give water without price from the fountain of the water of life.
He who conquers shall have this heritage, and I will be his God
and he shall be my son. (Revelation 21:3–7)

All becomes clear in John's mind: Operation Genesis is now fulfilled. All
of Jewish history, and therefore world history, has reached its goal.

But it's not clear for us. We moderns are startled by this description.
Heaven on Earth? This is not what we were expecting. And, moreover, a
city, a civilization? This is certainly not how we imagine Paradise!

First, we must try to get our heads around the fact that the Creator
intends to heavenize Planet Earth — yes, the biosphere, and not just humans. I can empathize with your astonishment. We moderns don't think
of the end of history in this way. Our imagination is of an otherworldly, ethereal, "spiritual" hereafter with Earth thrown on the junk heap of
history. We plan on going "upwards" to Heaven, abandoning the ship
of this world. Far from our thoughts is what John describes: "the holy
city Jerusalem coming down out of heaven from God" (Rv 21:10), a fact
which he repeats in Revelation 22 to make sure we get the message. Even
the visionary was apparently so hurled into numbing perplexity by what
he saw that the angel had to assure him that what he was viewing was
reliable (see Rv 21:5) and to urge him to start writing (Rv 1:19).

Our personal destination is the heavenized Earth via Heaven. Although in the intermediate state between our death and the Second
Coming of Jesus, God's plan is for us to "go up to" Heaven, this is not the
final place of arrival. It will be a stopover. Heaven at the end of history
will be amalgamated with Planet Earth, utterly transforming it. Therefore, salvation is, as N. T. Wright explains it, "not rescue from the present
world, but rescue and renewal within the present world."[4]

This completely rocks our sense of life's meaning. We begin to feel
at home in ourselves because we now recognize Earth as our homeland.
There is no longer a divide between "spiritual" and "material," "religion"
and "reality," my longings and God's longings. There is no longer a split
between our life's time and eternity because if we are living in closeness
to Jesus, we have begun our eternity! Therefore, death is but a doorway;
it has lost its power to terrify us. Our Creator-Lover-Rescuer wants us to

bond forever with him through *this* world, *this* life, *this* time. He wants us to use all our energies to make the ambitious prayer, "Thy Kingdom come, thy will be done *on Earth as it is in Heaven*" a reality. We begin to live futuristically, excited to create advance signposts of the type of life and society that will one day exist in the heavenized world. With the intensity and passion of pioneering frontiersmen and women, we aim to heavenize everything around us. A thrilling sense of meaning and mission spreads through all our thinking, relationships, careers, even hobbies. Every moment is purposeful. Everything matters. Every person matters. Every thought, word, and action has value — a value that will endure forever.

The upcoming chapters will unpack with theological and philosophical reasoning why this experience resonates with both the story of world history narrated in the divinely inspired texts and with the deepest longings of our psyche. Finally, we will see why the realities of civilization, culture, community, friendships, and creativity are integral to what the Bible means by *Heaven* and in harmony with what Catholicism states about the beatific vision.

CHAPTER 13

THE HEAVENIZED PLANET EARTH

*At the end of time, the Kingdom of God will come in its fullness.
After the universal judgment, the righteous will reign for ever
with Christ, glorified in body and soul. The universe itself will
be renewed: "The Church ... will receive her perfection only in
the glory of heaven, when will come the time of the renewal of all
things. At that time, together with the human race, the universe
itself, which is so closely related to man and which attains its
destiny through him, will be perfectly re-established in Christ."*

— *Catechism of the Catholic Church*, 1042

How can we be sure that this heavenizing of Earth is the divine plan?
The complex answer is that the final book in the Bible, through
its symbolic language, provides us with the big picture of world histo-

ry through the lens of the Jewish saga. In this optic we see that in the Creator's design, history is a movement directed to world renewal. If we moderns find this vision bizarre, it is not because there is anything impossible about it. It is because we ponder it through our fogged modern "glasses."

John, after his initial perplexity, knew that the vision was indeed reliable because it confirmed his Jewish worldview, as we will unpack in this chapter. Revelation 21–22 synthesizes the biblical worldview. The vision narrated in the Book of Revelation is not unprecedented in Jewish history. If it stuns us as new, it is because its newness is that of a synthesis and not of sheer novelty. Its images and words can be heard in the echo chamber of the entire Bible, from Genesis to Malachi. When John tells us that he saw a "new heaven and a new earth" (21:1), his Jewish listeners would immediately have heard echoes of the great worldwide renewal prophesied in Isaiah 65:17–25 and 66:9–22. It was a vision that fitted into the panoramic view of history that had been progressively revealed to the Jewish people over the millennia.[1] It thundered or whispered, even if mysteriously, in page after page of the sacred texts and in event after event, institution upon institution, and, not least, in prayer upon prayer. It was a vision of the final outcome of history that fulfilled the patterns encoded in nature and in the human bodymind. It confirmed those patterns disclosed by the Creator: Temple, land, and Kingdom of God. Through the rhythms of Sabbath and the motifs of exile, exodus, and Passover, John heard an ongoing, steady, repetitive beat, melodies and movements pointing to a unity in the vast complex movements of history and of human longings.

In the consciousness of the Jewish mind, especially from the sixth century BC when they had suffered the catastrophe of exile to Babylon, there was a deeply held conviction that their story as a nation — and therefore that of the entire world — was, as N. T. Wright expresses it, "a story in search of a conclusion."[2] It was a colossal, unfinished symphony awaiting a grand finale in which all its movements would converge. This story was a story about Planet Earth and everyone and everything on it. Communicating through the great intellectual leaders of Israel, the prophets, Yahweh had disclosed this final status of the Planet: "For behold, I create new heavens and a new earth; / and the former things shall not be remembered or come into mind. / But be glad and rejoice for ever in that which I create; / for behold, I create Jerusalem a rejoicing, and her people a joy. / I will rejoice in Jerusalem, and be glad in my people; / no more shall be heard in it the sound of weeping and the cry of distress" (Is 65:17–19).

But how are Earth and the spacetime cosmos to be transfigured? The Jewish mind had a vision of history as made up of two eras: the era of the millennia in which they were living, and a future endtime era in which all that is wrong with the world would be put right because God's sovereignty would be practically acknowledged by humans in the way they live their lives. This would be the way nature herself and the entire world would be brought to perfection. Planet Earth was to be mysteriously reshaped and renewed on the model of primeval Eden.

In the Jewish mind, the destiny of the world and the strategy for achieving it were intimately connected. The final victory would occur through the Jewish people because they were Yahweh's Chosen Nation, his spearheading movement for world renewal. Their understanding of how past, present, and future are interconnected kept them alert to this. By contrast, for us moderns, the past is of little interest. But for the Jews and the first Christians, the future could be read through the past. Like rowers who row forward by looking back, so they made their personal and national decisions in the light of past events. They understood that, as Peter J. Leithart states, "God can write with events and people and things as well as words, and the pattern of history itself is meaningful, full of foreshadowings, ironies, repetitions, analogies."[3] Thus they were alert to the providential patterns of exodus, exile, kingship, and Temple recorded in their sacred texts.

Land, especially the land of Israel, was one of the leitmotifs, a recurrent theme throughout the narrative, one that was pregnant with meaning for past, present, and future. For it was in their land that the Creator was intensively active in two ways: first, through the Temple, the scale model of the world; second, through the Sabbath, the rhythm of time that would exist in the forever-future. Indeed, they knew that Yahweh had given them the "promised land" (see Gn 12:7) for the sake of their mission. The land was a function of their vocation to fulfill the human vocation to image the Creator in lifestyle, culture, and civilization, and to expand the sacralizing of the land to the four corners of Planet Earth. As G. K. Beale notes:

> The land of promise, the land of Israel, was repeatedly called the "Garden of Eden" (cf. Gen 13:10; Isa 51:3; Joel 2:3; Ezek 36:35) partly perhaps because Israel was to expand the limits of the temple and of their own land to the ends of the earth in the same manner as should have Adam. That this was Israel's ultimate task is apparent from a number of OT passages prophesying that God will finally cause the sacred precinct of Israel's temple to expand and first encompass Jerusalem (see Isaiah 4:4–6; 54:2–3, 11–12; Jer 3:16–17; Zech 1:16–2:11), then the entire land of Israel (Ezek 37:25–28), and then the whole earth (Dan 2:34–35, 44–45; cf. also Isaiah 54:2–3).[4]

But by the first century AD, Jews knew, whether clearly or vaguely, that they themselves — whose mission was to rescue humanity — were in need of rescue. This recognition took the shape of a storyline in which they sensed themselves to be in exile. *Exile* was a loaded word for the Jewish mind. Indeed, they viewed the existential situation of humanity as a state of banishment from Eden, the paradigm of an integral, fully human existence in an ecological world. The word also provoked bitter memories of their time in Egypt and Babylon. The latter exile had partly come to an end in 538 BC, when the Persian ruler had allowed them to return to their homeland. But it was an incomplete restoration for two reasons: first, because only a remnant had made the journey home; second, because they remained under the political authority of Persia, and, in subsequent centuries (with only a brief interval), of the empires created by Alexander the Great and Rome.

When the Jews sought to understand how they, the Creator's Chosen People and the object of so many promises, could be in so humiliating a situation, they came up with a clear answer: sin. This sounds strange to our modern ears. For us, sin is a private matter without sociopolitical implications. But sin for the Jewish people was about betraying their vocation and mission to be world rescuers, the spearheading movement that would restore an Edenic existence on Planet Earth. Moses had made this clear to them more than a millennium earlier in his thundered final message to the nation before his death (see Dt 31).

The term most commonly associated with *sin* in both the Septuagint Greek version of the Old Testament and in the New Testament writings is the word group *hamartanō* (the verb "to sin") along with *hamartia* (the noun "sin") and *hamartōlos* (a "sinner"). These are the default Greek translations for the Hebrew terms in the Septuagint form of the Old Testament, where they appear 526 times. In the New Testament, the term appears 163 times.[5] Its root meaning is "to miss the mark," as in an arrow missing a target.

By the time Jesus was beginning his mission, this consciousness of the need for a Messianic liberator who would rescue them from being off target as a nation was at fever pitch. This was largely due to a prophecy in the Book of Daniel, which laid out a time clock:

> Seventy weeks of years are decreed concerning your people and your holy city, to finish the transgression, to put an end to sin, and to atone for iniquity, to bring in everlasting righteousness, to seal both vision and prophet, and to anoint a most holy place. Know therefore and understand that from the going forth of the word to restore and build Jerusalem to the coming of an anointed one, a prince, there shall be seven weeks. Then for sixty-two weeks it shall be built again with squares and moat, but in a troubled time. (9:24–25)

Seventy "sevens" is generally understood as seventy "weeks" of years, a period of 490 years. The prophecy then divides the 490 years into three units: one of forty-nine years, one of 434 years, and one of seven years. The first 483 years are generally calculated as beginning with the decree of King Artaxerxes I to rebuild Jerusalem (in 457 BC or thereabouts). Counting 483 years from 457 BC brings us to AD 27 (keeping in mind that because there is no year 0, we must add one year to the calculation). This brings us to the years of the Messianic campaigning of Jesus. His contemporaries were clearly aware of this timeline, as can be seen in several ways: in the movement of the Essenes, who believed themselves to be the faithful remnant who would spearhead the establishment of God's Kingdom, in the enthusiasm with which the crowds went to John the Baptist to be baptized in preparation for the Messiah's coming, and, somewhat later, in the violent revolt of AD 66. New Testament texts also point to this awareness in various individuals. In Luke 2, Simeon and Anna express their intense expectation for the restoration of Jerusalem and the ending of Israel's wretched sociopolitical-spiritual status. In John 1:41, Andrew goes to find his brother Simon and tells him, "We have found the Messiah," the Promised One. In Acts 1:6, the inner circle of Jesus asks the question foremost on their minds: "Lord, will you at this time restore the kingdom to Israel?'"

The Kingdom of God as a New World Order

As the Jewish people listened in their synagogues each week to the sacred texts, even the structure of the collection as it was organized in the first century pointed to their story as unfinished. The last book, the Book of Chronicles, in its narrative of the reign of King David, the symbol of the ideal Jewish political leader, subtly invited the Jews to long for the Messiah who would be his descendant.[6] This David-like personality, a liberating, royal personality, would bring about the forgiveness of sins and so end the exile. He would inaugurate national sovereignty and restore the land to the people, establishing a new era, the Sabbath era, in which Yahweh would be fully present and intensively active from the Temple, reigning over Israel and, eventually, through Israel, as "king over all the earth" (Zec 14:9). All the great symbols of Jewish national identity, world mission, and lifestyle resounded in their hearts as a cry for the inauguration of the Kingdom of God.[7]

We cannot emphasize enough the importance of this term, the *Kingdom of God*. If you were to pick one biblical concept to sum up what the entire Bible is about and what Jesus intended to achieve during his life's time in Israel, it would be the establishment of this Kingdom.

For the Jews, the Creator God by his omnipotence was the lord of the universe. But his lordship was not recognized outside of the frontiers of the tiny Jewish nation. Instead, idol worship reigned among the empires and kingdoms. The mission of the Jewish nation was therefore to bring about the universal reign of the Creator God among the nations of the world: to be a Kingdom of God movement. This would not be a coercive "Big State" as in Assyria, Babylon, and Egypt, but rather, as Scott Hahn states, a "liturgical empire" in which all the nations would acknowledge the Living God by coming to worship him in his Temple in Jerusalem and by obeying the Decalogue (Ten Commandments) — the laws that foster wisdom and a fully human lifestyle.[8]

The Kingdom of God was therefore going to be a kingdom for this world, for Planet Earth. Jesus said as much when he told Pontius Pilate that he most certainly was a royal figure with a kingdom, even if it was not from this world. His Kingdom did not originate in the patterns of thinking of the present era dominated by the "ruler of this world" (Jn 12:31), and it did not operate by the coercive methods of world empires like Rome. It was a counter-empire, a counter-civilization with a counterculture. But, most emphatically, it was about inaugurating a new type of society.[9] Implicit to the notion of kingdom is the notion of a social order, a political order, an economic system, a culture which, in a divine Kingdom, will consist of those things most favorable to human flourishing. This view of the Kingdom of God was the way the Jewish mind spontaneously connected its religion with reality. Unlike us moderns, the Jews thought holistically, treating everything as connected.

Because the establishment of the Kingdom of God was a political project, it was risk-laden. To struggle to inaugurate a nation under the rule of Yahweh implied the exclusion of other rulers, whether from Assyria, Babylon, Greece, or Rome. It also meant that even Jewish kings took second place; their role was to implement, interpret, and protect Yahweh's laws.

Constantly, the Bible speaks with what N. T. Wright calls "kingdom-of-God language."[10] Moreover, when we pray the words of the Lord's Prayer, "Thy kingdom come" (Mt 6:9–13), we are making a political statement. We are calling for a new world order that recognizes the rights of the Creator in every dimension of society. We are asserting that Jesus

Christ should be freely recognized as Lord by all humans. And we are also declaring that we will dedicate our lives to bring about this revolution.

The dramatic events of Jewish history throughout the millennia were the struggle to make this happen. For this goal the prophets spoke: to constantly recall to their compatriots, often at great personal sacrifice, that Yahweh must reign. This establishment of the Kingdom of Heaven was why the Second Person of the Blessed Trinity became human in Jesus. His three years of public life made this mission clear as they were a ceaseless campaigning, in word and symbolic action, for the inauguration of this Kingdom. In a sense, he acted like a subversive politician campaigning to inaugurate a new regime, as N. T. Wright argues:

> He called together a tight and symbolically-charged group of associates (in his world, the number twelve meant only one thing: the new Israel, the new people of God). And it wasn't very long before his closest followers told him that they thought he really was in charge, or ought to be. He was the king they'd all been waiting for. If we look for a parallel in today's world, we won't find it so much in the rise of a new "religious" teacher or leader as in the emergence of a charismatic, dynamic politician whose friends are encouraging him to run for president — and who gives every appearance of having what it takes to sort everything out when he gets there.[11]

Indeed, what we often consider to be his name is in reality his title, "Christ," which means Messiah, "anointed one," and, therefore, by implication, the royal descendant of King David. Thus, when we say, "Jesus Christ" we are saying, "King Yeshua," as Wright in his New Testament translation brings out.[12] To pronounce "Jesus Christ" is to name him as the ruler, legislator, and lord — who is lord of all or not at all.

If we were to sum up the entire story of Jesus' life on Planet Earth, we could do no better than to say it was all about, to borrow a phrase from Wright, "How God became King."[13] He fulfilled, even if in a most puzzling way to his contemporaries, the prophecies about the establishment of the Kingdom of God. He began his public campaigning with the clarion call: "The time is fulfilled, and the kingdom of God is at hand" (Mk 1:15). All his teaching was about the "Kingdom": "Jesus went about all the cities and villages, teaching in their synagogues and preaching the gospel of the kingdom" (Mt 9:35). Constantly, at great risk to his personal safety, he asserted that in his Person the Kingdom was being launched: "Today this Scripture has been fulfilled in your hearing" (Lk 4:21). It had been fulfilled not only in words but in symbolic actions. Jesus pointed to his miraculous actions as the fulfillment of the Messianic signs foretold centuries before by the prophets (see Mt 11: 4–5). He offered these signs as proof that he truly was "the coming one" (Heb 10:37).

Indeed, Jesus performed these healings and miracles, such as the multiplication of bread for the crowd, to give us advance signposts of a future transformed Planet Earth. By healing bodies, giving bread, giving importance to meals that were festive, and filling his teaching with references to landscapes, skyscapes, and seascapes, he was telling us that salvation is about all: all of you, your body and mind, and all of the biosphere. He showed himself opposed to everything that dehumanizes humans: not only sin but also sickness, pain, and death. Thus, he wept at the tomb of Lazarus. When a sick man beseeched him, "Lord, you have the power to heal me if you want," his reply was "I want to heal you. Be healed!" (see Lk 5:12–13).

If we straitjacket the mission of Jesus to the "spiritual," we misunderstand him just as some of his contemporaries did. For them, he was too earthly: He didn't fast enough, he drank wine, he accepted invitations to festivities, he was sensitive to the bodily needs of his apostles, and he was sociable with all who were not hypocrites. Of course, we know that he did fast (forty days in one session), he spent whole nights in prayer, and he worked to the point of exhausting his inner circle. But he emphatically showed that the body as well as the mind and the biosphere mattered to him.

For this reason, he entered into combat with the counter-Kingdom political powers of Rome, Herod, and the Temple elite who were dehumanizing the masses. However, to the dismay of all, he did so not directly but indirectly — by assaulting and triumphing over the powers behind these puppets: the idols, and behind them, Satan, as he showed by his exorcisms. All these words and gestures witnessed to the Kingdom of Heaven that the Jews were waiting for. For them, this was no otherworldly Heaven, but the land of Israel, their promised land, which they wanted to see completely liberated from alien domination.

Of course, Jesus went far beyond their expectations. He reconfigured them in a totally unexpected style. He conquered the anti-Kingdom forces in the most unpredictable of ways: by allowing the satanic powers and their pawns (Pilate, the Temple elite, and the mob) to use the ultimate weapons of all political tyrannies: torture and the death penalty. Jesus willingly underwent all, and thus conquered death itself, as his resurrected body confirmed. In this way, he reconstituted the twelve tribes of Israel as a Kingdom around the Twelve Apostles for the global mission of world transformation.[14] Therefore, in his Person was fulfilled the historic mission of the nation of Israel, even if in a most radically disconcerting way.

Even more puzzling to his inner circle was the strategy of a two-stage movement for the achieving of the new world order. Instead of fixing everything immediately, he continued with the Creator's non-coercive, wanting-to-work-through-humans policy. Beginning at the Ascension, he inaugurated the Kingdom of God movement with its universal ("catholic") mission: "Go therefore and make disciples of all nations, baptizing them in the name of the Father and of the Son and of the Holy Spirit" (Mt 28:19). Thus the Church is the spearheading movement for the inauguration of the Kingdom of God. As the human-divine synthesis, her mission is to create colonies with advance signposts of the future civilization throughout the world. Yes, indeed, we are all alert to the fact that the Church is filled with flawed humans. Nevertheless, in her innermost reality, she is the sublime, Mystical Body of the God-Man. To understand our mission, we will first turn our attention to the vision enlightening it: the description of life on the heavenized Planet Earth provided by the divine revelation given to John on Patmos.

CHAPTER 14

YOUR FOREVER HOME

Nature is not a place to visit. It is home.

— *Gary Snyder*, The Practice of the Wild

John, in his mystical vision on the island of Patmos, comes to the awareness that the fulfillment of the Creator's cosmic project will take the shape of an "in-Godded" civilization for human flourishing on Planet Earth:

> And in the Spirit he carried me away to a great, high mountain, and showed me the holy city Jerusalem coming down out of heaven from God, having the glory of God, its radiance like a most rare jewel, like a jasper, clear as crystal. It had a great, high wall, with twelve gates. … The city lies foursquare, its length the same as its breadth; and he measured the city with his rod, twelve thousand stadia; its length and breadth and height are equal. …

The wall was built of jasper, while the city was pure gold, clear as glass. The foundations of the wall of the city were adorned with every jewel. ... And the twelve gates were twelve pearls, each of the gates made of a single pearl, and the street of the city was pure gold, transparent as glass. And I saw no temple in the city, for its temple is the Lord God the Almighty and the Lamb. And the city has no need of sun or moon to shine upon it, for the glory of God is its light, and its lamp is the Lamb. By its light shall the nations walk; and the kings of the earth shall bring their glory into it, and its gates shall never be shut by day — and there shall be no night there; they shall bring into it the glory and the honor of the nations. (Revelation 21:10–12, 16, 18–19, 21–26)

The language of this description is symbolic language, which, however, refers to real-world realities. Such metaphorical language is the only adequate lingo for expressing multi-dimensional, complex, mysterious facts. Werner Heisenberg recognized that metaphors are also necessary for describing the subatomic level: "Quantum theory provides us with a striking illustration of the fact that we can fully understand a connection though we can only speak of it in images and parables."[1] The Creator who inspired these images in the Book of Revelation meant us to understand them according to the holistic, earthy, concrete mentality of the Jewish authors, and not according to our modern tendency to spiritualize, changing the concreteness of these images into abstractions that falsify them.

Metaphors and symbols are about the real. As Iain McGilchrist has noted, "Metaphor is the crucial aspect of language whereby it retains its connectedness to the world."[2] Modernity's privileging of scientific language, which has mathematics as its standard, reduces realities to one-dimensional things. Although excellent for explaining parts, math does a poor job at explaining wholes. In seeking to understand John's description of life on the heavenized Planet Earth, we need to abandon the left-brain, analytical thinking of modernity and instead use the ultramodern dual-hemisphere approach, utilizing both our right and left brain.

Above all, we must cease "spiritualizing" everything in the description into abstract notions. Life in Heaven is going to be earthy, concrete, sense-impacting, and palpable. To ensure we understand this, we need to read the text of Revelation with a professional historian's eyes. We must see with the first-century Jewish-Christian eyes of the inspired author and not through our modern eyes heavily influenced by centuries of "idealizing" the biblical message. If we can begin to see in this way, we will become futurists, excited about Heaven and energized to begin heavenizing ourselves and society here and now.

The first remarkable fact about the city in John's vision is its unprecedented size. Its base is about half the size of Europe. As biblical expert T. Desmond Alexander writes: "Its dimensions alone set it apart. Each side of its length, breadth, and height measures some 1,380 miles or 2,220 kilometers, far exceeding in size any known city, ancient or modern."[3] Second, it is a cosmopolitan city, insinuating that the future Planet Earth will be home to a global civilization. However, it will not be a homogenized, one-size-must-fit-all structure, but an atmosphere in which not only individuals but nations glory in their national grandeur while learning from each other's complementary diversity.

A "Green" Civilization[4]

Reading John's description, one immediately imagines a "green city": "Then he [the angel] showed me a river containing the water of life, bright as crystal, flowing from the throne of God and of the Lamb through the middle of the street of the city; also, on either side of the river, the tree of life with its twelve kinds of fruit, yielding its fruit each month; and the leaves of the tree were for the healing of the nations" (Rv 22:1–2). At this point in the description, Leithart states:

> We seem to move from city to countryside, as the angel shows John a river and an orchard. Yet this is clearly a continuation of the vision of the holy city. It has a street (22:2), like Jerusalem (21:21); the Lamb is in it, as he is in the city. … Yet the imagery changes. From chapter 21, we would not know that there was any living thing in the city other than human beings. It is all stone and metal, precious gems and gold. In the final stage of the

vision, we discover Jerusalem is a garden city, glorified Eden.[5]

This Eden contains a river of life-giving, crystalline waters and a tree of life as in the primeval Paradise, but now both are in the city center, on either side of the river. The Garden of Paradise has become Paradise City, a civilization so ecologically excellent that it brings healing to the nations of Planet Earth. All of nature is now joined harmoniously to all of human, artistic, scientific, and technological genius in a civilization that resembles a picturesque hamlet amid a nature preserve. All the nations, formerly in competition and conflict with each other and the biosphere, are now healed. The description points to an ecological civilization. As Alexander notes, the "New Jerusalem" is a "Garden City."[6] A garden is a magnificent metaphor because it is where we find the splendor of nature and the biosphere harmoniously united to the grandeur of culture — of humans fulfilling their mission as cocreators by cultivating the environment in such a way that an ecological civilization is birthed.

This vision of an ecological civilization is not suddenly sprung upon us in the last book of the Bible; rather, it had always been present in divine Revelation, as Leithart notes:

> John's final vision is of a city that looks a lot like Eden — tasty fruit, tree of life, water, purity (Rev 21:22—22:5). These aren't visions of a return to Eden. They're visions of a built-up Eden, an urban Eden, the world subdued so as to become a garden-city. … New Jerusalem isn't a garden or simply a city. It's a garden-city and also a temple. It's a house for God and the Lamb, a house for His images, the saints who populate the city. … The garden is also a temple. Every other sanctuary in the Bible is modeled after the garden. Each sanctuary is a well-watered place. Every one is a place of festivity. Yahweh speaks with Adam in the garden, and each sanctuary is a dwelling place for Yahweh, centered on Yahweh's Word.[7]

As we allow the implications of John's description to sink in, we understand that we are seeing the fulfillment of Jesus' words: "Truly, I say to you, in the new world, when the Son of man shall sit on his glorious throne, you who have followed me will also sit on twelve thrones, judging the twelve tribes of Israel. And every one who has left houses or brothers or sisters or father or mother or children or lands, for my name's sake, will receive a hundredfold, and inherit eternal life" (Mt 19:28–29). Breathtakingly, he speaks of the renewal of all things! In the Greek term used here — *palingenesia*, "beginning again" — we hear echoes of Genesis ("Beginnings"). He does not intend to make a new world but to make the world new. It will not be a strange, ghostly environment, as we so often imagine Heaven to be, but a recognizable, concrete, physically delightful world filled with all that we cherish in this one. Nothing that is of value will be lost.

As embarrassing as it is for the "spiritual" way we so often imagine Heaven, it doesn't look as if there is any way out of facing the fact that God intends us to live on a very earthy Earth. It seems that all his remarks about "houses" and "fields" are to be taken seriously. Both human achievement and the grandeur of nature are to be splendidly fulfilled, renewed, and enjoyed. This should not surprise us. In the biblical worldview, all of nature is dear to the Creator-Lover. Through the metaphors with which God inspired the biblical authors, we see how bonded he is to humans and to the comprehensive biosphere.[8] The Creator is described as forming humans as individuals (Is 49:5; Jer 1:5). The same birthing metaphor is used when describing the divine inauguration of Israel as an identifiable people and nation (Dt 32:18) and in the descriptions of God's passionate desire for the renewal of Israel and of all humanity (Is 42:14). This highly maternal language is also used for God's creation of non-human living beings. The Creator lovingly causes plants to grow,[9] and he is personally committed to his ongoing care for the biosphere. He portrays himself as the farmer tenderly caring for his vineyard, Israel (Is 5:1–2; 27:2–6; Jer 2:21; Hos 10:1; Ps 80:8–9, 14–15), as the viniculturalist wanting Israel to become the New Israel, blossoming, filling the Earth with her shoots (Is 27:6; Hos 14:5–7), as the shepherd watching over his lambs (Ez 34:15–16).

And he intends his bondedness with nature to last forever. Indeed, throughout the centuries, the prophets, especially Isaiah, constantly communicated that the Creator intended to make his creation brand new again in some mysterious way. Yahweh will do a new thing, will remake creation itself so that the desert blossoms like a rose, and then his glory will be revealed and "all flesh shall see it together" (Is 35:2; 40:5; 60:1).

The Book of Revelation points to this renewal of everything in the final, forever era as the climax of history. In a dramatic scene, countless powerful, pure spiritual beings (popularly called *angels*) are joined not only by humans but by all of nature in a thunderous, majestic symphony of praise resounding throughout the universe to Jesus the Rescuer and to the Father and the Creator-Spirit: "'Worthy is the Lamb who was slain, to receive power and wealth and wisdom and might and honor and glory and blessing!' And I heard every creature in heaven and on earth and under the earth and in the sea, and all therein, saying, 'To him who sits upon the throne and to the Lamb be blessing and honor and glory and might for ever and ever!'" (Rv 5:12–13).

Thus, finally, all of nature — stars, oceans, trees, birds, and animals — is connected directly to the Trinity by functioning as it should: naturally. This is its worship and liturgy. It occurs even during this era but will attain a glorious crescendo on the heavenized Planet Earth, where all will function to perfection.

Therefore, we can expect animals to be present. In the divinely inspired utterances, we discover a Creator-Lover who shows a keen interest in caring for animals. It seems that we are going to have dogs, goats, lambs, cats, leopards, cows, lions, and bears in the new Heaven and new Earth. Those animals that are presently predatory will be friendly and gentle, as we read in the Book of Isaiah: "The wolf shall dwell with the lamb, and the leopard shall lie down with the kid" (11:6).

Perhaps you wonder why we should need animals on the heavenized Earth. Well, we as humans are not lone rangers. We are relational: humans-in-the-biosphere. You and I survive and thrive because of a myriad of connections between ourselves and plants, animals, sunlight, soil, and so many others. In the words of Dietrich Bonhoeffer, animals and every reality in nature "constitute the world in which I live, without which I cease to be. ... I am not free from [them] in any sense of my essential being, my spirit, having no need of nature, as though nature were something alien to the spirit. On the contrary, in my whole being, in my crea-tureliness, I belong wholly to this world; it bears me, nurtures me, holds me."[10] Bonhoeffer notes that only insofar as we see ourselves as within an ecosystem do we act in a fully human way: "The reason why we fail to rule [as we should], however, is because we do not know the world as God's creation and do not accept the dominion we have as God-given but seize hold of it for ourselves."[11]

In the instance of animals, it is not difficult to see that we and they are made for each other. Indeed, animals in a certain sense make us who we are.[12] For centuries we depended on them for traveling, and we still depend on them for agriculture. How often have we found solace in the company of a beloved horse, dog, or cat? And why couldn't coyotes be-come beloved pets? Already, in this era, we see this happening in histori-cally verified stories, such as St. Francis of Assisi and the wolf of Gubbio.[13] So, we should look forward to spending eternity even with animals! In the future heavenized landscape, we will be able to experience the delight of falling asleep under starlit skies with a tiger cub at our feet.

Another reason in favor of this conclusion is the divine disclosure that the Creator-Lover intends the well-being of humans to be linked to his desires for the thriving of "every living thing" (Gn 6:19). This is dra-matically portrayed in God's insisting that Noah bring representatives of every species of animal and bird onto the ark. Moreover, after the Flood, the Creator makes solemn promises to "every living creature":

> Then God said to Noah and to his sons with him, "Behold, I establish my covenant with you and your descendants after you, and with every living creature that is with you, the birds, the cat-tle, and every beast of the earth with you, as many as came out of the ark. I establish my covenant with you, that never again shall all flesh be cut off by the waters of a flood, and never again shall there be a flood to destroy the earth." (Genesis 9:8–11)

The Creator-Lover-Rescuer empowers us to remain ever aware of his bondedness to all of the biosphere through the rainbow, "the sign of the covenant" he makes with "every living creature" (Gn 9:12).

In the biblical descriptions of the renewal of Planet Earth, the absence of predatory animals is one indicator that all the deadly forces impeding a perfect biosphere will be eliminated. But these will disappear because all evil, whether physical or moral, will have been expelled, and all the potential for destructiveness ended. This is the meaning of the cryptic phrase "the sea was no more" (Rv 21:1) because "sea" in the Jewish mind symbolized the forces of chaos amid nature. Such events as earthquakes, tsunamis, harmful climate changes, and imbalances in the ecosystem will be noticeable by their absence. Likewise, all the destructive forces that have their origin in humans will no longer exist because such humans will not be present. This is the meaning of Revelation 22:3, "There shall no more be anything accursed." The evils resulting from faulty human relationships due to moral disorder, psychological disturbance, and physical defects will be eliminated. No temptations. No disorder. Instead, there will be serenity, peace. We will be able to trust everyone. We will be able to trust ourselves. Likewise, the destruction inflicted upon the environment by humans when we rupture the fundamental relationship necessary for an ecological system — the bond with God — will be no more.[14]

Most significantly, death, the reality standing for all the deadly forces in reality, will have been annihilated: "And I heard a great voice from the throne saying, 'Behold, the dwelling of God is with men. ... Death shall be no more'" (Rv 21:3–4). Not only will all chaotic and destructive forces be eliminated, but everything that is in any way flawed will be absent. On the heavenized Earth, Isaiah's prophecy will be fulfilled: "The former things shall not be remembered or come into mind" (Is 65:17). This includes even unhappy memories: Sadness will have no entry into the new world. Sheer beauty will be around you, sheer joy within you.

A Fully Alive You amid a Flourishing Ecosystem

These prophecies about a future flourishing biosphere show that nature's flourishing is going to be an integral dimension of the new type of civilization on the heavenized Earth. The evidence for this is the unity in John's description between the urban and rural landscapes. This points to the harmonious unity between human creativity and nature's spontaneous grandeur. It is clear from the entire description that God wants a fully ecological civilization. In the future city, the New Jerusalem, humans and nature will relate naturally as the Creator had always intended.[15]

In the era of Christendom, this naturality was omnipresent. Catholics were simply in love with nature. Throughout the European continent, the monks led the way in practicing sustainable agriculture because they viewed themselves as nature's stewards. The Catholic builders of Gothic cathedrals practiced "biomimesis" (from the Greek words *bios* meaning life and *mīmēsis* meaning "imitation"), learning from and imitating nature's way of functioning to solve design challenges and foster human flourishing. Thus, they created what John Ruskin (1819–1900) the English polymath, philosopher, and art critic, called a "foliated architecture … that has been derived from vegetation,"[16] with Gothic curves imitating different species of leaves.[17] Gothic is a "vitalized geometry,"[18] not only in its style but in every dimension. It exemplified an organic relationship between nature, the Creator, and humans, between the stonemasons and other workmen with their guilds, their community, and their love of God. The Gothic style even encouraged initiative and enterprise in its architects and in the humblest workmen, wanting them to express their human nature in creating beauty to express their sense of the divine loveliness. This was because it was an architecture whose "father," Abbot Suger (1081–1151), modeled it on the vision of "the holy city, new Jerusalem, coming down out of heaven from God, prepared as a bride adorned for her husband" (Rv 21:2).[19]

Why would the Creator want the future civilization to be a garden city? Because a fully ecological civilization in which humans are living is the fully natural way to be fully human. From the beginnings, the Creator-Lover-Rescuer revealed that this was the plan: Genesis shows the original human environment as a garden, and the human vocation was to be a gardener in the widest, deepest, and most sublime sense:

> And the LORD God planted a garden in Eden, in the east; and there he put the man whom he had formed. And out of the ground the LORD God made to grow every tree that is pleasant to the sight and good for food, the tree of life also in the midst

of the garden, and the tree of the knowledge of good and evil. A river flowed out of Eden to water the garden, and there it divided and became four rivers. (Genesis 2:8–10)

The entire Bible from beginning to end unfolds the Creator's ecological vision and man's mission to create a garden civilization. As Peter J. Leithart explains:

World, garden, and temple overlap and interpenetrate. If we read of a garden, we should also taste the hints of a fruitful land and the temple and the world itself as potential garden. ... The garden is the template (pun initially unnoticed), the little taste of heaven that anticipates what Adam will achieve on earth. Adam's task in the world is to glorify the world until it's a civic Eden and a dwelling of God. This is Israel's task as well. ... History is the gardenification of creation, the Edenification of the planet, the new-Jerusalemification of the cosmos, the temple-ization of the original cosmic temple, the heavenization of earth.[20]

Although the vision of the heavenized world had stunned John because no one in all of Jewish history had ever imagined Heaven and Earth amalgamating in one reality, the great prophets such as Isaiah and Ezekiel had received visions of an ultimate liberation of the world from anti-ecological, dehumanizing forces.[21] They had spoken of a planetary second exodus and of a promised land with a new Temple that would encompass all nations. John, therefore, as he put ink to papyrus, used the language of texts such as Isaiah 11:6–9 and Ezekiel 40–48. These ancient Jewish visionaries had been privileged by divine inspiration to foresee humans living amid a perfect biosphere. They had understood that all of the Earth's potential for grandeur ever longed for by poets, artists, and musicians would one day be reality. Indeed, the entire Book of Revelation is a weaving together of these ancient Jewish longings, but within a new synthesis provoked by the crucified, risen, and ascended Jesus, Lord of History.

It is in the biblical references to "land," especially to the "land of Israel," that we are to see this resolve of the Creator to bring about an ecological civilization. "Land" referred not only to the soil but also to the sociocultural-political reality of Israel and to the human connectedness to soil and place. Moreover, "land [of Israel]" was a term that functioned as a pattern: What God wanted for this tiny Mediterranean territory he wanted to extend throughout the entire world.[22]

In this worldview, therefore, we are called to see ourselves as bonded, like the Creator, to the biosphere. Even our name and our human identity — "Adam" from *adamah* ("soil") — discloses this connectedness. Our Jewish and Christian forefathers lived this connectedness with zest. They treasured their closeness to certain places, to a particular land and soil, to certain landscapes, and to their own nation. They experienced places in their bones! As the English writer Owen Barfield remarked: "The world was more like a garment men wore about them than a stage on which they moved."[23] The places — lands, soil, mountains, lakes, farms, homesteads — in which they or their forefathers had lived were felt to be part of themselves. They felt themselves to flourish more humanly through their connectedness to them. They felt that these places more than others impacted them existentially. They identified with the place, the land, the soil, the nation.

It is in this sense of the biosphere as home that we should read the great Jewish prophets foreseeing "the land" holistically flourishing at some time in the future — a time now seen by John to be fulfilled on the heavenized Earth. Thus, the ecological environment in the new Heaven and new Earth fulfills the prophecies of the Earth becoming like the primordial Garden of Eden.[24] For instance, in Ezekiel's communication of Yahweh's words to the mountains of Israel:

> But you, O mountains of Israel, shall shoot forth your branches, and yield your fruit to my people Israel; for they will soon come home. For, behold, I am for you, and I will turn to you, and you shall be tilled and sown; and I will multiply men upon you, the whole house of Israel, all of it: the cities shall be inhabited and the waste places rebuilt; and I will multiply upon you man and beast; and they shall increase and be fruitful; and I will cause you to be inhabited as in your former times, and will do more good

to you than ever before. Then you will know that I am the Lord. (Ezekiel 36:8–11)

But why a *city* lifestyle? In the popular way of imagining life in Heaven, we tend to think of it as us alone with God, even if other humans and angels are around. But far different is the biblical view. We will not be lone individuals but people enjoying a fully social lifestyle in a pulsating-with-excitement civilization amid a captivating ecological biosphere. It will be a highly social, active life lived on a most earthy Earth, in a Garden City immersed in nature. This will be the subject of the next chapter.

CHAPTER 15

THE VISION OF THE FUTURE CIVILIZATION IN WHICH HUMANS THRIVE

God is not dependent on anything for His beauty; His beauty
is not limited to certain times or aspects; but He is beautiful by
himself, through himself, and in himself. He is eternal beauty
— not changing from one moment to the next — constantly the
same beyond all change or alteration, increase or addition.

— St. Gregory of Nyssa

"But," you insist, "surely, Heaven is about me and God?" Well, yes, certainly, but *who are you*? As Christians we possess a much different and deeper sense of human identity than that of modernity. Yes, of course, we are unique among living realities because of our intelligence, freedom, and highly adaptive nature, but that's rather basic.[1] Through the divine disclosure we discover that we are gloriously much, much more. Genesis reveals that the Eternal One personally gets involved in the creation of each human.[2] As we read in Genesis, Adam (each one of us) comes from *adamah* (the soil) because God scoops soil from Planet Earth, sculpts the human shape from it, and breathes life into his nostrils. Thus, our humanness is a combination of divine breath and earthiness: "Then the Lord God formed man of dust from the ground, and breathed into his nostrils the breath of life; and man became a living soul" (Gn 2:7). But even more amazingly, the Creator created humans with the capacity to be mirrors of his own identity: "So God created man in his own image, in the image of God he created him; male and female he created them" (1:27).

Consequently, you, in your "insidest inside," are called to be a reflection of the Trinitarian God who is the highly social and sociable God. The Triune Lover is not a loner but sheer, dynamic relating. The three Divine Persons are ever knowing, loving, acting in torrential self-outpouring both within the Trinity and in the cosmos. You are therefore designer-made to flourish through intense relationships of self-giving. Genesis confirms this when God says, "It is not good that the man should be alone" (2:18). You are never more your true self than when you are building up and bettering others. The Creator made it clear that he wants you to see your connectedness to him happening through, in, and with your bondedness to others, as we see plainly in the prayer Jesus taught his followers, which begins "Our Father" (Mt 6:9–13).

The Creator further emphasized this by the strategy of his rescue operation after the Fall of man. His liberation of individuals from the dehumanizing forces of this world occurs through their membership in a society wherein his power is active. From Genesis to Revelation, we hear the divine determination to bring into existence a community that is meant to birth a civilization[3] — first within the nation of Israel, then inside the New Israel, the Mystical Body of the God-Man, the Church, called to be the corporate reality, the social milieu through which we reach human fulfillment: salvation.

But the nation of Israel was a nation centered on a city: Jerusalem.

Jewish life and lifestyle were centripetal and centrifugal from what went on in its Temple. Daily, they faced three times toward it. It was the Temple-city embodying their identity and their mission: "a city set on a hill" (Mt 5:14) in order to be "a light to the nations" (Is 42:6). In the divine strategy it was patterned on the Eden of the past and the New Jerusalem of the future, as Ezekiel 40–48, the prophecies of Zechariah and Isaiah, and the Book of Revelation make clear.

Therefore, there will be a civilization amidst a heavenized Earth, not for some arbitrary reason, but because of who man is: a social being, made to live and thrive in the company of others, called to fulfill his identity as a creator of culture, and therefore needing inspiration and giving inspiration. All of this requires, for its maximal expression, a city. And not just any type of city, but an authentically human city in which all relationships flourish: between humans, between humans and the biosphere, and above all and through all, between humans and the Creator-Lover. It is to be, therefore, a sacred civilization, a sacralized civilization. Only one such civilization existed before the coming of Jesus: that of Israel, with its capital in Jerusalem. Now it is the New Israel, the Mystical Body of Jesus, the Jewish God-Man who fulfilled the mission of his noble nation. Both Israel and the New Israel are the fractal patterns, the scale models of the final forever society on the heavenized Planet Earth.

Before the arrival of Jesus, humans connected to the Creator through the Temple of Jerusalem with its sacrifices — the place of his intensive personal presence on Planet Earth. Because of Jesus, this connection now occurs through the Temple of the Mystical Body with its mystical enactment of the Sacrifice. Not only individual well-being but civilizational flourishing, including the thriving of the biosphere, depend on it. The great Jewish prophets constantly communicated that human and social prosperity and agricultural fruitfulness are linked to "the height of Zion" (Jer 31:12), which is Jerusalem, the place of the Temple. This mysterious, complex connection applies analogously to the new Temple:

> And in that day the mountains shall drip sweet wine, and the hills shall flow with milk, and all the stream beds of Judah shall flow with water; and a fountain shall come forth from the house

of the LORD and water the valley of Shittim. (Joel 3:18)

Also:

> They shall come and sing aloud on the height of Zion, and they
> shall be radiant over the goodness of the LORD, over the grain,
> the wine, and the oil, and over the young of the flock and the
> herd; their life shall be like a watered garden, and they shall lan-
> guish no more. (Jeremiah 31:12)

Agricultural superabundance is promised, not in isolation, but as part of
the ecological network in which everything functions because humans
have connected themselves to the Creator:

> I will summon the grain and make it abundant and lay no fam-
> ine upon you. I will make the fruit of the tree and the increase of
> the field abundant, that you may never again suffer the disgrace
> of famine among the nations. ... On the day that I cleanse you
> from all your iniquities, I will cause the cities to be inhabited,
> and the waste places shall be rebuilt. And the land that was des-
> olate shall be tilled. ... And they will say, "This land that was
> desolate has become like the garden of Eden; and the waste and
> desolate and ruined cities are now inhabited and fortified." (Eze-
> kiel 36:29–30, 33–35)

However, besides speaking about the immediate future, the giants of
Israel's history also kept pointing to the final era of world history. The
prophets spoke of a future renewal of Planet Earth in which a renewed
biosphere would have at its center a renewed civilization. This is the implication of the constantly repeated message that the city of Jerusalem
would, notwithstanding her failure to fulfill her mission, be part of the
renewed world. It had to be like that because of the divine strategy backed
up by promises. The Creator intended Heaven and Earth to be joined at
that place on Planet Earth where heavenly and earthly spacetime inter-
locked and interacted: the Temple of Jerusalem. And the promise holds

firm in this present era for the Temple of the Mystical Body of Christ, the Church. Both are anticipations of what God will one day achieve throughout Planet Earth. This was always on the agenda. Even when Jerusalem didn't fulfill her role — and even now when we Catholics do not fulfill our role — the divine plan remains in operation.

Where Your Longing to Live in a Society of Friendships Is Fulfilled

There is another powerful argument for life on the heavenized Earth as a civilizational life. When you listen to the secret longings of your heart, isn't explosively joyful friendship what you've always wanted? Haven't you always desired to be surrounded by flourishing bonds to family, neighbors, local community, and nation? A bondedness wherein not only you cherish them, but they cherish you?

Moreover, the Creator created you to be his cocreator. This implies that you become yourself by acting creatively, by changing the world around you for the better. In the widest sense of the word, even in everyday actions, he wants you to be artistic — a designer, an architect, a builder, a solutionologist. Because the civilization on the heavenized Planet Earth will be highly developed, it will require humans to be creative. This is not spelled out in John's account of his vision of the future, but it is everywhere implied by his references to such texts as Isaiah 65:21, "They shall build houses and inhabit them; / they shall plant vineyards and eat their fruit," or Revelation 21:24: "By its light shall the nations walk; and the kings of the earth shall bring their glory into it." The first Christians, whose knowledge of the biblical texts was the equivalent of our pop culture savvy today, would have seen this effortlessly.

On the heavenized Planet Earth, everyone will be unleashing all of their God-given potential to build upon all they achieved in this life. We can hope to hear music surpassing the work of the greatest composers, along with folk songs and popular music of electrifying sensitivity. It will be a world in which everyone in varying degrees and with extraordinary diversity will be beautifying the world. Everyone, in every action, will build others up and birth new wonders in art, music, literature, architecture, gardening, and, above all, in human relationships. There will be an explosion of creativity because relationships unleash the best within each of us.

The human existence of the future is life in a city, and this is not simply an add-on but one of its central characteristics. It fulfills the designs for human flourishing laid out in Genesis. For it is by means of living in community that the Creator-Lover intends to bring humans to completion. In the social environment the Trinity will manifest and imbue us maximally with his own relational vitality and beauty. Thus, Leithart writes, "God's glory pervades the city; more accurately, the city is the visibility of the glory of God."[4] As Saint Irenaeus remarked, "The glory of God is the living man, and the life of man is the vision of God."[5]

The stunning magnificence of the New Jerusalem's architecture, as John beheld it in his vision, shows this divine glory acting through glorious humans for the birthing of a society of human flourishing. Breathtaking sights are everywhere you turn: a city wall of jasper, gates each made of a single pearl, the city center of pure gold like clear glass, foundations of precious minerals from sapphires to emeralds (Rv 21:18–20). Here, as everywhere in the Book of Revelation, we must strike a balance between the language used and the reality to which it refers. We must not put on our modern, left-brain way of reasoning and dismiss the descriptions as mere fantasy. Symbolic language is necessary because only through it can these multilayered, complex realities of the future be disclosed to us. We should approach these visions with all our powers of intuition. Thus, for instance, in the description of the city's architecture, the biblical scholar Ian Boxall recommends that we allow ourselves to feel what the visionary sensed: sheer grandeur, excellence, brilliance, "a powerful visual reflection of her origin in the God of glory."[6] And when the divinely inspired visionary states that "its radiance [was] like a most rare jewel, like a jasper, clear as crystal" (Rv 21:11), his choice is insightful. It tells us why the city is so glorious: The crystal transparency of jasper enables the city to be, as Boxall states,

> resplendent with God's glory. ... Her splendor, radiance and brilliance — dazzling to the eye — are a powerful visual reflection of her origin in the God of glory. Because God is within her, the mediated divine presence of the earthly tabernacle and

Temple have given way to immediate, unmediated access to the divine Presence, the glory or *kavod* of the Hebrew Bible (e.g., Ex 16:7, 24:16; 1 Kgs 8:11; Is 60:1).

Thus, we see that the civilization on the heavenized Earth is not a distraction from the vision of the Triune Creator-Lover. Besides our immediate vision of the Blessed Trinity, our eyes will also thrillingly behold him *through the civilization and its beauty*. John communicates this through his choice of the same translucent stone to characterize both the One seated on the throne (see Rv 4:3) and also the entire city.[7] Thus, the entire civilization is one immense, transparent window unto the Triune God. It is the metaphor that expresses the fact that now "God [is] everything to every one" (1 Cor 15:28). As two Yale theologians, Miroslav Volf and Ryan McAnnally-Linz, note: "Consequently, God is not mainly an 'external' object of worship, whether that worship happens through specific liturgical acts or through ordinary activities. Instead, God is mainly the indwelling presence in all and each, the source of all liveliness, holiness, and agency. People live and act not so much toward God as with God (Rv 21:3)."[8]

In the time before Christ, God had dwelt "among" his people (Ex 29:45–46). But Jesus inaugurated a new level and intensity of presence in those who would unite with him. Indeed, he declared it to be his mission: "That the love with which you have loved me may be in them, and I in them" (Jn 17:26). With Jesus, through him, and in him, the Christian is united in the Spirit to the Father.[9] Now on the heavenized Earth comes the complete realization of this mutual indwelling: You will experience yourself living in him!

The verb used for *dwelling* literally means "to pitch one's tent" or "tabernacle."[10] It is the same used at the opening of John's Gospel: "And the Word became flesh and dwelt [tabernacled/pitched his tent] among us" (Jn 1:14). With his embodiment so tenderly visible in the Christmas event, we now see its awe-inspiring completion, as Leithart remarks: "When Jerusalem descends and God dwells among his people, pitching his tent not in the personal flesh of Jesus but among us, in the body of the Bride,"[11] and in the depths of your psyche.

"Behold, the dwelling of God is with men. He will dwell with them, and they shall be his people, and God himself will be with them" (Rv 21:3). This text shows us God as Emmanuel, the God who is so intensely with us that he "has taken his people into his own identity and name."[12] As Leithart points out, in some of the original Greek manuscripts, the word *God* is repeated at the end of verse 3, "forming a little word picture": "Himself God / with them / is / their / God." He continues, "'God' protectively surrounds the sentence as God encircles his holy city and bride. The first part of the sentence mimics the Hebrew 'Emmanuel,' God with them, and at the center of the sentence is the verb of being: The God who is the God who is with them; the God who is has determined he will not be God without them."[13]

Thus, while having a more vivid awareness of your own uniqueness than you ever had during your mortal lifetime, you will simultaneously feel your soul flow into intimacy with your Triune Creator-Lover-Rescuer as you experience him cosmically inside you and all around you: in the warmth and soft light of the summer morning, in the freshness of the breeze, in the smile on the other's face, in the grandeur of the mountains; at the sight of turquoise-blue streams, in the aromas of the oak- and pine-vaulted forest where wafts the scent of mint, in the rich, fruity, orchard-sweet taste of the blackberries picked off the hedge, in the soothing lapping of sea waters on the sunrise-gold sands, in the orchestral symphony of the birds, in moonshine-clear Alpine lake waters. In all our surroundings, we will intuitively see God's face, hear the resonance of his voice, experience the heat of his love. He will radiate his presence to us through the exercising of our own creativity and by the delighted experience of other people's creativity. In the sight of the perfection of the craftsmanship of our fellow humans, we will sense the inner fire of their authors. In works of art, architecture, and music, we will sense not only the supreme creative power of the Creator but, in a way beyond our present power to imagine, we will see God himself.

Ultimately, we will experience the Creator-Lover-Rescuer through everything around us because that is the way we will know him as he really is. God is the most personal and personable of lovers, who wants others to echo and resound his love. He is a Father who delights and rejoices when those who are his daughters and sons act as completely natural humans in a completely natural way, using the talents he gave them (whether ten, five, or one), all of which he intends to multiply exponentially on the heavenized Earth. He is the Powerful One who is a power-sharer and wants others to exercise power as he does: for the sake of love. By seeing all of nature, ourselves, and others "charged with the grandeur of God,"[14] we will know and love him, know and love nature, and know and love others — we will know and love Love.

Moreover, we will discover that his love transforms, glorifies, beautifies, and energizes the one in whom it is present. His love is light-filled, and one of the properties of light is to make visible the unique qualities of the reality enlightened. It manifests and radiates its individuality. Thus, we will discover that the sweet obligation, "You shall love the Lord your God with all your heart, and with all your soul, and with all your mind, and with all your strength" (Mk 12:30–31), requires us also to love the world loved by him — and with the type of love with which "God so loved the world" (Jn 3:16). As Volf and McAnnally-Linz remark: "If this idea appears startlingly 'worldly,' that's because the holy and transcendent God is surprisingly worldly — desiring to make a home and be at home in the beloved creation."[15]

Nevertheless, even after writing all of the above, a doubt nags me. When I see the Lord Jesus still bearing the marks of those wounds by which I have been healed (see Is 53:5), I still strongly suspect that I will forget everything else except him — forever. It is easy to empathize with our Jewish forefather when he wrote: "Whom have I in heaven but you? / And there is nothing upon earth that I / desire besides you. / My flesh and my heart may fail, / but God is the strength of my heart and / my portion for ever" (Ps 73:25–26).

Ecological and Sacralized Civilization

To the amazement of John, the heavenly Jerusalem, the new heavenized civilization, descends to Earth without a temple: "And I saw no temple in the city." It is only upon reflection that he realizes why not: "For its temple is the Lord God the Almighty and the Lamb" (Rv 21:22). The entire world has become temple because every square mile and every nano-moment are filled with the intense and intensive Presence of the Triune

Lover-Creator.[16]

What millennia of Jewish history had murmured or shouted in prophecy after prophecy, event after event, has now been fulfilled: The Creator's intention to become intensely present, to make himself at home on Earth and with humans, is achieved.[17] All of the meaning loaded into the institutions of Sabbath and Temple now explodes, as the theologian Jürgen Moltmann states: "The hidden, anticipatory indwelling of God in the Temple and among his people shall be universally fulfilled at the consummation of creation."[18] Sabbath and Temple, contrary to our modern split-world view, were the two symbols asserting that the cosmos was a unified whole in which the two dimensions of Heaven and Earth intersected and interacted. They did so chiefly through the time of Sabbath and the other festivals and in the space of the Temple wherein the heavenly presence of the Creator became intensively active on Earth for bringing it to fulfillment. But in the new Heavens and the new Earth, all the transformational purpose of both Sabbath and Temple will be embodied in each individual and in civilization. The result will be a total change of atmosphere on Planet Earth. It will be the atmosphere of Sabbath in the Temple: sheer, overwhelming fulfillment and ecstatic joy.

John's description woven out of the old prophecies outlining the final outcome of Planet Earth shows how the world in its entirety is Temple. His description of the city's shape points to it: a cube, massive in size, about 2,400 kilometers on each side and located on "a great, high mountain" (Rv 21:10).[19] The city is therefore the fulfillment of the only other cube-shaped place referred to in Jewish history: the holy of holies, the inner sanctuary in the tent of meeting, and, later, in the Jerusalem Temple. This was the symbol of the bipartite cosmos, the advance signpost that one day they would become a unified reality, when the entire planet would become Temple.

Thus, in the final era of history, Operation Genesis is achieved. The place of the divine indwelling has invaded the entire world: All space has become not merely Temple, but the holy of holies because of the all-pervasive Divine Presence. Thus, as St. John Damascene states, we are to see "the indwelling God as a dwelling place."[20]

There is no secular space in the New Jerusalem: In its entirety, it is a temple. Consequently, just as everything in the holy of holies and at its entrance — the menorah symbolizing the purpose of time, the Bread of the Presence symbolizing Israel, the staff of Aaron symbolizing the Jewish priesthood — was sacred, so now everything within the walls of the new city has been sacralized. Goodbye, secularism and secularization.

The vision therefore shows us the Jewish and Christian view of a civilization organically growing out of the fundamental relation coordinating all others: the relationship with God. It is the counter-civilization, the counter-empire to all the empires of this world that model themselves on Babel, the paradigm of the civilization that is human-centered, in denial of the Creator's authority, and therefore antihuman.

Israel throughout her history, at least in a remnant of those faithful to the vision, was alert to this mission of creating a radically new civilization utterly different from those of its powerful dominators: Babylon, Assyria, Greece, and Rome. This would be, as Dr. Scott Hahn expresses it, a "liturgical empire,"[21] wherein the prayer of Jews through the millennia would be fulfilled: "Praise the LORD, all nations!" (Ps 117:1). The mission is the same today: We Christians, like our Jewish fathers, know that our mission is to honor the Triune God by doing all in our power to make him known and loved to the ends of the Earth because, as Sigmund Mowinckel, a biblical theologian, remarks, "The song of praise 'increases God's power and renown,'"[22] enabling him to achieve what he desires: fully flourishing humans. This is because when we honor God, we become more fully human. So, when we create a society that honors him, we facilitate this interconnected double goal.

A "liturgical empire" brings into existence in the present world God-centered and therefore pro-human politics, economics, and arts,[23] all of which enable humans to become fully human. All, of course, will be flawed during this era, the first stage of the building of the theocentric civilization, but all will be achieved in the final stage in the new Heaven and new Earth, when the ancient prophecy will be realized: "For the earth will be filled with the knowledge of the glory of the LORD, as the waters cover the sea" (Hb 2:14). Then the entire Earth, all of the biosphere and all the nations, will be in direct contact with God, adoring him in and through all of reality. "The earth shall be full of the knowledge of the

LORD as the waters cover the sea" (Is 11:9). Now, in the vision of the final outcome of history, we understand its beginning as portrayed in Genesis. As Old Testament scholar John Walton states:

> Genesis 1 can now be seen as a creation account focusing on the cosmos as a temple. It is describing the creation of the cosmic temple with all of its functions and with God dwelling in its midst. This is what makes day seven so significant, because without God taking up his dwelling in its midst, the (cosmic) temple does not exist. The most central truth to the creation account is that this world is a place for God's presence. Though all of the functions are anthropocentric, meeting the needs of humanity, the cosmic temple is theocentric, with God's presence serving as the defining element of existence. This represents a change that has taken place over the seven days. Prior to day one, God's spirit was active over the nonfunctional cosmos; God was involved but had not yet taken up his residence. The establishment of the functional cosmic temple is effectuated by God taking up his residence on day seven.[24]

Because of the Divine Presence, we will be living in an ecological world with an ecological culture and an ecological civilization. All of which are meant to be inaugurated here and now by us living out our fundamental relationship with the Triune Creator-Lover. How? Through sacralizing our life's time by living within the Temple of the Mystical Body, the Church. For it is within her sanctuary, through participation in the Sacrifice of the Mass, which is the mystical enactment of the central event of history, that we become empowered to transform Planet Earth. We will sketch the dynamism by which we can achieve this in the final chapter, after we examine why the biblical description of the future is in sync with our own deepest longings.

CHAPTER 16

YOUR DEEPEST LONGINGS

The sweetest thing in all my life has been the longing — to reach the Mountain, to find the place where all the beauty came from — my country, the place where I ought to have been born. Do you think it all meant nothing, all the longing? The longing for home? For indeed it now feels not like going, but like going back.

— _C. S. Lewis_, Till We Have Faces

Your experience on the heavenized Earth will in some ways feel like a continuation, intensified and made sublimely beautiful, of your experience during your mortal life's time. C. S. Lewis captured this well in the last book of the Chronicles of Narnia, _The Last Battle_: "The difference between the old Narnia and the new Narnia was like that. The new one was a deeper country: every rock and flower and blade of grass looked as if it meant more. I can't describe it any better than that: if ever you get there you will know what I mean."[1]

All around you the splendid beauty of the new world will be physical, concrete, tangible, palpable. Nothing we can imagine on Earth comes close to the level of concreteness that exists in Heaven. The sunrises will be more radiant; the sunsets more poignant; the ocean waves frothier; the breezes fresher; the star-filled nights more pregnant with meaning. Your own senses will seem to be turbo-powered as they touch the green leaves; hear the waters of a whirruping waterfall toppling with a thunderclap into a hollowed-out paradise-blue pool; smell the nectar-sweet smell of spring flowers; listen to the humming of a swarm of bees; contemplate a jeweled night sky. Sounds, sights, touches, tastes will seem to enter within you, swell your soul, and unite you spontaneously to him who is their source. We will discover the answer to the question, expressed so well by the novelist E. M. Forster, that ever unsettles us in this lifetime: "What is the good of your stars and trees, your sunrise and the wind, if they do not enter into our daily lives?"[2]

You sense music everywhere. Indeed, it is like a symphony played by nature's orchestra in which all the instruments play harmoniously: the murmuring breeze, the cracking-snapping of the grasshopper, the rushing stream, the *thunk*-ing of ripe nuts falling, and the whispering of the leaves. Best of all, there is music inside you. The symphony is playing within as all your senses, intuition, memory, and affection play in splendid harmony. The thought hits you: "But, of course, it has to be like this — he promised!" The Creator-Lover had always spoken about a mysterious "new song" that we would one day sing. He had disclosed time and again that the presence of music was the signal of his renewing presence: "He put a new song in my mouth" (Ps 40:3). Indeed, as ultramodern mathematicians from Pythagoras to Edward Frenkel point out, the universe has a musical dimension: "There is geometry in the humming of the strings, there is music in the spacing of the spheres."[3] Along with genuine laughter, music is a symbol of harmony, one of the surest expressions of joy, and it immerses us in beauty. St. John Henry Newman once wrote, "Music, I suppose ... has an object of its own. ... It is the expression of ideas greater and more profound than any in the visible world, ideas, which center indeed in Him whom Catholicism manifests, who is the seat of all beauty, order, and perfection whatever."[4] The entire Planet Earth will fulfill what its Creator had called for eons before: "O sing to the Lord a new song; / sing to the Lord, all the earth!/ Sing to the Lord, bless his name; / tell of his salvation from day to day. / Declare his glory among the nations, / his marvelous works among all the peoples!" (Ps 96:1–3).

You will feel at home! We will all sense what C. S. Lewis's unicorn in *The Last Battle* experienced:

> It was the Unicorn who summed up what everyone was feeling. He stamped his right fore-hoof on the ground and neighed, and then he cried:
>
> "I have come home at last! This is my real country! I belong here. This is the land I have been looking for all my life, though I never knew it till now. The reason why we loved the old Narnia is that it sometimes looked a little like this. Bree-hee-hee! Come further up, come further in!"[5]

The atmosphere on the heavenized Planet Earth will be that of home. Home is where you are surrounded by acceptance, where no one judges you, and where you are fully known, and, simultaneously, loved for who you are, not for what you have achieved. Home is where you are yourself. As some of the best ultramodern psychologists confirm, home is the soil that provides the sap for the vitality rushing through the veins of your psyche. It is the air and atmosphere, the ideal biosphere designed for you, the climate in which you thrive.

Let me clarify this by an analogy from the science of viniculture first developed by the monks of St. Bernard of Clairvaux amid the Rhinelands, Burgundy, and the Auvergne during the era of Christendom.[6] These Cistercians, who produced some of the most appreciated wines and liqueurs in Europe, developed the concept of *terroir* to explain what is required for great wines. They discovered that the distinctive excellence of any great wine (its cru) is due to the fact that it has come from that unique place where sunlight, soil type, altitude, land surface, and location (including hills and rivers, winds and breezes, and times of seasons) all converge for a unique quality of wine with its own distinctive color, flavor, and body.

This is how you will experience Heaven as home. It is not by chance that the Creator-Lover constantly described both Israel and the New Is-rael, the Church, as vineyards. Very deliberately, he wanted us to think of him as a vineyard farmer, an agriculturalist tenderly caring for his vine lands (Is 5:1–2, 27:2–6; Jer 2:21; Hos 10:1; Ps 80:8–9, 14–15), wanting Israel to blossom into the New Israel, filling the Earth with her shoots (Is 27:6; Hos 14:5–7). Indeed, he explained the dynamism for human fulfillment through the metaphor of the vine. Because we are within his Mystical Body, his heavenly vitality flows through us like lifeblood, like the sap of a vine that flows into its branches: "I am the vine, you are the branches. He who abides in me, and I in him, he it is that bears much fruit" (Jn 15:5).

By means of his first public miracle at Cana, he wants us to recog-nize that he desires to turn the water of our existence into wine. Wine in the Mediterranean world was the drink of excellence, the beverage of rulers. And it was for ruling that the Creator had authored humans: to rule Planet Earth like vineyard owners seeking to inaugurate a garden civilization in which every human would discover his homeland amid a splendidly cared for biosphere. In Heaven, finally, you will be in the ideal spot. There, you will be unhampered by all the frustrating limitations of your previous life's time. You will have the ideal conditions for produc-ing a harvest of the most exquisite vintage wine — a wine that can only come from you. A wine that everyone around you — and, above all, your Triune Creator-Lover-Rescuer — will rejoice to drink.

Feeling Fully at Home in Your Own Skin

Home and homeland are where you will achieve beyond your wildest dreams all the longings that ever filled your heart — all the yearnings for beauty, goodness, genuineness, and flawless joy that artists, poets, dra-matists, architects, musicians, and sculptors through the millennia have sought to express. The restlessness of the human heart will find on the heavenized Earth what it had searched for: that desire underlying all de-sires, the aspiration for a oneness in self, with others, with the biosphere, and, in and through all, with the Creator-Lover-Rescuer. Here, finally, all our relationships will function as they should.

In the Creator's mind, known to us through the divine disclosure of

Genesis, the world was created to be his home with humans. The refrain is heard through the millennia: "My dwelling place shall be with them; and I will be their God, and they shall be my people" (Ez 37:27). "Sing and rejoice, O daughter of Zion; for behold, I come and I will dwell in the midst of you, says the LORD" (Zec 2:10). Until, finally, the refrain thunders at the grand finale as the final era of history begins: "And I heard a great voice from the throne saying, 'Behold, the dwelling of God is with men. He will dwell with them, and they shall be his people, and God himself will be with them'" (Rv 21:3). This is the grand finale, made possible because "the Word became flesh and dwelt among us, full of grace and truth; we have beheld his glory, glory as of the only-begotten Son from the Father" (Jn 1:14). It is also possible because of his dwelling in the sanctuaries of Jerusalem and the Mystical Body of the Church: "And let them make me a sanctuary, that I may dwell in their midst" (Ex 25:8).

For God, homemaking is the serious business of life. He wants a family! "For those whom he foreknew he also predestined to be conformed to the image of his Son, in order that he might be the first-born among many brethren" (Rom 8:29). And he "from whom every family in heaven and on earth is named" (Eph 3:15) requires a home, because his adopted daughters and sons are not angels but body-plus-mind bipeds who need to live in a world of trees, rivers, and sunrises if they are to be integrally human as he designed them to be.

As C. S. Lewis recognized, throughout our lifetime we are always in search of this elusive home:

> I am trying to rip open the inconsolable secret in each one of you — the secret which hurts so much that you take your revenge on it by calling it names like Nostalgia and Romanticism and Adolescence; the secret also which pierces with such sweetness that when, in very intimate conversation, the mention of it becomes imminent, we grow awkward and affect to laugh at ourselves; the secret we cannot hide and cannot tell, though we desire to do both.
>
> We cannot tell it because it is a desire for something that has never actually appeared in our experience. We cannot hide it

because our experience is constantly suggesting it, and we betray ourselves like lovers at the mention of a name. ... These things — the beauty, the memory of our own past — are good images of what we really desire; but if they are mistaken for the thing itself they turn into dumb idols. ... For they are not the thing itself; they are only the scent of a flower we have not found, the echo of a tune we have not heard, news from a country we have never visited.[7]

This seeking is the secret source of all our drives. Relentlessly and passionately, it is behind our every action. As Lewis notes elsewhere:

Even in your hobbies, has there not always been some secret attraction which the others are curiously ignorant of — something, not to be identified with, but always on the verge of breaking through, the smell of cut wood in the workshop or the clap-clap of water against the boat's side? Are not all lifelong friendships born at the moment when at last you meet another human being who has some inkling (but faint and uncertain even in the best) of that something which you were born desiring, and which, beneath the flux of other desires and in all the momentary silences between the louder passions, night and day, year by year, from childhood to old age, you are looking for, watching for, listening for? You have never had it. All the things that have ever deeply possessed your soul have been but hints of it. ... But if it should really become manifest — if there ever came an echo that did not die away but swelled into the sound itself — you would know it. Beyond all possibility of doubt you would say "Here at last is the thing I was made for."[8]

We will experience ourselves in a civilization that feels like home because we will experience ourselves as connected to who we should be in our "insidest inside." We will feel a oneness and a wholeness inside us because we will sense a oneness with others, with nature, with who we are, and with who we were — all because we are one with the One.

The Creator-Lover assures us of the achievement of all natural desires on the heavenized Earth. "To the thirsty I will give water without price from the fountain of the water of life. He who conquers shall have this heritage, and I will be his God and he shall be my son" (Rv 21:6–8). Then, the living waters of divine vitality will flow through the center of the civilization and through our psyche, creating the Forever Paradise that will slake our thirst for beauty, genuineness, and joy.

Indeed, God has never ceased to assure us that our longings would be fulfilled in this way. Fractal patterns of these divinely irrigating waters have ever existed. "A river flowed out of Eden to water the garden, and there it divided and became four rivers" (Gn 2:10). Through the millennia, Yahweh's prophets kept urging us to look forward to the fulfillment of these promises: "They shall not hunger or thirst, neither scorching wind nor sun shall strike them, for he who has pity on them will lead them, and by springs of water will guide them" (Is 49:10). And, further developing this idea, "Ho, every one who thirsts, come to the waters; and he who has no money, come, buy and eat! Come, buy wine and milk without money and without price" (Is 55:1).[9] It was the Creator who had encrypted these desires in the human heart; indeed, he had made it a characteristic of being fully alive, a requirement for journeying on the way to fulfillment. In the psalms, the prayers the Spirit had inspired, he fanned these longings into a flame. "As a deer longs for flowing streams, so longs my soul for you, O God" (Ps 42:1). Further on, the psalmist expressed how, within the depths of these divinely inspired longings, he himself mysteriously experienced his Creator: "Deep calls to deep at the thunder of your cataracts; all your waves and your billows have gone over me" (42:7). Ezekiel had seen in his vision of the future Temple — the future heavenized world — with waters flowing from it (Ez 47:1–12; see also Rv 22:1–2).

Jesus himself, on the feast of Tabernacles, had "stood up and proclaimed, 'If any one thirst, let him come to me and drink. He who believes in me, as the Scripture has said, "Out of his heart shall flow rivers of living water"' (Jn 7:37–38). In his Mystical Body, the Church, whose mission is to inaugurate advance signposts of the future world, the river of life from him has continued to flow through the Sacrifice, the sacraments, and the sacramentals to simultaneously quench and increase our thirst.

However, let us ever be alert to the fact that this river is "flowing from the throne of God and of the Lamb" (Rv 22:1).[10] This means that all our joy will come from the Triune God through the Lamb. The Lamb is Jesus, who sacrificed himself on that Friday afternoon at the same hour as the Passover lambs were being sacrificed in the Temple. So, all our joy comes from the Crucified One: "By his wounds we are healed" (Is 53:5, NIV). Now, in this era, this occurs through the Mass, the ritual mystically enacting the impact of that Friday, and through the sacraments, which empower us to participate more intensely in it. In the future, in the Forever Paradise, "the leaves of the tree ... for the healing of the nations" (Rv 22:2) will be therapeutic because they grow on the Tree of Life, whose soil is rich because it is drenched in the blood that flowed on that Friday afternoon from the Tree of the Cross.

"Here at Last Is the Thing I Was Made For"[11]

Sheer vitality! That was why He, the Second Person of the Trinity, had become embodied in Jesus: "I came that they may have life, and have it abundantly" (Jn 10:10). This abundant life is finally achieved in all its magnificence on the heavenized Earth. The first instance of this super-human vitality was in Jesus' own resurrected body.

This is why the forever civilization will be marked by exuberant live-liness, excitement, and creativity. The atmosphere will be that of a wedding banquet. Rightly so, because what will occur in the new world is, in its deepest meaning, a marriage. As Leithart remarks, John's vision in Revelation, when seen as the continuation of his Gospel, "can be read as a grand divine romance, an apocalyptic expansion of the Song of Songs."[12] Heaven and Earth are married because the Crucified-Resurrected-Ascended Jesus is fully united to his perfected Bride, his Mystical Body. The announcement of the nuptials is made amid dramatic scenes pointing to it as the climax of world history:

> And from the throne came a voice crying, "Praise our God, all you his servants, you who fear him, small and great." Then I heard what seemed to be the voice of a great multitude, like the sound of many waters and like the sound of mighty thunder-

peals, crying, "Hallelujah! For the Lord our God the Almighty reigns. Let us rejoice and exult and give him the glory, for the marriage of the Lamb has come, and his Bride has made herself ready; it was granted her to be clothed with fine linen, bright and pure" — for the fine linen is the righteous deeds of the saints. And the angel said to me, "Write this: Blessed are those who are invited to the marriage supper of the Lamb." (Revelation 19:5–9)

The meaning of the analogy of marriage is disclosed by the voice in Revelation 21:3: "Behold, the dwelling of God is with men. He will dwell with them, and they shall be his people, and God himself will be with them." The greatest love story ever told, which began before the days began, is now brought to a magnificent conclusion that is simultaneously the beginning that will have no ending.

This wedding is a joyful event marked by festivity, the thrill of new beginnings, and the delight of a bright future. That is why the metaphor of a wedding feast — among the Jews the festivities lasted seven days — constantly occurs throughout Jewish history. Jesus' own presence at many festive meals and banquets was a symbolic gesture announcing that in his person the eschatological banquet had arrived in its inaugural stage. Moreover, he had portrayed the forever life as festive: "And men will come from east and west, and from north and south, and sit at table in the kingdom of God" (Lk 13:29).

There, you will feel the joy expand within you and around you, for his words will have become your reality: "Enter into the joy" (Mt 25:23). All that our Jewish forefathers had ardently longed for will be a reality: "I … will set my sanctuary in the midst of them for evermore. My dwelling place shall be with them; and I will be their God, and they shall be my people" (Ez 37:26–27). "For behold, I create new heavens and a new earth; / and the former things shall not be remembered or come into mind. / But be glad and rejoice for ever in that which I create; / for behold, I create Jerusalem a rejoicing, and her people a joy" (Is 65:17–18).

This bridal relationship of humans with God will create the climate for all other relationships in the heavenized civilization. You will feel an atmosphere of self-sacrificing love everywhere in the city! As Volf and

McAnnally-Linz note, the "politics" of the heavenized civilization will be that of "a community governed by internalized love, each willing to attune their behavior to others' needs, and all together inhabiting a space of common belonging."[13]

In Heaven you will fall in love with Love in a way that only you are capable of. As Lewis states:

> Your soul has a curious shape because it is a hollow made to fit a particular swelling in the infinite contours of the divine substance, or a key to unlock one of the doors in the house with many mansions. For it is not humanity in the abstract that is to be saved, but you — you, the individual reader. ... Blessed and fortunate creature, your eyes shall behold Him and not another's. All that you are, sins apart, is destined, if you will let God have His good way, to utter satisfaction. ... Your place in heaven will seem to be made for you and you alone, because you were made for it.[14]

From "the day the days were born,"[15] you had been a thought in God's mind. He knew you before he formed you in your mother's womb (Jer 1:5). Your name was "written before the foundation of the world in the book of life of the Lamb" (Rv 13:8). All because he desired to have a uniquely intimate relationship with you, as astounding as this is to our ears. As Lewis remarks, "He died not for men, but for each man. If each man had been the only man made, He would have done no less."[16] In Heaven you will ever remain alert to this fact because you will see on his resurrected body the marks of his wounds. So unique will be this relationship of yours with him that no one else will ever be privy to its secrets: "He who has an ear, let him hear what the Spirit says to the churches. To him who conquers I will give some of the hidden manna, and I will give him a white stone, with a new name written on the stone which no one knows except him who receives it'" (Rv 2:17).

In this intimate relationship, God fully knows you and, amazingly, you immediately know him. "For now we see in a mirror dimly, but then face to face. Now I know in part; then I shall understand fully, even as

I have been fully understood" (1 Cor 13:12). We will inhabit him as he inhabits us. Knowing us fully, he will renew us fully by renewing even our past: "He will wipe away every tear from their eyes, and death shall be no more, neither shall there be mourning nor crying nor pain any more, for the former things have passed away" (Rv 21:4). As John Eldredge remarks, "What tender intimacy is foretold when we are promised that our loving Father will wipe every tear from our eyes personally — not only tears of sorrow, but all the tears of shame, guilt, and remorse. That moment alone will make the whole journey worth it."[17]

While still on the journey, we make our own the prayer of our Jewish forefather: "One thing have I asked of the Lord, that will I seek after; / that I may dwell in the house of the Lord all the days of my life, / to behold the beauty of the Lord, and to inquire in his temple" (Ps 27:4). This gazing on the beauty of the Lord is the beatific vision. Endlessly, in a crescendo of excitement, awe, wonder, and joy, we will discover depths upon depths of Love and Beauty — a forever ecstasy. Indeed, "What no eye has seen, nor ear heard, nor the heart of man conceived, what God has prepared for those who love him" (1 Cor 2:9).

CHAPTER 17

TRAILBLAZER FOR A NEW CIVILIZATION

Life — a great adventure toward the light.

— Paul Claudel[1]

W e have traveled a long journey from the materialistic city of modernity with its vision of a meaningless world in which we see ourselves as disconnected from each other, nature, the past, the forever-future, and the Creator. Along the way, we have discovered that there is no need for this disconnectedness and lack of deep relationships. The breakthroughs of the new physics and numerous discoveries (and rediscoveries) in disciplines from astrophysics to microbiology confirm Catholicism's synthesis of rational thought with the divinely revealed biblical message. When we reached the peaks of the biblical worldview, we discovered the truth of philosopher Martin Buber's statement, "All journeys have secret destinations of which the traveler is unaware." Indeed, we found that we had tracked down our own identity.

We want to remain on these peaks. We want to ever keep in sight its panorama of life's meaning. However, as we are well aware, this is quite a challenge in contemporary society, where interruptions and distractions have become a lifestyle.[2] But what if landscapes, starry skies, the circadian rhythm, and the seasons were to become the means of not only remembering but even intensifying our alertness to the panoramic vision?

There is a mysterious moment each day when we can become more sensitive to the life-changing impact caused by living inside the magnetic field of influence of the Lord of History: the twilight before sunrise. In those moments, when the sun is deeply below the horizon, we experience an in-between time, a "thin time." At this hour, one reality alone is moving, growing, intensifying in the landscape and in our inscape: Light! In Hebrew the word for "twilight" is *neshef*, one meaning of which is "movement toward the light." We cannot overemphasize the role of light — the first reality created by the Creator, he who "is the Love that moves the sun and other stars,"[3] and who indeed wants us to know him as "the light of the world" (Jn 8:12). As Scripture scholar John Phillips remarks:

> God said, "Light be," and light was. Nobody, even today, can tell us what light is. We know what light does, but not what light is. It is one of the most mysterious entities in the universe. In physics it has become the new absolute. As such, it is at the heart of the famous equation $E = mc^2$ (energy equals mass multiplied by the speed of light squared) which, in turn, ushered in the atomic age.[4]

At dawn we can look forward to both the sunrise and the Son's "resurrection" of Earth. We live in the epoch between the past event of Easter and the future era of the heavenized Earth. But, already, we experience the Resurrection's power inaugurating that future. Now! Inside us. In a resurrected mind. Dawn as the time between night and day gives us insight into the sense of time that we who are in Christ experience. For we live at the overlap of two time zones: that of the everyday, death-headed time and that of the forever, heavenized time that will reign one day on Earth.

Amid the intimate atmosphere of those moments before sunrise, when semidarkness covers the landscape, stillness and timelessness reign. It is when you *really* feel, hear, see. You discover that you are not quite alone. He, your Creator-Lover-Rescuer, is present. You hear him murmur: "Be still, and I know that I am God" (Ps 46:10). He alerts you to his approach through the doorway of dawn: "Behold, I stand at the door and knock; if any one hears my voice and opens the door, I will come in to him and eat with him, and he with me" (Rv 3:20). "I am your deliverance" (Ps 35:3). And with every fiber of your being, you cry out: "O Lord, who is like you?" (Ps 35:10), and "In your light do we see light" (Ps 36:9).

The distinctive steely-blue shade of light just before sunrise and after sunset has given these times of twilight each day the name "blue hour." The golden hours immediately following dawn and preceding sunset both have a characteristic warm glow. Both "hours" swiftly pass, sometimes lasting for just fifteen minutes.

But how they mesmerize us! Artists, poets, novelists, and photographers have found inspiration for creativity in this atmosphere in which nature and self are recreated, reborn, reenergized. Henry David Thoreau remarked, "Every morning was a cheerful invitation to make my life of equal simplicity and, I may say, innocence, with Nature herself." Paul Valery, the French poet, often known as the "poet of the dawn," for much of his life woke before sunrise and began his creative work during the hours he described as "between the lamp and the sun."[5]

The golden hour of sunrise is glorious, but the blue hour before it is perhaps even more wonderful. It is she, described by John Ruskin as the "transparent Blue passing into Gold,"[6] who provokes the thrilling sense of expectancy in our psyche. We feel nature and ourselves pulsating, readying to birth light, vitality, and energy. Then, in the sunrise, the magnificence of the new day's beauty arrives. Nature is reborn; the silhouettes begin to be filled with a soft glow; all of the landscape acquires the inscape of identity; trees, plants, and flowers seem to begin breathing and send forth their fragrance into our psyche.

In this "temporary Paradise at the frontier of the day,"[7] as amid a flash of lightning, you intuit the future heavenized Earth. You are filled with a longing for it, as for home. This is due to the distinctive effect of twilight's blue hour, with its absence of shadows and the transfixing of the landscape into silhouettes showing us shapes but not features. An aura of mystery envelops you. Mystery! You are in the era of "the mystery hidden for ages and generations but now made manifest to his saints" (Col 1:26). This is the mystery of the glorious destiny for humans to "become partakers of the divine nature" (2 Pt 1:4) and to live on the heavenized Earth where the Creator-Lover will be "everything to every one" (1 Cor 15:28). In dawn's atmosphere, surrounded by nature's mystery, the Great Mystery is better able to enrapture you. It fills you with the sense of wonder and expectation so necessary for holistic connectedness to reality.

When his Mystery resurrects your mind, meaning begins to encircle you and penetrate you. This is because the sense of mystery births wonder, the starting point for all of history's breakthrough discoveries — and it births wonder-full people. As Chesterton remarked, "We have grown accustomed to the unaccountable. Every stone or flower is a hieroglyphic of which we have lost the key; with every step of our lives we enter into the middle of some story."[8] Through the deepening sense of mystery and wonder you can see all of reality with new eyes. You can "stare at a tree in an infinite leisure; but we know all the time that the real difference is between a stillness of mystery and an explosion of explanation."[9] Chesterton was right: "The object of the artistic and spiritual life was to dig for this submerged sunrise of wonder; so that a man sitting in a chair might suddenly understand that he was actually alive, and be happy."[10]

We are still amid the dusk, but the light is growing inside us. It is inaugural time, threshold time: the time of potential for new beginnings, the opportunity for breakthroughs. As at daybreak, when we have enough light to see the silhouettes of mountains, trees, landscapes, and people, but not enough to visualize their features, light is meant to grow inside us and around us. For as the moments go by, the silhouettes are filled with light. As Oscar Wilde described, "Veil after veil of thin dusky gauze is lifted, and by degrees the forms and colors of things are restored to them and we watch the dawn remaking the world in its antique pattern"[11] — the ancient pattern disclosed from Genesis to Revelation.

The biblical texts reveal to us the patterns of nature, life, and lifestyle that will occur on the heavenized Planet Earth. In their light, we can better understand everything in the present era. In landscapes and ourselves we perceive inaugural versions of what the Creator intends them to be on the heavenized Earth. Then, nature will be flawlessly beautiful, but it will still be the mountains, seas, trees, animals, flora, and fauna that we know and love here and now. Those who arrive at the future heavenized Earth will experience immediately how different and yet how similar the renewed Earth is to what they knew in their mortal lifetime.

Even in this age in which we live now, we are called to see everything futuristically. This is not flight from reality but flight *into* reality. Seeing in this way allows us to recognize the sublime potential in others, in the biosphere, and in civilization because we have seen the Divine Architect's blueprints for the world, and we know that they are beauty-filled beyond imagination. For we have stood on the mountain peak of Calvary at the dawn of Resurrection time. This is the experience that has made so many of our great Jewish and Christian forefathers into people who risked all to build a new world order.

In every dawn, we experience the emergence of the new world inaugurated at Jesus' resurrection. As Chesterton stated: "On the third day the friends of Christ coming at daybreak to the place found the grave empty and the stone rolled away. In varying ways, they realized the new wonder; the world had died in the night. What they were looking at was the first day of a new creation, with a new heaven and a new earth; and in a semblance of a gardener God walked again in the garden, not in the cool of the evening, but in the dawn."[12]

Now, in this era, as we live in him who described himself as "the root and the offspring of David, the bright morning star" (Rv 22:16), we begin to enter into this light and it begins to enter into us. We know that "if any one is in Christ, he is a new creation; the old has passed away, behold, the new has come" (2 Cor 5:17). The newness is not complete in us, however; we are in the inaugural stage, as an embryo in the womb. But we experience it in the same way we experience the dawn: with utter certainty, because "we have the prophetic word made more sure. You will do well to pay attention to this as to a lamp shining in a dark place, until the day dawns and the morning star rises in your hearts" (2 Pt 1:19).

Now we experience the beginning of its light, but one day we will be so intimately flooded with its light that we will — here we are at the borders of language — become like it. For this is his promise: "And I will give him the morning star" (Rv 2:28). Again, we can be confident of this, for he who speaks the promise is "he who made the Pleiades and Orion, and turns deep darkness into the morning, and darkens the day into night, who calls for the waters of the sea, and pours them out upon the surface of the earth, the LORD is his name" (Am 5:8).

Resurrectionists!

Just as we recognize the dawn of the final era in every daybreak, we can sense that every moment of beauty is tinged by Heaven's forever loveliness. In each sunrise, we see the forever sunrise. In the thrilling moments of joy, the forever joy. In the rush of wind, we are alert to the presence of the Creator Spirit — the Wind who once "was moving over the face of the waters" (Gn 1:2), resolved to bring his universe to fulfillment. In every newness at the birth of a child, in springtime, at the recovery of health, in the new year, we rejoice at the newness of supernatural vitality throbbing in our veins, and we are confident that in him we can live forever. The dawn reminds us that a new beginning can occur at any moment because we live in him who resurrected "toward the dawn of the first day of the week" (Mt 28:1). Because our own geographical location is now "in Christ," we are ever within the sphere of radiance of his resurrected power. Our past can never drown us. Every new day is a flash of vision, vitality, and energy for starting all over again.

We are thus a "dawn people," and as we immerse ourselves in the experience of light ever so gradually vanquishing darkness, we realize that our life's time in Christ is likewise a movement into light. Our movement through time replicates the Creator's transformation of the universe from the darkness of chaotic and shapeless non-identity into an ordered and beautiful cosmos. As dawn people, we have the mission to enter into the movement of world history, to act as agents of Operation Genesis: to bring light where there is darkness. Because we have experienced the "light of the world" (Jn 8:12) through our experience of living in dawn time, we are called to "let [our] light so shine" (Mt 5:16), to be light, indeed, to be "sons of light" (1 Thes 5:5). In this way, we will have the vision and energy to create cities of light. Because, since "we walk in the light, as he is in the light, we have fellowship with one another" (1 Jn 1:7) and we are called to create a civilization that breathes the "fragrance of Christ" (2 Cor 2:15, NASB). We are called to be revolutionaries of the Light! Our shout is "I will awake the dawn" (Ps 57:8)[13] — the dawn of the new era when the Creator-Lover-Rescuer will be "everything to every one" (1 Cor 15:28) *because he will be all in all.*

Resurrectionists are meant to be revolutionists! By allowing him who is the "light of the world" (Jn 8:12) to metamorphose us into radiant people, we enter inside the mysterious dynamism of light. Light drives beauty! This is because, as the philosopher Georg Gadamer remarks, "Beauty has the mode of being of light."[14] It is the shining, the radiance of any reality that empowers it to become beautiful for us. As Gadamer writes, "Without light nothing beautiful can appear" and therefore without light "nothing can be beautiful."[15] This requires that our mind be capable of seeing the radiance. Therefore, the mind itself needs its own light, which has been given it by him who is the Light of the World, through whom all things were made (Jn 1:3). Light was the first reality created, the light through which the shapeless chaos of raw material became the identifiable universe in which we live. Light in the biblical worldview symbolizes the energy, vitality, genuineness, and goodness which together empower beauty. It is darkness-destroying: "The light shines in the darkness, and the darkness has not overcome it" (Jn 1:5).

As image bearers of the Creator-Lover-Rescuer, we are called to create beauty inside ourselves and all around us. But how? By allowing the dynamism of beauty to function as designed. As Gadamer states, "The beauty of a beautiful thing appears in it as light, as a radiance. It makes itself manifest. In fact the universal mode of being of light is to be reflected in itself in this way. Light is not only the brightness of that on which it shines; by making something visible, it is visible itself, and it is not visible in any other way than by making something else visible."[16] In other words, to create beauty we must be creators who desire not our own beauty but the beauty of others and of civilization. We must want to make others "visible." We must desire others to become radiantly alive, and this means we must want a beautiful world more than a beautiful self. Above all, through all, and in all, we must want to make the Way, the Truth, and the Life visible and radiant to the world. Like John the Baptist, our shout will be "He must increase, but I must decrease" (Jn 3:30). We resolve to be like Jesus himself, who became the supremely beautiful human by being supremely self-sacrificing. When we allow his passionate, resurrectionist dynamism to seize hold of us, we also will discover — to our amazement — that in the apparent loss of self, we gain more, infinitely more.

This is the starting point for Catholicism's civilization-building. Our divinely inspired blueprints for changing the world require us to view it as a project of beautifying culture and society. We discover how to do this by recognizing the Creator's patterns and rhythms of beauty encoded into reality. And we intensify our experience of beauty by gazing on Jesus. Consequently, we become people who want to beautify everything around us. We Catholics are called to fight for beauty, everywhere and in every moment. The banal must and can become sublimely beautiful through him, with him, and in him who is Beauty itself. We are called to battle to bring beauty — the synthesis of genuineness and goodness — into our way of being human and our way of building civilization. As Thomas Dubay notes:

> In his masterpiece, *The Brothers Karamazov*, Fyodor Dostoyevski placed on the lips of one of his characters the observation that "beauty is the battlefield where God and Satan contend with each other for the hearts of men." The one is supreme Glory (the biblical name for supereminent beauty); the other is supreme ugliness. Though our free wills make the choice, it is beauty that provides the powerful attraction to the only victory that ultimately matters in this peak of all combats.[17]

Pioneers for a Civilization Radiating Beauty

Because we live in Christ, we are resurrectionists. Our faces are turned toward the sunrise "through the tender mercy of our God, when the day shall dawn upon us from on high to give light to those who sit in darkness and in the shadow of death" (Lk 1:78–79). And we have his certainty that the dawn of newness will always be possible for ourselves and civilization, even when delayed by the cosmic forces of evil: "If it seem slow, wait for it; it will surely come, it will not delay" (Hb 2:3). As "sons of light" (1 Thes 5:5), we know that we are called to free minds, hearts, and social structures from the darkness which is the source of the deadly. To achieve this liberation requires combativeness against the dehumanizing forces within us and around us. We are called to strike blows for freedom every day of our lives, everywhere! "I will awake the dawn!" is ever the shout resounding in our hearts.[18]

This freedom is meant to organically breathe forth from individuals into lifestyle, culture, politics, and economics. The New Israel, like the Israel of old, is called to create a "liturgical empire," freeing the nations from all dehumanizing tyrannies in all shapes, from addictions to economic policies.[19] Constantly, in the psalms and elsewhere, the Spirit alerts us to our mission to change the world: "I will give thanks to you, O LORD, among the peoples, / I will sing praises to you among the nations. / For your steadfast love is great above the heavens, / your faithfulness reaches to the clouds. / Be exalted, O God, above the heavens! / Let your glory be over all the earth!" (Ps 108:3–5). These texts, which speak of the theophany of divine glory as a revelation of God's right to be recognized as ruler of Planet Earth, imply that, as biblical scholars Frank-Lothar Hossfeld and Erich Zenger have stated, "The nations will achieve their authentic politicosocial form only when they acknowledge and accept YAHWEH as the world's king."[20]

By living as dawn people, we become who we should be: people living in the circadian rhythm of the Forever-Day with its forever light and forever vitality. As day breaks, we sense our mission to change ourselves and the world around us, carrying forward the revolution that began on that Friday afternoon and the first Easter Sunday. The Christ-follower is called to be like a poet of light, in the sense that, as the writer Aberjhani remarks, "a poet is a verb that blossoms light / in gardens of dawn, or sometimes midnight. ... / Like vines of flaming truth they embrace and renew, / squeezing hope out of fears once poisonous and blue."[21]

We pray for God's light in us to grow so we can shatter darkness inside us and around us to create a civilization of dawn. This is the mission he has given us. And we are capable of it, for, as Jesus told his followers, "You are the light of the world. A city set on a hill cannot be hidden. Nor do men light a lamp and put it under a bushel, but on a stand, and it gives light to all in the house. Let your light so shine before men, that they may see your good works and give glory to your Father who is in heaven" (Mt 5:14–16). We work therefore to inaugurate a civilization filled with the light and beauty of him who is the world's light.

The vision of the heavenized Earth in the Book of Revelation is the vision of the world transfigured by beauty. The "New Jerusalem," the civilization of the future, with its walls of transparent jasper, its foundations all jeweled, and its gates of pearl, is presented as a radiant splendor emanating from the divine beauty who is everywhere present. This is the vision that can inspire us to inaugurate advance signposts of this beauty: in the arts, economics, politics, in designing new neighborhoods and decorating our own homes, and in everyday gestures and actions of genuine humanity filled with kindness, loveliness, generosity, and goodness. Thus every action becomes sublime and contributes to beautifying others and society as a whole. Thus, by every glance of our eyes, word of our lips, and action of our limbs, implicitly and explicitly we will strive to attract everyone around us to him who is "the way, and the truth, and the life" (Jn 14:6) and who can be experienced in all of his grandeur within his Mystical Body, the Church.

Thus, we will act futuristically. As our Jewish forefathers built the Temple as the inaugural scale model of the heavenized Earth, and as our Catholic forefathers built Christendom for the same reason, so will we also, emulating them, seek to build a futuristic civilization with a Christian soul because of our enthusiasm for the vision given us.

We are called to create this civilization of light organically, by allowing Jesus' light within us to radiate outwards. That was how Christendom came into existence. As Joseph Pearce states, "It is, therefore, hardly surprising that the heart of Christendom — its theology, its philosophy, its painting, its architecture, its sculpture, its music, its literature — is the very incarnation of the integrated harmony, wholeness and oneness, of its Founder."[22]

This resolve to play our role in changing the world around us has characterized the heroines and heroes of Catholicism through the ages. As faithful followers of the God-Man, they were alert to the fact that because of the creation and the redemption, history is mysteriously both God's story and ours. We know that the world has a story — Operation Genesis — and therefore, as the writer and convert to Catholicism Richard John Neuhaus states, "We perceive a dignity to the world that is grounded in a destiny from eternity to eternity; we see a story of the world that the world does not begin to suspect is part of its integral identity."[23]

Indomitable Romantics

In this story, everyone has a role, everyone is important, and there are no banal actions. Every act of yours is sublimely important and matters. This is because we are in Christ, in the God-Man's Mystical Body, sharing in his resurrected power to transfigure the world around us. The tumultuous Parisian writer Léon Bloy, in his own inimitable style, expressed it as follows:

> The smallest action is heavy with necessary significance: Our freedom is linked to the balance of the world, and this is what must be understood in order not to be surprised by the deep mystery of Reversibility which is the philosophical name of the grand dogma of the Communion of Saints. Every man who produces a free act projects his personality into infinity. If he reluctantly gives a penny to a poor person, this penny pierces the hand of the poor, falls, pierces the earth, pierces the suns, crosses the firmament and compromises the universe. If he performs an impure act, he may darken thousands of hearts which, although unknown to him, are nevertheless mysteriously connected to him and who need this man to be pure, as a traveler dying of thirst needs the glass of water of the gospel. A charitable act, a movement of true pity sings for him the divine praises from Adam until the end of the centuries; it heals the sick, consoles the despairing, calms the storms, redeems the captives, converts those without faith, and protects the human race. The entirety of Christian philosophy is in the inexpressible

importance of the free act and in the notion of an enveloping and indestructible solidarity.[24]

The young genius Novalis (1772–1801), polymath and poet, arguably the father of Romanticism, who greatly impacted European literature and philosophy, once asked a question that was startling considering he was a Protestant: "What proves that Catholicism was the true religion?"[25] In his book *Christendom or Europe*, he answers in a most surprising way:

> Christianity has three forms. One is the creative element of religion, the joy in all religion. Another is mediation in general, the belief in the capacity of everything earthly to be the wine and bread of eternal life. Yet a third is the belief in Christ, his mother and the saints. … The old catholic faith, the last of these forms, was applied Christianity come to life. Its omnipresence in life, its love for art, its deep humanity, the sanctity of its marriages, its philanthropic sense of community, its joy in poverty, obedience and loyalty, all make it unmistakable as genuine religion and contain the basic features of its constitution. It is purified through the stream of time … it will bless the earth.[26]

Novalis, a poetic genius alert to the beauty of divine and human love, sensed that at the center of Catholicism's Christendom there lay the transforming power of self-sacrificing love. With astonishing foresight, he saw the very problem for which contemporary postmodern philosophers, ecologists, poets, and artists now critique modernity: the "progressive disenchantment of the world."[27] But he also identified its cause: the destruction of the enthralling vision of the world brought by Christianity because it had affirmed that the world and everything in it is the outcome of Love. This colored the mindset of the Catholics of Christendom with what can only be called a "romantic" view of the world. They recognized that the story of the world is a great romance between the Creator-Lover-Rescuer and his beloved that reaches its climax in the drama of the passionate event of Good Friday. Consequently, a new world order must begin with the restoration of this type of love. In an unpublished note,

Novalis remarked: "The world must be romanticized. Only in that way will one rediscover its original senses. Romanticization is nothing less than a qualitative raising of the power of a thing ... I romanticize something when I give the commonplace a higher meaning, the known the dignity of the unknown, and the finite the appearance of the infinite."[28]

Christendom was romanticized through its romantic central ritual that mystically imbued the passionate love of the Second Person of the Trinity in its participants: the Sacrifice of the Mass. On the foundation of the Great Hero's self-sacrificing love, individuals became self-sacrificing lovers. Christendom was a civilization characterized by self-sacrificing love because it was born at the altar of the Sacrifice of the Mass, the mystical enactment of the God-Man's passionate love empowering humans to become free.

This ethos of self-sacrificing love brought to birth the civilization of Christendom. Unlike other civilizations which came into existence from the top down by the "will to power" of elites, Christendom was born organically from transfigured people who thought and lived by the self-sacrificing commitment of their resurrected minds.[29] It was a grassroots movement, a voluntary, freedom-filled reality. This spirit created a "climate" in which the genuinely human values thrived and the dehumanizing were stifled. As G. K. Chesterton wrote:

> At the beginning of the Dark Ages the great pagan cosmopolitan society now grown Christian was as much a slave state as old South Carolina. By the fourteenth century, it was almost as much a state of peasant proprietors as modern France. ... This startling and silent transformation is perhaps the best measure of the pressure of popular life in the Middle Ages, of how fast it was making new things in its spiritual factory. ... The Catholic type of Christianity was not merely an element, it was a climate; and in that climate the slave would not grow.[30]

Watchmen of the Dawn

So, therefore, like that fiery, empathic woman Mary Magdalene "toward the dawn of the first day of the week" (Mt 28:1), we too resolve to live in dawn time, the place where the resurrection of our minds will occur now in preparation for the resurrection of our complete body and psyche in the future.

We are called to the mission of being watchmen of the dawn: "I wait for the LORD, my soul waits, / and in his word I hope; / my soul waits for the LORD / more than watchmen for the morning, / more than watchmen for the morning" (Ps 130:5–6). It is a mission for the well-being and protection of the world, which is dependent on the Mystical Body of Christ. The Hebrew word for "watchman" is *tsâphâh*, which means "to lean forward, to peer into the distance."[31] Historically, the guardians of Jerusalem, who took turns during the night to mount guard upon its parapets, were styled "watchmen": "Upon your walls, O Jerusalem, I have set watchmen; all the day and all the night they shall never be silent" (Is 62:6). They symbolized Yahweh's watchfulness but also the mission of his Chosen People to be mediators between him and humanity through liturgy, prayer, and the spreading of the Kingdom of God. That is why historically the first Christians kept vigil, especially before Easter Sunday, and why monks rise during the night to pray Matins and before dawn to pray Lauds.

The followers of the resurrected Lord share in the light of his Person, which became evident in his Transfiguration. Throughout history there have been so many historically verified instances of committed Christians radiating a mysterious light, not only in their words and actions but even from their physical bodies, that artists have expressed it with the symbol of the disc halo, a universal symbol of holiness.

To give just one example of an occurrence of this mysterious radiance, when Nicholas Motovilov (1809–32) visited the saintly hermit Seraphim of Sarov (1754–1833), he asked the holy man how one could be sure that the Holy Spirit was present and active in one's life. The two men were sitting on tree stumps in a wood. It was a cloudy day. Motovilov narrates what happened:

Then Father Seraphim gripped me firmly by the shoulders and said: "My friend, both of us, at this moment, are in the Holy Spirit, you and I. Why won't you look at me?" "I can't look at you, Father, because the light flashing from your eyes and face is brighter than the sun and I'm dazzled!"

"Don't be afraid, friend of God, you yourself are shining just like I am; you too are now in the fullness of the grace of the Holy Spirit, otherwise you wouldn't be able to see me as you do." Then I looked at the holy man and was panic-stricken. Picture, in the sun's orb, in the most dazzling brightness of its noon-day shining, the face of a man who is talking to you. You see his lips moving, the expression in his eyes, you hear his voice, you feel his arms round your shoulders, and yet you see neither his arms, nor his body, nor his face, you lose all sense of yourself, you can see only the blinding light which spreads everywhere, lighting up the layer of snow covering the glade, and igniting the flakes that are falling on us both like white powder. "What do you feel?" asked Father Seraphim. "An amazing well-being!" I replied. … "I feel a great calm in my soul, a peace which no words can express. … A strange, unknown delight. … An amazing happiness. … I'm amazingly warm. … There's no scent in all the world like this one!" "I know," said Father Seraphim, smiling. "This is as it should be, for divine grace comes to live in our hearts, within us."[32]

Yet we experience a conflict inside ourselves and all around us in society as we live at this intersection of the time zones of Heaven and Earth, striving to fulfill our freedom-fighting mission. Tchaikovsky's 1812 Overture provides us with a musical "picture" of this very real conflict. Written to commemorate Russia's defense against the invading armies of Napoleon in 1812, the clash is represented musically by the opposition between the Christian hymn, the "Troparion of the Holy Cross," and the secular "La Marseillaise," France's national anthem. The former, softly played by violas and cellos, is in jarring contrast with the latter, which is stridently worldly. For much of the overture, the invaders' anthem dominates over the defenders' prayer, growing ever stronger, threatening to drown it out. But then comes the climactic moment, which beautifully expresses all of history's conflicts between good and evil, truth and lies. First, we hear the tumultuous sound of five cannon shots, so loud that all seems definitively lost for the defenders of truth, goodness, and freedom. This is followed by music that sounds like the blowing of winter winds. Yet at this moment of desperation, all begins to change. For it is when the sound of the enemy is loudest, shrillest, and most deafening, that his defeat begins. The invading army's retreat is expressed by a plunging, descending scale now heard in counterpoint to the hymn, which is played by the entire orchestra. At this moment, we hear bells, a Christian symbol of victory, representing the voice of God. The sound of "La Marseillaise" begins to fade away as the harmony of the Christian hymn grows louder, more vibrant, and more beautiful, until, in the grand finale, we hear the total victory of the prayer-filled hymn, symbolized by eleven powerful cannonades.

So likewise in our life as followers of Christ. Paradoxically, the longer we live in the radiant light of his dawn — notwithstanding the cacophonic clamor of the anti-Christ, anti-human forces inside us and around us — the more we experience within ourselves a crescendo of the mysterious light that brings with it supernatural energies for changing the world. We can now see our lifetime with new eyes, as the beginning of the story of our life on the heavenized Earth in which, as C. S. Lewis has reminded us, "every chapter is better than the one before."[33]

ACKNOWLEDGMENTS

For my introduction to modern and postmodern worldviews, I am grateful to the brilliant minds — and dedicated hearts — I came into contact with at the Gregorian University. These "blackrobes" included the Jesuit Raniero Selvaggi, Fr. Vittorio Marcozzi, and Fr. Eduard Huber. I studied modernity's mind-shapers, from Kant and Hegel to Nietzsche, Derrida, and Foucault, under Peter Henrici, later bishop of Chur in Switzerland. From a brief encounter with Jesuit Johannes Baptist Lotz, who had been close to Heidegger, I came to know more of this intellectual whose influence has penetrated Catholic theology. The Irishman Francis O' Farrell taught me transcendental Thomism. Although I would later see its shortcomings while studying under Antonio Livi, certainly it was as clear a presentation of this influential current as one could desire. To the Jesuit Kevin Flannery, the director of my dissertation, a specialist in Aristotle, I am grateful for his demanding logic. For an introduction to cybernetics and the relationship between body and mind in the light of neurophysiology, I am in debt to Gianfranco Basti.

In an extraordinary way, I am grateful to the man whose shout on October 14, 1978, has never ceased to resound in my memory: "Open wide the doors for Christ! To his saving power open the boundaries of States, economic and political systems, the vast fields of culture, civilization and development. Do not be afraid! Christ knows 'what is in man.' He alone knows it."[1] I was a seventeen-year-old listening to the newly elected Polish pope, little realizing that he would ordain me to the priesthood in St. Peter's Basilica over the tomb of Saint Peter twelve years later. He lived with intense alertness to the fact that civilization was at a crossroads; that a new civilization could be built out of the rubble of modernity.

I thank the audiences throughout the United States, English-speaking Canada, Quebec, France, and Ireland, where I have given lectures, directed summer schools, and preached retreats. Recently, I have been energized by the dedicated staff and missionaries at Damascus and so many of the twenty thousand participants, by my students at the Franciscan University of Steubenville, by the young people at Saint Paul's Outreach at Ohio State University, and by the people at Hard as Nails Ministries. I thank Fr. Tim Hayes and Nicholas Ganis for reading the manuscript and for their suggestions. My thanks also in a special way to Fr. PeterClaver Kasasa Kiviiri; and to Fr. Dave Sizemore.

I have loudly thanked Heaven for my editor, Mary Beth Giltner. She is any author's dream reviewer. A woman who has thought deeply about the great questions and with her finger on the pulse of the target audience, ever so thoroughly and tactfully she gets you to re-write and clarify, and indeed she provokes new insights.

Special thanks to Bishop Earl Fernandes for his encouragement of my writing.

Finally, I thank the Most Holy Trinity, first for leading me to become fluent in Gaelic, French, Spanish, Italian, and Latin, and to live and work on three continents, which liberated me from an exclusively Anglo-Saxon way of thinking about the world. And, sublimely, for having brought me to encounter some years ago a mysterious ancient ritual on a summer's afternoon hike amid the Swiss Alps at two thousand meters. Ever since, it has resonated within me, re-enchanting my entire existence, enlightening all that appears in these pages, bonding me as I murmur, "I will go to the altar of God, to God my exceeding joy" (Ps 43:4).

NOTES

Introduction

Arnold Toynbee, quoted in Mary Anne Perkins, Christendom and European Identity: The Legacy of a Grand Narrative since 1789 (Walter de Gruyter, 2004), Kindle Locations 178-184.

1. Roger Kimball, *The Long March: How the Cultural Revolution of the 1960s Changed America* (Encounter Books, 2000), 14–15. The slogan was coined by the socialist student-activist Rudi Dutschke in the 1960s to describe his strategy for putting in place the conditions for revolution. The phrase "long march" calls to mind the physical march of the Chinese communist army across China.

2. See David K. Naugle, *Worldview: The History of a Concept* (Eerdmans, 2002). For the role of worldviews in understanding Christianity, see N. T. Wright, *Christian Origins and the Question of God, vol. 1: The New Testament and the People of God* (SPCK, 1992), pt. 2.

3. Derek H. Davis, *Religion and the Continental Congress, 1774–1789: Contributions to Original Intent* (Oxford University Press, 2000), 144.

4. Quoted in Christopher Partridge, *The Re-enchantment of the West, vol. 1: Alternative Spiritualities, Sacralization, Popular Culture, and Occulture* (Bloomsbury Academic, 2004), 8. The phrase was coined by Friedrich Schiller.

5. Zygmunt Bauman, *Modernity and the Holocaust* (Cornell University Press, 2002).

6. Jean-François Lyotard, *The Differend: Phrases in Dispute*, trans. Georges Van Den Abbeele (University of Minnesota Press, 1988), 91.

7. Klaus Schwab and Thierry Malleret, *COVID-19: The Great Reset* (Forum, 2020).

8. The term "new world order" was used toward the end of the First World War about President Woodrow Wilson's international vision. For a contemporary book using the term, see Anne M. Lovell, et al., eds., *Global Health and the New World Order: Historical and Anthropological Approaches to a Changing Regime of Governance* (Manchester University Press, 2020).

9. Alan Ware, *Political Parties and Party Systems* (Oxford University Press, 1996), 60.

10. See the official website of the World Economic Forum, "World Economic Forum Annual Meeting," https://www.weforum.org/events/world-economic-forum-annual-meeting-2023.

11. Schwab and Malleret, *COVID-19*, Kindle loc.s 1887–1891. The two academics cited are Carl Benedikt Frey and Michael A. Osborne, "The Future of Employment: How Susceptible Are Jobs to Computerisation?," *Technological Forecasting and Social Change* 114 (January 2017): 254–280.

12. Ibid., Kindle loc.s 136–138.

13. Klaus Schwab, "Now Is the Time for a 'Great Reset,'" World Economic Forum, June 3, 2020, https://www.weforum.org/agenda/2020/06/now-is-the-time-for-a-great-reset.

14. Paul de Man, "Literary History and Literary Modernity," in *Blindness and Insight* (Oxford University Press, 1971), quoted in Zina O'Leary, *The Social Science Jargon-Buster: The Key Terms You Need to Know* (Sage, 2007), 171.

15. Klaus Schwab, *The Aftermath of the Covid-19 Pandemic* (Independently Published, 2020).

16. See the interview with the pastor of the Catholic parish in Davos: "Das katholische

Element kommt auch zum Tragen," Domradio.de, January 22, 2020, https://www
.domradio.de/artikel/das-katholische-element-kommt-auch-zum-tragen-pfarrer
-davos-ueber-das-weltwirtschaftsforum.

17. "The Great Reset: Remarks to World Economic Forum, Kristalina Georgieva,
Managing Director, IMF," June 3, 2020, https://www.imf.org/en/News/Articles/2020
/06/03/sp060320-remarks-to-world-economic-forum-the-great-reset.

18. Klaus Schwab, *The Fourth Industrial Revolution* (Crown, 2017), 3.

19. Klaus Schwab, *Stakeholder Capitalism: A Global Economy That Works for Progress,
People and Planet* (Wiley, 2021); Schwab and Malleret, *COVID-19*, Kindle loc.s 1108–
1109.

20. This was a proposal of a 2010 World Economic Forum report titled "Global
Redesign." See Markus Kaltenborn, Markus Krajewski, and Heike Kuhn, eds., *Sustainable
Development Goals and Human Rights* (SpringerOpen, 2020), 209ff; see also Adam Jezard,
"Who and What Is 'Civil Society?,'" World Economic Forum, April 23, 2018, https://www.
weforum.org/agenda/2018/04/what-is-civil-society/.

21. Schwab and Malleret, *COVID-19*, Kindle loc. 1093.

22. Ibid., Kindle loc.s 1361–1362.

23. See the classic account of twentieth-century Marxism, David T. McLellan,
Marxism after Marx, 4th ed. (Palgrave Macmillan, 2007).

24. Perry Anderson, *Considerations on Western Marxism* (Verso Books, 2016).

25. Kimball, *The Long March*, 14–15.

26. Thomas Wheatland, *The Frankfurt School in Exile* (University of Minnesota
Press, 2009).

27. Rather astonishing in the light of Freud's own self-evaluation. In a letter to
Wilhelm Fliess, February 1, 1900, he declared: "I am actually not at all a man of science,
not an observer, nor an experimenter, nor a thinker. I am by temperament nothing
but a conquistador — an adventurer, if you want it translated — with all the curiosity,
daring, and tenacity characteristic of a man of this sort." In Brian McHale and Randall
Stevenson, eds., *The Edinburgh Companion to Twentieth-Century Literatures in English*
(Edinburgh University Press, 2006), 12.

28. Craig Calhoun, *Critical Social Theory: Culture, History, and the Challenge of Difference* (Blackwell, 1995).

29. Wheatland, *The Frankfurt School in Exile* (University of Minnesota Press, 2009),
342.

30. *A Critique of Pure Tolerance* is the 1965 book authored by Herbert Marcuse together with Robert Paul Wolff and Barrington Moore Jr., in which the authors examine
the political role of tolerance.

31. Joe Kincheloe and Shirley Steinburg, *Changing Multiculturalism* (Open University Press, 1997). 24.

32. David Horowitz, *Barack Obama's Rules for Revolution: The Alinsky Model* (David
Horowitz Freedom Center, 2009).

33. "The Left Is Remaking the World," *The New York Times* July 11, 2020, a https://
www.nytimes.com/2020/07/11/opinion/sunday/defund-police-cancel-rent.html.

34. "The Left Is Remaking the World."

35. A term used by Paul Ricoeur, *Freud & Philosophy: An Essay on Interpretation,*

trans. Denis Savage (Yale University Press, 1970), 32–36.

36. A phrase coined by Cardinal Joseph Ratzinger in the last homily he gave before becoming Pope Benedict XVI. See Homily of His Eminence Cardinal Joseph Ratzinger, Vatican Basilica, April 18, 2005, Vatican.va.

37. Quoted in Paul R. Sponheim, *The Pulse of Creation*: *God and the Transformation of the World* (Fortress Press, 1999), Kindle loc. 36.

38. For politics in the era of Christendom, see the groundbreaking work of Andrew Willard Jones, *Before Church and State*: *A Study of Social Order in the Sacramental Kingdom of St. Louis IX* (Emmaus Academic, 2017). For economics, see chap. 10, "Founders of Free-Market Economics," in William J. Slattery, *Heroism and Genius: How Catholic Priests Helped to Build — and Can Help Rebuild — Western Civilization* (Ignatius Press, 2017).

39. Slattery, *Heroism and Genius*.

40. Daniel Cohen, *Homo Economicus: The (Lost) Prophet of Modern Times* (Wiley, 2014).

41. Charlene Spretnak, *The Resurgence of the Real*: *Body, Nature, and Place in a Hypermodern World* (Routledge, 1999) Kindle loc. 222.

42. See Norberto Bobbio, *Left and Right*: *The Significance of a Political Distinction* (Wiley, 2016).

43. Conservatism as a political philosophy began with the publication of the work of Edmund Burke, *Reflections on the Revolution in France* in 1790. See Michael Freeman, *Edmund Burke and the Critique of Political Radicalism* (Blackwell, 1980); James Burnham, *Suicide of the West: An Essay on the Meaning and Destiny of Liberalism* (Encounter Books, 2014); and Patrick J. Deneen, *Why Liberalism Failed* (Yale University Press, 2019).

44. Werner Heisenberg, *Physics and Beyond*: *Encounters and Conversations* (Harper and Row, 1971), 146.

45. Rodney Stark, *How the West Won*: *The Neglected Story of the Triumph of Modernity* (ISI Books, 2014); and Slattery, *Heroism and Genius*.

46. Michael Allen Gillespie, *The Theological Origins of Modernity* (University of Chicago Press, 2008) and Catherine Wilson, *Epicureanism at the Origins of Modernity* (Oxford University Press, 2008). Also see Peter Gay, *The Enlightenment*: *An Interpretation*: *The Rise of Modern Paganism* (Norton, 1966).

Chapter 1: Catholicism Is About Reality, Not Religion

1. "Constitution of Ireland," Government of Ireland, January 2020, https://www.irishstatutebook.ie/eli/cons/en/html, preamble.

2. Joseph Mary Plunkett, quoted in Padraic Colum and Edward J. O' Brien, eds., *Poems of the Irish Revolutionary Brotherhood* (The Red Hedgehog Press, 2020), 55–56.

3. For instance, to see the metaphysical and divine implications in math, see the work of the Jewish professor of mathematics at the University of California Berkeley, Edward Frenkel, *Love and Math: The Heart of Hidden Reality* (Basic Books, 2013).

4. Bernardo Bertolucci, quoted in "Leading Nine Awards at the 60th Oscars, 'The Last Emperor' Constructed a More Three-dimensional Puyi," 2024, https://daydaynews.cc/en/entertainment/280524.html.

5. Gillespie, *The Theological Origins of Modernity*, x, in the preface. Also see: Peter Gay, *The Enlightenment: An Interpretation*; Anthony Giddens, *The Consequences of Moder-*

nity (Stanford University Press, 1990); and Rémi Brague, *The Kingdom of Man: Genesis and Failure of the Modern Project* (University of Notre Dame Press, 2018).

6. For instance: Spretnak, *The Resurgence of the Real.*

7. Jon D. Levenson, *Sinai & Zion* (HarperCollins, 2013), 15.

8. Werner Heisenberg, *Physics and Philosophy: The Revolution in Modern Science* (HarperPerennial Modern Classics, 2007); Wolfgang Smith, *Physics: A Science in Quest of an Ontology* (Philos-Sophia Initiative Foundation, 2022); Robert C. Koons and George Bealer, eds., *The Waning of Materialism* (Oxford University Press, 2010). See also the classic, David C. Lindberg, *The Beginnings of Western Science: The European Scientific Tradition in Philosophical, Religious, and Institutional Context, Prehistory to A.D. 1450*, 2nd ed. (University of Chicago Press, 2007), and J. P. Moreland, *Scientism and Secularism: Learning to Respond to a Dangerous Ideology* (Crossway, 2018).

9. William T. Cavanaugh, *The Myth of Religious Violence: Secular Ideology and the Roots of Modern Conflict* (Oxford University Press, 2009), 59.

10. Richard Kroner, *The Primacy of Faith* (Macmillan, 1943), 47.

11. C. S. Lewis, "Is Theology Poetry?" *The Weight of Glory* (1944), par. 24, quoted in Jerry Root and Wayne Martindale, eds., *The Quotable Lewis* (Tyndale House, 2012), 99.

12. Klyne R. Snodgrass, *You Need a Better Gospel: Reclaiming the Good News of Participation with Christ* (Baker, 2022), Kindle loc. 16.

13. Pope Pius XII, *Mystici Corporis* (Vatican City State, 1943); Emile Mersch, *The Whole Christ: The Historical Development of the Doctrine of the Mystical Body in Scripture and Tradition* (Dobson, 1938).

14. Christopher Dawson, "Why I Am a Catholic," *Catholic Times*, May 21, 1926. Reprinted in *Chesterton Review* 9 (May 1983): 112–113, quoted in Adam Schwartz, *The Third Spring: G.K. Chesterton, Graham Greene, Christopher Dawson, and David Jones* (The Catholic University of America Press, 2005), 222.

15. John T. Graham, *The Social Thought of Ortega y Gasset: A Systematic Synthesis in Postmodernism and Interdisciplinarity* (University of Missouri Press, 2001), 125.

16. See Warren Breckman, *European Romanticism: A Brief History with Documents* (Hackett, 2015), Kindle loc. 218. Among the most outstanding figures of the Romantic movement were Beethoven, Blake, Wordsworth, Coleridge, Keats, Byron, Shelley, Walter Scott, Mary Shelley, Caspar David Friedrich, Jane Austen, Victor Hugo, Carlyle, Mendelssohn, Schumann, and Wagner. See also, Gerard G. Steckler, S.J., *The Triumph of Romanticism* (Os Iusti Press, 2023) and Louis Dupré, *The Quest of the Absolute: Birth and Decline of European Romanticism* (University of Notre Dame Press, 2013).

17. For a brief description of the organic nature of Christendom's society, see Christopher Dawson, *The Formation of Christendom* (Ignatius Press, 2008); also, for keen insights see Carolyn Merchant, chap. 3, "Organic Society and Utopia," in *The Death of Nature: Women, Ecology, and the Scientific Revolution* (HarperCollins, 2020).

18. My thanks to Yasmin Mogahed for this metaphor of visiting art galleries. See Yasmin Mogahed, *Reclaim Your Heart: Personal Insights on Breaking Free from Life's Shackles* (Lightning Source, 2015), 24.

19. Spretnak, *The Resurgence of the Real*, Kindle loc. 130.

20. Spretnak, 130.

21. Saint Irenaeus, *Adversus haereses*, bk. 4, chap. 34, no.1, quoted in John Behr, *The*

Way to Nicaea (St. Vladimir's Seminary Press, 2001), 116.

22. N. T. Wright, *The Kingdom New Testament* (Zondervan, 2011), Kindle loc. 370.

23. Heinrich Heine in *The French Stage* (1837), chap. 9, quoted in Fred R. Shapiro, ed., *The New Yale Book of Quotations* (Yale University Press, 2021), 368.

Chapter 2: Thrilling Times to Be Alive

1. Charlene Spretnak, *Relational Reality: New Discoveries of Interrelatedness That Are Transforming the Modern World* (Green Horizon Books, 2011), 71. I am grateful to Spretnak, whose ideas have shaped this chapter.

2. Edward M. Hallowell, M.D., quoted in Ellen Michaud, "Reconnect," *Prevention*, December 2000, 124.

3. James C. Whorton, *Nature Cures: The History of Alternative Medicine in America* (Oxford University Press, 2004), 19.

4. Cited in Alzheimer's Association Report, "2020 Alzheimer's Disease Facts and Figures," *Alzheimer's & Dementia* 16, no. 3 (March 2020): 391–460, https://doi.org/10.1002/alz.12068. See also Jason Karlawish, *The Problem of Alzheimer's: How Science, Culture, and Politics Turned a Rare Disease into a Crisis and What We Can Do About It* (St. Martin's, 2021).

5. See, for instance, Carol Graham, "The Economics of Happiness," in *The New Palgrave Dictionary of Economics*, 2nd ed. (Palgrave Macmillan, 2008).

6. Hui-Xin Wang et al., "Late-Life Engagement in Social and Leisure Activities Is Associated with a Decreased Risk of Dementia: A Longitudinal Study from the Kungsholmen Project," *American Journal of Epidemiology* 155, no. 12 (June 2002): 1081–1087, https://doi.org/10.1093/aje/155.12.1081.

7. See Kathleen Taylor, *The Fragile Brain: The Strange, Hopeful Science of Dementia* (Oxford University Press, 2016); see also Stephen G. Post, ed., *Altruism and Health: Perspectives from Empirical Research* (Oxford University Press, 2007).

8. Anthea Innes, *Dementia Studies: A Social Science Perspective* (Sage, 2009); Jennifer J. Perion, "The Effect of the Reciprocal Nature of Friendship on the Experience of Malignant Social Psychology in Community Dwelling Persons with Mild to Moderate Dementia" (master's thesis, University of Toledo, 2016).

9. Spretnak, *Relational Reality*, Kindle loc. 192.

10. See J. Maas et al., "Morbidity Is Related to a Green Living Environment," *Journal of Epidemiology and Community Health* 63, no. 12 (December 2009): 967–973, https://pubmed.ncbi.nlm.nih.gov/19833605/.

11. Magdalena M. H. E. Van den Berg et al., "Autonomic Nervous System Responses to Viewing Green and Built Settings: Differentiating between Sympathetic and Parasympathetic Activity," *International Journal of Environmental Research and Public Health* 12, no. 12 (2015): 15860–15874, https://doi.org/10.3390/ijerph121215026.

12. Gordon Neufeld, PhD, and Gabor Maté, M.D., *Hold On to Your Kids: Why Parents Need to Matter More than Peers* (Ballantine Books, 2005). See "Relational Factors in Learning" in Charlene Spretnak, *Relational Reality*, Kindle loc. 971ff.

13. Mark Bauerlein, *The Dumbest Generation Grows Up: From Stupefied Youth to Dangerous Adults* (Regnery Gateway, 2022).

14. Richard Louv, "Leave No Child Inside," *Sierra*, July/August 2006, quoted in

Spretnak, *Relational Reality*. See also, Richard Louv, *Last Child in the Woods: Saving Our Children from Nature-Deficit Disorder* (Algonquin Books, 2008).

15. Jeremy Rifkin, *The Empathic Civilization: The Race to Global Consciousness in a World in Crisis* (Polity Press, 2009), 164.

16. David Pearson, *New Organic Architecture: The Breaking Wave* (University of California Press, 2001).

17. Howard Zehr, *The Little Book of Restorative Justice: Revised and Updated* (Good Books, 2015).

18. See Gina Barton, "Community Plays a Role in Helping Ex-prisoners," *Journal Sentinel*, May 14, 2016, https://archive.jsonline.com/news/crime/community-plays-a-role-in-helping-ex-prisoners-b99718342z1-379536211.html; Mark S. Umbreit, "Restorative Justice through Victim-Offender Mediation: A Multi-site Assessment," *Western Criminology Review* 1, no. 1 (June 1998), 1–28, https://www.ojp.gov/ncjrs/virtual-library/abstracts/restorative-justice-through-victim-offender-mediation-multi-site; and Spretnak, *Relational Reality*, chap. 5.

19. City Slicker Farms, X, https://x.com/cityslickerfrms?lang=en.

20. "After 2 consecutive years of declines in suicide (47,511 in 2019 and 45,979 in 2020), 2021 data indicate an increase in suicide to 48,183, nearly returning to the 2018 peak (48,344) with an age-adjusted rate of 14.1 suicides per 100,000 population (versus 14.2 in 2018)." In D. M. Stone, K. A. Mack, and J. Qualters, "*Notes from the Field*: Recent Changes in Suicide Rates, by Race and Ethnicity and Age Group — United States, 2021," *Morbidity and Mortality Weekly Report* 72, no. 6 (2023): 160–162, 2024, http://dx.doi.org/10.15585/mmwr.mm7206a4.

21. "Teen Suicide in United States," America's Health Rankings, United Health Foundation, https://www.americashealthrankings.org/explore/measures/teen_suicide.

22. "Harvard Youth Poll," Institute of Politics at Harvard Kennedy School, April 23, 2021, https://iop.harvard.edu/youth-poll/spring-2021-harvard-youth-poll.

23. Gregg Easterbrook, *The Progress Paradox: How Life Gets Better While People Feel Worse* (Random House, 2003) and Giovanna Moneta, *Positive Psychology: A Critical Introduction* (Bloomsbury, 2013).

24. David Herzberg, *Happy Pills in America: From Miltown to Prozac* (The Johns Hopkins University Press, 2010).

25. Centers for Disease Control and Prevention, *Suicide Was the Tenth Leading Cause of Death in the United States*, https://www.cdc.gov/policy/polaris/healthtopics/suicide/index.html#:~:text=Economic%20Burden,and%20work%2Dloss%20costs%20alone.

26. Y. E. Yegorov et al., "The Link between Chronic Stress and Accelerated Aging," *Biomedicines* 8, no. 7 (2020): 198, https://pmc.ncbi.nlm.nih.gov/articles/PMC7400286/. See also David Perlman, "Early Aging Tied to Chronic Stress," *San Francisco Chronicle*, November 30, 2001.

27. Stephen R. Barley, Debra E. Meyerson, and Stine Grodal, "E-mail as a Source and Symbol of Stress," *Organization Science* 22, no. 4 (August 2011): 887–906, https://psycnet.apa.org/record/2011-15803-005. See also Adam Alter, *Irresistible: The Rise of Addictive Technology and the Business of Keeping Us Hooked* (Penguin, 2018).

28. S. Bhaskar, D. Hemavathy, and S. Prasad, "Prevalence of Chronic Insomnia in

Adult Patients and Its Correlation with Medical Comorbidities," *J Family Med Prim Care* 5, no. 4 (October–December 2016): 780–784, https://pubmed.ncbi.nlm.nih.gov /28348990/.

29. Tanya J. Peterson, "Learning Disabilities Statistics and Prevalence," *HealthyPlace*, January 17, 2022, https://www.healthyplace.com/parenting/learning-disabilities /learning-disabilities-statistics-and-prevalence.

30. Donald C. Goff, M.D. et al., "The Long-Term Effects of Antipsychotic Medication on Clinical Course in Schizophrenia," *American Journal of Psychiatry* 174, no. 9 (September 2017): 840–849, https://doi.org/10.1176/appi.ajp.2017.16091016.

31. E. Varimo et al., "New Users of Antipsychotics among Children and Adolescents in 2008–2017: A Nationwide Register Study," *Front. Psychiatry* 11, no. 316 (2020), https://doi.org/10.3389/fpsyt.2020.00316.

32. Hyuna Sung, PhD, et al., "Global Cancer Statistics 2020: GLOBOCAN Estimates of Incidence and Mortality Worldwide for 36 Cancers in 185 Countries," *CA: A Cancer Journal for Clinicians* 71, no. 3 (May/June 2021): 209–249, https://doi .org/10.3322/caac.21660.

33. Merzenich H, Zeeb H, and Blettner M., "Decreasing sperm quality: A global problem?" *BMC Public Health* 10, no. 24 (2010), https://doi.org/10.1186/1471-2458-10 -24.

34. "Infertility: Frequently Asked Questions," Centers for Disease Control and Prevention, https://www.cdc.gov/reproductive-health/infertility-faq.

35. "What are PFAS?," Agency for Toxic Substances and Disease Registry. Centers for Disease Control and Prevention, https://www.atsdr.cdc.gov/pfas/health-effects /overview.html.

36. Guomao Zheng et al., "Per- and Polyfluoroalkyl Substances (PFAS) in Breast Milk: Concerning Trends for Current-Use PFAS," *Environmental Science & Technology* 55, no. 11 (2021): 7510–7520, https://doi.org/10.1021/acs.est.0c06978. Quoted in Tom Perkins, "Study Finds Alarming Levels of 'Forever Chemicals' in US Mothers' Breast Milk," *Guardian*, May 13, 2021, https://www.theguardian.com/environment/2021 /may/13/pfas-forever-chemicals-breast-milk-us-study.

37. "Adult Obesity Rates," IBISWorld, January 17, 2023, 2024, https://www .ibisworld.com/us/bed/adult-obesity-rate/112885.

38. "Dirt Poor: Have Fruits and Vegetables Become Less Nutritious?" *Scientific American*, April 27, 2011, https://www.scientificamerican.com/article/soil -depletion-and-nutrition-loss/.

39. Marianne McGinnis, "Breaking News: Skip the Soda, Turn Off the TV — Modern Life is Bad for Kids' Bones," *Prevention*, June 2004, 146.

40. Susan Vitale, PhD, M.H.S., Robert D. Sperduto, M.D., and Frederick L. Ferris III, M.D., "Increased Prevalence of Myopia in the United States between 1971–1972 and 1999–2004," *Arch Ophthalmol* 127, no. 12 (2009): 1632–1639, https://doi.org/10.1001 /archophthalmol.2009.303.

41. Mary Midgley, *The Myths We Live By* (Taylor and Francis, 2003), Kindle loc. 18.

42. *Encyclopaedia Britannica Online*, s.v. "Taylorism," https://www.britannica.com /science/Taylorism.

43. Midgley, *The Myths We Live By*, Kindle loc. 18–19.

44. Karl Marx, *Das Kapital* (1867), vol. 1, trans. by Ben Fowkes, chap. 25, quoted in Marcello Musto, *Karl Marx's Writings on Alienation* (Springer Nature Switzerland, 2021), 150. Italics added.

Chapter 3: Why the Status Quo?

1. Spretnak, *Relational Reality*, Kindle loc. 2.

2. Stephen Jay Gould, "Nonoverlapping Magisteria," *Natural History* 106, no. 2 (March 1997): 16–22, https://philpapers.org/rec/GOUNM; Stephen Jay Gould, *Rocks of Ages: Science and Religion in the Fullness of Life* (Ballantine Books, 1999), 5.

3. Galileo, *The Essential Galileo*, ed. and trans. Maurice A. Finocchiaro (Hackett, 2008), 119.

4. Donald MacKay, *The Clockwork Image: A Christian Perspective on Science* (Inter-Varsity Press, 1978), 51–55.

5. Marx, *Dass Kapital*, quoted in Shlomo Avineri, *The Social and Political Thought of Karl Marx* (Cambridge University Press, 1968), 120.

6. Marx, *Das Kapital*, quoted in Musto, *Karl Marx's Writings on Alienation*, 150.

7. Spretnak, *Relational Reality*, Kindle loc. 1.

8. See the book by the Pulitzer Prize–winning author Douglas Hofstadter and the French psychologist Emmanuel Sander, *Surfaces and Essences: Analogy as the Fuel and Fire of Thinking* (Basic Books, 2013).

9. See Frederick Copleston, SJ, *A History of Philosophy* (Doubleday, 1994), 63–152.

10. Michael Friedman, *Kant's Construction of Nature: A Reading of the* Metaphysical Foundations of Natural Science (Cambridge University Press, 2013), 239.

11. Michael Friedman and Alfred Nordmann, eds., *The Kantian Legacy in Nineteenth-Century Science* (MIT Press, 2006).

12. Richard G. Olson, *Science and Scientism in Nineteenth-Century Europe* (University of Illinois Press, 2008).

13. Midgley, *The Myths We Live By*, Kindle loc. 1.

14. "Une maison est une machine-à-habiter." Quoted in Shapiro, *The New Yale Book of Quotations*, Kindle loc. 477.

15. Midgley, *The Myths We Live By*, Kindle loc. 1.

16. George Lakoff and Mark Johnson, *Metaphors We Live By* (University of Chicago Press, 1980), 3. George Lakoff is the professor of Cognitive Science and Linguistics at the University of California at Berkeley and is one of the authors of the *New York Times* bestseller *Don't Think of an Elephant! Know Your Values and Frame the Debate: The Essential Guide for Progressives*, and is America's leading expert on the framing of political ideas.

17. Midgley, *The Myths We Live By*, Kindle loc. 18.

18. See the refutation of determinism by Michael Egnor, "Have Science and Philosophy Refuted Free Will?," chap. 18 in William A. Dembski, Casey Luskin, and Joseph M. Holden, eds., *The Comprehensive Guide to Science and Faith: Exploring the Ultimate Questions About Life and the Cosmos* (Harvest House, 2021), 197–210.

19. Konrad Lorenz, quoted in Jakob Schwichtenberg, *No-Nonsense Quantum Field Theory: A Student-Friendly Introduction* (n.p.: No-Nonsense Books, 2020), 513.

20. Arnold Lunn, *The Flight from Reason* (Longmans, Green, 1931).

21. Friedrich Nietzche, quoted in Peter Poellner, *Nietzsche and Metaphysics* (Oxford

University Press, 2000), 103.

22. G. K. Chesterton, *The Well and the Shallows*, quoted in Joseph Pearce, *Wisdom and Innocence: A Life of G. K. Chesterton* (Ignatius Press, 2015), 465.

23. G. K. Chesterton, *Orthodoxy*, quoted in Kevin L. Morris, *The Truest Fairy Tale: A Religious Anthology of G. K. Chesterton* (The Lutterworth Press, 2017), 215.

24. C. S. Lewis, "The Poison of Subjectivism," in Walter Hooper, ed., *Christian Reflections* (Eerdmans, 1995), 73.

25. C. S. Lewis, *The Abolition of Man* (Macmillan, 1947) and *Perelandra* (Macmillan, 1950), 150.

26. Marcel de Corte, *De la dissociété* (Rémi Perrin, 2002).

27. Charles Taylor, *A Secular Age* (Harvard University Press, 2009).

28. Friedrich Nietzche, *The Will to Power* (n.p.: Jovian Press, 2018).

29. Herbert Spencer coined the phrase after reading Charles Darwin's *On the Origin of Species*. In his *Principles of Biology* (1864), he writes: "This survival of the fittest, which I have here sought to express in mechanical terms, is that which Mr. Darwin has called 'natural selection', or the preservation of favoured races in the struggle for life." Quoted in Karolina Broś, *Survival of the Fittest: Fricative Lenition in English and Spanish from the Perspective of Optimality Theory* (Cambridge Scholars, 2015), 9.

30. A saying usually associated with Thomas Hobbes, who wrote "Man is a god to man, and man is a wolf to man," although the phrase can be found already in the 1500s in the writings of Erasmus, quoted in Nicholas Williams, *Thomas Hobbes: Philosophy's Bad Boy Reassessed* (Grin, 2005), 3.

31. See chap. 10, "Founders of Free-Market Economics" in William J. Slattery, *Heroism and Genius*.

32. Quoted in Katrine Marcal, *Who Cooked Adam Smith's Dinner?* (Pegasus Books, 2016), 11, a humorous and thought-provoking examination of the myth of the "economic man." The term "invisible hand" first appeared in Adam Smith's *The Wealth of Nations* as a description of how a free-market economy brings to birth a society in which individuals produce what is necessary for it by acting in their own self-interest. For the difference between the type of economics birthed by Catholicism — free-enterprise economics — and the capitalism of Adam Smith, see Slattery, *Heroism and Genius*, 211–239.

33. Quoted in David Midgley, ed., *The Essential Mary Midgley* (Routledge, 2005), 292.

34. Midgley, 292.

35. "Counting the Costs of Industrial Pollution," European Environment Agency, September 29, 2021, https://www.eea.europa.eu/publications/counting-the-costs-of -industrial-pollution.

36. Philip J. Landrigan, M.D. et al., "The *Lancet* Commission on Pollution and Health," *The Lancet* 391, no. 10119 (2018): 462–512, https://www.thelancet.com/journals /lancet/article/PIIS0140-67361732345-0/fulltext?code=lancet-site.

37. Kathryn Milun, *Pathologies of Modern Space: Empty Space, Urban Anxiety, and the Recovery of the Public Self* (Taylor and Francis, 2013).

38. Charles Baudelaire, *Oeuvres Completes* (Gallimard, 1961), 1163, quoted in Alberto Acereda and Rigoberto Guevara, *Modernism, Rubén Darío, and the Poetics of Despair*

(University Press of America, 2004), 38.

39. Taylor, *A Secular Age*, Kindle loc. 629.

40. Oswald Spengler, *The Decline of the West*, quoted in Hans Sedlmayr, *Art in Crisis* (Routledge, 2017), Kindle loc. 173.

41. Olive Schreiner (1855–1920), *The Story of an African Farm* (1883), pt. 2, chap. 4, quoted in Shapiro, *The New Yale Book of Quotations*, Kindle loc. 723.

Chapter 4: The Face of Modernity's God

1. Terry Eagleton, *Culture and the Death of God* (Yale University Press, 2014), 44, quoted in Steven D. Smith, *Pagans and Christians in the City: Culture Wars from the Tiber to the Potomac* (Eerdmans, 2018), Kindle loc. 307–308.

2. Smith, *Pagans and Christians in the City*, Kindle loc. 9–10.

3. Christopher Hitchens, *God Is Not Great: How Religion Poisons Everything* (McClelland & Stewart, 2007).

4. Michael Allen Gillespie, *The Theological Origins of Modernity*, 15.

5. See Brandon D. Short, *The Cartesian Split* (Routledge, 2021).

6. See video of the lecture by Edward Frenkel titled "Cartesianism as the Effect of Our Collective Childhood Trauma, Edward Frenkel," Science and Nonduality, December 17, 2015, YouTube video, 25:55, https://www.youtube.com/watch?v=t_iE04ggR9w.

7. Gillespie, *The Theological Origins of Modernity*, "Luther's Metaphysics" in chap. 4, "Luther and the Storm of Faith," Kindle loc. 101.

8. Gillespie, *The Theological Origins of Modernity*, 114.

9. Ibid., 205.

10. Ibid., 205.

11. Ibid., 204–205.

12. J. G. Fichte, *On the Ground of Our Belief in a Divine World-Governance* (1798), quoted in J. G. Fichte and F. W. J. Schelling, *The Philosophical Rupture between Fichte and Schelling: Selected Texts and Correspondence (1800–1802)*, ed. and trans. Michael G. Vater and David W. Wood (State University of New York Press, 2012), 10.

13. Gillespie, *The Theological Origins of Modernity*, Kindle loc. 339–340.

14. N. T. Wright, *History and Eschatology: Jesus and the Promise of Natural Theology* (Baylor University Press, 2019), chap. 1, "Natural Theology in Its Historical Context," especially sec. 1, "The Fallen Shrine Lisbon 1755 and the Triumph of Epicureanism."

15. Samuel Taylor Coleridge, *Biographia Literaria*, 1, quoted in Dennis Danielson, *Paradise Lost and the Cosmological Revolution* (Cambridge University Press, 2014), xiii.

16. Meister Eckhart, quoted in *Meister Eckhart, Teacher and Preacher*, ed. Bernard McGinn (Paulist Press, 1986), 278.

17. This is a phrase that appears in the writings of the Dutch ethicist Hugo Grotius, (1583–1645), notably in *De iure belli ac pacis*, prolegomena 11, quoted in Andrew Davison, *The Love of Wisdom: An Introduction to Philosophy for Theologians* (SCM Press, 2013), 111. Likewise, Dietrich Bonhoeffer was convinced that God would have modern Christians live "as men who manage our lives without him," Dietrich Bonhoeffer, *Letters and Papers from Prison* (SCM Press, 1971), 360, quoted in Andrew Davison, *The Love of Wisdom*, 111.

18. Taylor, *A Secular Age*, 300.

19. John T. Graham, *The Social Thought of Ortega y Gasset*, 125.

20. Quoted in Sachin Jain, "A Treatment for Loneliness," *Harvard Medicine*, Autumn 2018, https://hms.harvard.edu/magazine/imaging/treatment-loneliness. See also Vivek H. Murthy, *Together: The Healing Power of Human Connection in a Sometimes Lonely World* (HarperCollins, 2020) and *Our Epidemic of Loneliness and Isolation: The U.S. Surgeon General's Advisory on the Healing Effects of Social Connection and Community* (Department of Health and Human Services, 2023), https://pubmed.ncbi.nlm.nih.gov /37792968/.

21. Dr. Alison Hulme, "Loneliness in a Globalised World," University of Northampton, June 11, 2021, https://www.northampton.ac.uk/news/loneliness-in-a -globalised-world/.

22. Jerry Carroll and Laura Evenson, "The Sage of Cyberspace / Paul Saffo, Mapper of Uncertainty, Seems to Know Everything in the Whole Wired World," *San Francisco Chronicle*, June 9, 1996, https://www.sfgate.com/news/article/The-Sage-of-Cyberspace -Paul-Saffo-mapper-of-2979529.php.

23. Paul Veyne, *When Our World Became Christian* (Polity Press, 2010), 20.

24. For the distinctions between first and secondary causes, see Étienne Gilson, *The Spirit of Mediaeval Philosophy* (University of Notre Dame Press, 1991), chap. 7, "Analogy, Causality, and Finality."

25. Pope Benedict XVI, Sermon of the Mass for the Inauguration of His Pontificate, April 24, 2005, Vatican.va.

26. Herbert McCabe, *God Matters* (Continuum, 1987), 59–60.

27. St. Thomas Aquinas, *Summa Theologiae*, I; Gilson, *The Spirit of Medieval Philosophy*.

28. Iain McGilchrist, *The Master and His Emissary: The Divided Brain and the Making of the Western World* (Yale University Press, 2018), 170, Kindle. For Catholics, McGilchrist's excellent point requires clarification due to the novel terminology he uses. In order to avoid misunderstandings, I want to affirm that Catholicism's truths are certainties, as the Council of Trent stated. See the section "The Acceptance of Revelation (Faith)" in Henry Denzinger and Karl Rahner, eds., *The Sources of Catholic Dogma*, trans. Roy J. Deferrari (Herder, 1954).

29. Among a growing group of thinkers convinced that a mechanical worldview is dehumanizing is Jeremy Lent, *The Patterning Instinct: A Cultural History of Humanity's Search for Meaning* (Prometheus Books, 2017).

Chapter 5: Feeling at Home as You Gaze on the Night Sky

1. G. K. Chesterton, *A Short History of England*, chapter 3, quoted in Kevin L. Morris, *The Truest Fairy Tale: A Religious Anthology of G. K. Chesterton* (The Lutterworth Press, 2017), 192.

2. Quoted from the scientist's conference at Prato, Italy, *Gli Uomini e il Cielo* [Men and the Heavens], April 13, 1970, shortly after Apollo 13, available in Italian on audio at the website http://www.internetsv.info/Discorsi.html.. My translation. See also Antonino Gliozzo, *Enrico Medi: Lo scienziato di Dio* (Casa Editrice Leardini e Centro Missionario Francescano, 2021).

3. Enrico Medi, quoted in Acts of the Second International Catechetical Congress,

Rome, September 20–25, 1971 (Studium, 1972), 449–450.

4. Heisenberg, *Physics and Philosophy*, 175–176.

5. F. W. H. Myers, quoted in Emil Carl Wilm, *The Problem of Religion* (Rumford Press, 1912), 114. The question is often attributed to Einstein.

6. Oscar Milosz, quoted in Sayyed Hossein Nasr, *Religion and the Order of Nature* (Oxford University Press, 1996), 153.

7. As St. Thomas Aquinas wrote, "Now it is evident from what has been said that the teaching of the Christian faith treats of creatures in so far as they reflect a certain likeness of God, and forasmuch as *error concerning them leads to error about God.*" *Summa Contra Gentiles* (London: Burns, Oates, & Washbourne, 1924), bk. 2, chap. 4.

8. Iain McGilchrist, *The Master and His Emissary: The Divided Brain and the Making of the Western World* (New Haven, CT: Yale University Press, 2018), Kindle loc. 356.

9. Rudolf Otto, *The Idea of the Holy*, trans. John W. Harvey (Wipf & Stock, 2021), 25. Translation is mine.

10. Huston Smith, *Beyond the Postmodern Mind: The Place of Meaning in a Global Civilization* (Quest Books), Kindle loc. 122–123.

11. Smith, *Beyond the Postmodern Mind*, 134.

12. C. S. Lewis, *Studies in Medieval and Renaissance Literature* (HarperCollins, 2013), Kindle loc. 47–48.

13. Ibid., 48.

14. Ibid., 105.

15. Ibid., 105.

16. Ibid., 105.

17. Ibid., 47–48.

18. Guillermo Gonzalez and Jay W. Richards, *The Privileged Planet: How Our Place in the Cosmos Is Designed for Discovery* (Regnery, 2004).

19. Quoted in David Deutsch, *The Beginning of Infinity: Explanations that Transform the World* (Penguin Books, 2011), Kindle loc. 792. This physicist explains why the principle of mediocrity is false both from the viewpoint of humanity's place in the universe and its characteristics as a species.

20. Stephen Hawking, quoted in David C. Catling, *Astrobiology: A Very Short Introduction* (Oxford University Press, 2013), 126.

21. Gonzalez and Richards, *The Privileged Planet*, 271.

22. Ibid., 272.

23. Ibid.

24. Ibid., 85.

25. Ibid., 146.

26. Ibid., 2592.

27. Michael Denton, *Nature's Destiny: How the Laws of Biology Reveal Purpose in the Universe* (Free Press, 1998), 262.

28. See Gonzalez and Richards, *The Privileged Planet*, chap. 9, "Our Place in Cosmic Time."

29. Ibid., 3157.

30. Lawrence J. Henderson, *The Fitness of the Environment* (Macmillan, 1913), 272 and 211.

31. Guillermo Gonzalez, "Do We Live on a Privileged Planet?," chap. 24 in Dembski, Luskin, and Holden, eds., *The Comprehensive Guide to Science and Faith*, 240.

32. Gonzalez and Richards, *The Privileged Planet*, 334.

33. Wolfgang Smith, *Cosmos and Transcendence: Breaking Through the Barrier of Scientistic Belief* (Philos-Sophia Initiative Foundation, 2021), 165.

34. C. S. Lewis, *The Discarded Image* (HarperCollins, 2013), 11.

35. Lewis, *Studies in Medieval and Renaissance Literature*, Kindle loc. 48.

36. Lewis, "Imagination and Thought," in *Studies in Medieval and Renaissance Literature*, Kindle loc. 48.

37. Ibid., 48.

38. Ibid., 48.

39. Quoted in Wolfgang Smith, *The Quantum Enigma: Finding the Hidden Key* (Sophia Perennis, 2005), 113.

40. Aquinas, *Summa Theologiae*, I, q.10, a.5, corp.

41. Wolfgang Smith, *The Wisdom of Ancient Cosmology: Contemporary Science in Light of Tradition* (Foundation for Traditional Studies, 2009), Kindle loc. 2538.

42. Quoted in "Are Superliminal Connections Necessary?" *Nuovo Cimento B* 40 (1977): 191.

43. Smith, *The Wisdom of Ancient Cosmology*, Kindle loc. 2453–2455.

44. Smith, *Cosmos and Transcendence*, 165.

45. C. S. Lewis, *Out of the Silent Planet*.

Chapter 6: A Designer-Made Universe

1. See James Hannam, *The Genesis of Science: How the Christian Middle Ages Launched the Scientific Revolution* (Washington, D.C.: Regnery, 2011); Seb Falk, *The Light Ages: The Surprising Story of Medieval Science* (Norton, 2020); David C. Lindberg, ed., *Science in the Middle Ages* (University of Chicago Press, 1978).

2. Richard Dawkins, *River Out of Eden: A Darwinian View of Life* (Basic Books, 1995), 133.

3. Dembski, Luskin, and Holden, eds., *The Comprehensive Guide to Science and Faith*, Kindle loc. 299.

4. Michael Behe, *Darwin's Black Box: The Biochemical Challenge to Evolution* (Simon and Schuster, 1996), 257.

5. The term appears in Herbert Spencer, *The Principles of Biology* (1864).

6. Darwin, quoted in William A. Dembski and Jonathan Wells, *The Design of Life: Discovering Signs of Intelligence in Biological Systems* (ISI, 2008), 193.

7. See pt. 3 in the book by physicist Stephen M. Barr, *Modern Physics and Ancient Faith* (University of Notre Dame Press, 2003), Kindle.

8. See Jonathan Wells, *The Politically Incorrect Guide to Darwinism and Intelligent Design* (Regnery, 2006).

9. William Dembski, *The Design Inference,* quoted in Wells, *The Politically Incorrect Guide to Darwinism and Intelligent Design*, 84.

10. *The Free Dictionary*, s.v. "Design," https://www.thefreedictionary.com/design, quoted in Dembski, Luskin, and Holden, eds., *The Comprehensive Guide to Science and Faith*, Kindle loc. 602.

11. Smith, *The Wisdom of Ancient Cosmology*.

12. Dembski, Luskin, and Holden, eds., *The Comprehensive Guide to Science and Faith*, Kindle loc. 146–147.

13. See William A. Dembski, *No Free Lunch: Why Specified Complexity Cannot Be Purchased without Intelligence* (Rowman & Litttlefield, 2006).

14. See chaps. 20–23 in Dembski, Luskin, and Holden, eds., *The Comprehensive Guide to Science and Faith*.

15. "Building bridges," *Nature* 442, 110 (2006), https://doi.org/10.1038/442110a. See also Nicanor Pier Giorgio Austriaco, OP, et al, *Thomistic Evolution: A Catholic Approach to Understanding Evolution in the Light of Faith* (2019), and Christopher T. Baglow, *Faith, Science, and Reason* (Midwest Theological Forum, 2019).

16. Joseph Ratzinger, *In the Beginning: A Catholic Understanding of the Story of Creation and the Fall* (1995), 50.

17. D. Bohm and B. Hiley, "On the Intuitive Understanding of Nonlocality as Implied by Quantum Theory," *Foundations of Physics* 5 (March 1975): 93–109, https://link.springer.com/article/10.1007/BF01100319, 96.

18. Smith, *The Quantum Enigma*, 78.

19. A paraphrase of Nicholas Murray Butler's "An expert is one who knows more and more about less and less," quoted in Susan Ratcliffe, ed., *Oxford Treasury of Sayings and Quotations*, 4th ed. (Oxford University Press, 2011), 248.

20. Gonzalez and Richards, *The Privileged Planet*. See also part 4 in Barr, *Modern Physics and Ancient Faith*. For consideration of teleology in nature, Dembski, Luskin, and Holden, eds., *The Comprehensive Guide to Science and Faith*.

21. Quoted in Dembski, Luskin, and Holden, eds., *The Comprehensive Guide to Science and Faith*, Kindle loc. 182.

22. Dembski, Luskin, and Holden, eds., *The Comprehensive Guide to Science and Faith*, 195.

23. Thomas Nagel, *Mind and Cosmos: Why the Materialist Neo-Darwinian Conception of Nature Is Almost Certainly False* (Oxford University Press, 2012), 9, quoted in Dembski, Luskin, and Holden, eds., *The Comprehensive Guide to Science and Faith*, Kindle loc. 309–310.

24. Nagel, *Mind and Cosmos*, 92, quoting Roger White, "Does Origins of Life Research Rest on a Mistake?" *Noûs* 41, no. 3 (2007): 453–477; quoted in Douglas Axe, "Can New Proteins Evolve?"; in Dembski, Luskin, and Holden, eds., *The Comprehensive Guide to Science and Faith*, Kindle loc. 310.

25. Dembski, Luskin, and Holden, eds., *The Comprehensive Guide to Science and Faith*, Kindle loc. 310, referencing Thomas Nagel, *The Last Word* (Oxford University Press, 1997), 130–131.

26. Aquinas, *Summa Theologiae*, I, q.44: "Since God is the efficient, the exemplar and the final cause of all things, and since primary matter is from Him, it follows that the first principle of all things is one in reality." Quoted in Rudi te Velde, *Aquinas on God: The "Divine Science" of the* Summa Theologiae (Ashgate, 2006), Kindle loc. 143.

27. The article "Form" in Bernard Wuellner, *Dictionary of Scholastic Philosophy* (Germany: Editiones Scholasticae, 2011), 47.

Chapter 7: Quantum Physics and the "Big Bang" God

1. Albert Einstein, *The Einstein Reader* (Citadel Press, 1984), 35.

2. Barr, *Modern Physics and Ancient Faith*, Kindle loc. 39f.

3. Ibid., 41.

4. Barr, 43.

5. Ibid.., 43. See also the section "Was the Big Bang Really the Beginning?," 47ff.

6. "Sometime between 1666 and 1668, in an unpublished manuscript that we refer to by its opening words, *De gravitatione*, Newton wrote that an 'infinite and eternal' divine power coexists with space, which 'extends infinitely in all directions' and 'is eternal in duration.'" Quoted in Edward Harrison, "Newton and the Infinite Universe," *Physics Today* 39, no. 2 (1986): 24–32, https://doi.org/10.1063/1.881049.

7. Quoted in Barr, *Modern Physics and Ancient Faith*, Kindle loc. 43.

8. Barr, *Modern Physics and Ancient Faith*, Kindle loc. 227. I highly recommend this book by this physicist who was elected a fellow of the American Physical Society for original contributions to grand unified theories. See also "Stephen M. Barr's Personal Website," https://stephenmbarr.weebly.com/, and the website of the Society of Catholic Scientists at https://catholicscientists.org/.

9. Richard P. Feynman, Robert B. Leighton, and Matthew Sands, *The Feynman Lectures on Physics, vol. 1: Mainly Mechanics, Radiation, and Heat* (Basic Books, 2015), 1–3.

10. Tim van Leent et al., "Entangling Single Atoms over 33 km Telecom Fibre," *Nature* 607 (2022): 69–73, https://doi.org/10.1038/s41586-022-04764-4.

11. See Smith, chap. 4, "Bell's Theorem and the Perennial Ontology," in *The Wisdom of Ancient Cosmology*, Kindle loc. 2351.

12. Quoted in Ben Brubaker, "How Bell's Theorem Proved 'Spooky Action at a Distance' is Real," *Quanta*, July 20, 2021, https://www.quantamagazine.org/how-bells-theorem-proved-spooky-action-at-a-distance-is-real-20210720/.

13. Sheldon Goldstein et al., "Bell's Theorem," *Scholarpedia* 6, no. 10 (2011): 8378, http://www.scholarpedia.org/article/Bell%27s_theorem.

14. Dan Hooper, PhD, "Quantum Universe: Fundamentally Probabilistic, not Deterministic" from the lecture series *What Einstein Got Wrong*.

15. Werner Heisenberg, "On the Perceptual Content of Quantum Theoretical Kinematics and Mechanics" (1927), quoted in Shapiro, *The New Yale Book of Quotations*, Kindle loc. 369.

16. Like many other "modern" convictions, it originated in ancient times, with origins in the pre-Socratic Greek philosophers such as Heraclitus and Leucippus, between the seventh and eighth centuries BC and popularized by the Stoics.

17. Hooper, "Quantum Universe."

18. Albert Einstein in a letter to Max Born, March 3, 1947, quoted in Arkady Plotnitsky, *The Principles of Quantum Theory, From Planck's Quanta to the Higgs Boson* (Springer, 2016), 33.

19. Einstein in a letter to Max Born, March 3, 1947 quoted in Plotnitsky, *The Principles of Quantum Theory*, 33.

20. Albert Einstein, quoted in Emilio Segrè, *From X-rays to Quarks: Modern Physicists and Their Discoveries* (Dover, 2012), 73.

21. Albert Einstein in a letter to Max Born, April 29, 1924, quoted in Shapiro, *The*

New Yale Book of Quotations, Kindle loc. 240.

22. Albert Einstein in a letter to Max Born, December 4, 1926. Usually quoted as "God does not play dice with the universe." Quoted in Shapiro, *The New Yale Book of Quotations*, Kindle, loc. 240.

23. Niels Bohr, "Discussion with Einstein on Epistemological Problems in Atomic Physics," in Paul Arthur Schilpp, ed., *Albert Einstein, Philosopher-Scientist* (Princeton University Press, 1983), 117.

24. Niels Bohr, quoted in Heisenberg, *Physics and Beyond*, 206.

25. Quoted in S. M. Blinder, *Introduction to Quantum Mechanics* (Academic Press, 2021), 337.

26. Quoted in B. Rosenblum and F. Kuttner, *Quantum Enigma* (Duckworth Books, 2011), 6.

27. Richard P. Feynman, "Simulating Physics with Computers," in *International Journal of Theoretical Physics* 21, nos. 6/7 (1982): 467–488, 471.

28. Cited from Art Hobson, *Tales of the Quantum: Understanding Physics' Most Fundamental Theory* (Oxford University Press, 2017), 233.

29. See Smith, *Physics and Vertical Causation*, Kindle loc. 260.

30. Alfred North Whitehead, quoted in Smith, *Physics and Vertical Causation*, Kindle loc. 292.

31. Nick Herbert, *Quantum Reality* (Doubleday, 1987) Kindle loc. 329.

32. Elizabeth Heisenberg, *Inner Exile: Recollections of a Life with Werner Heisenberg* (Birkhäuser, 1984), 157.

33. Barr, *Modern Physics and Ancient Faith*, Kindle loc. 257.

34. Werner Heisenberg, "Positivism, Metaphysics, and Religion," in Timothy Ferris, ed., *The World Treasury of Physics, Astronomy, and Mathematics* (Little, Brown, 1991), 826.

35. See William J. Slattery, *The Logic of Truth*: *St. Thomas Aquinas's Epistemology and Antonio Livi's Alethic Logic* (Leonardo da Vinci, 2015).

36. Walter Freeman, "Nonlinear Brain Dynamics and Intention according to Aquinas," *Mind and Matter* 6, no. 2 (2008): 207–234, https://philpapers.org/rec/FRENBD.

37. Werner Heisenberg, cited in Sebastian De Haro, "Science and Philosophy: A Love–Hate Relationship," *Foundations of Science* 25, no. 2 (2020): 297–314, https://link.springer.com/article/10.1007/s10699-019-09619-2.

38. Heisenberg, *Physics and Philosophy*, 54.

39. Werner Heisenberg, quoted in Ken Wilber, ed., *Quantum Questions: Mystical Writings of the World's Greatest Physicists* (Shambala, 2001), 52.

40. Heisenberg, *Physics and Philosophy*, 160.

41. Werner Heisenberg, quoted in Herbert, *Quantum Reality*, Kindle loc. 534.

42. Wolfgang Smith graduated from Cornell University at the age of eighteen with majors in physics, philosophy, and mathematics. He received his master's degree in theoretical physics from Purdue University and then worked at Bell Aircraft Corporation as an aerodynamicist. His pioneering work on the effect of diffusion fields was a theoretical solution to the re-entry problem for space flight. After taking his PhD in mathematics from Columbia University, Smith held positions at MIT, UCLA, and Oregon State University. Among his published works is *Physics and Vertical Causation*. His thought is a meeting place between contemporary science and Thomistic metaphysics.

43. Aristotle, *Metaphysics*, 1017a.

44. See Smith, *Physics and Vertical Causation*, Kindle loc. 383. See also Herbert, *Quantum Reality*, 23, 187.

45. Smith, *Physics: A Science in Quest of an Ontology*, 41.

46. Heisenberg, *Physics and Philosophy*, cited in Smith, *Physics: A Science in Quest of an Ontology*, 11.

47. Smith, *Physics: A Science in Quest of an Ontology*, 66, a view first proposed by Werner Heisenberg.

48. See also Herbert, *Quantum Reality*, 193–195.

49. Smith, *The Quantum Enigma*, 119.

50. Max Planck, "Das Wesen der Materie" (The nature of matter, speech at Florence, Italy, 1944). Archiv zur Geschichte der Max-Planck-Gesellschaft, abt. va, rep. 11 Planck, nr. 1797, quoted in Manfred Bauer, *Quantum Physics and God* (BoD, 2022), 63–64. See the citation of Max Planck in chap. 11.

51. See Smith, *Physics and Vertical Causation*, Kindle loc. 401ff.

52. Smith, chap. 7.

53. See Edward Feser, *Aquinas: A Beginner's Guide* (OneWorld, 2009), Kindle loc. 315.

54. Bernard Wuellner, *Dictionary of Scholastic Philosophy* (2011), s.v. "Form," 48.

55. Ibid..

56. See St. Thomas Aquinas, *De Potentia*, q.7, a.2, ad 9, quoted in John F. X. Knasas, *Thomistic Existentialism and Cosmological Reasoning* (Washington, DC: The Catholic University of America Press, 2019), 58.

57. Aquinas, *Summa Theologiae*, I, q.2, a.3, in *The Summa Theologiae of St. Thomas Aquinas*, 2nd rev. ed., trans. Fathers of the English Dominican Province (1920; online ed. Kevin Knight, New Advent, 2019), https://www.newadvent.org/summa/1002.htm.

58. See Reinhard Hütter, *Bound for Beatitude: A Thomistic Study in Eschatology and Ethics* (The Catholic University of America Press, 2019), 228.

59. Étienne Gilson, *God and Philosophy* (Yale University Press, 2002), 69–70.

60. Bruce Gordon, "How Does the Intelligibility of Nature Point to Design?" chap. 24 in Dembski, Luskin, and Holden, *The Comprehensive Guide to Science and Faith*, Kindle loc. 260.

61. See Smith, *Physics and Vertical Causation*, Kindle loc. 583.

62. Phil Mason, *Quantum Glory: The Science of Heaven Invading Earth* (New Earth Tribe, 2010), Kindle loc. 123.

63. Paul Davies and John Gribbin, *The Matter Myth: Dramatic Discoveries That Challenge Our Understanding of Physical Reality* (Simon & Schuster, 2007), 142–143.

64. Ibid., 309.

65. Fred Hoyle, "The Universe: Past and Present Reflections," *Science and Engineering* 20 (September 1982): 1–36.

66. Quoted in Barr, *Modern Physics and Ancient Faith*, 257.

Chapter 8: New Math and Restored Wonder

1. Slattery, *The Logic of Truth*.

2. James J. Gibson, *The Ecological Approach to Visual Perception* (Erlbaum, 1986);

articles by E. S. Reed and R. K. Jones, "Gibson's Theory of Perception: A Case of Hasty Epistemologizing?" *Philosophy of Science* 45, no. 4 (1978): 519–530, https://philpapers. org/rec/REEGTO; and "James Gibson's Ecological Revolution in Psychology," *Philosophy of the Social Sciences* 9, no. 2 (1979): 189–204, https://philpapers.org /rec/REEJGE. In addition to *The Ecological Approach to Visual Perception*, Gibson's most important writings include *The Perception of the Visual World* (1950) and *The Senses Considered as Perceptual Systems* (1966). His followers founded the International Society for Ecological Psychology in 1981.

3. Gibson, *The Ecological Approach to Visual Perception*. See also Wolfgang Smith, *Science and Myth* (Angelico Press/Sophia Perennis, 2012), chapter 4.

4. Gibson *The Ecological Theory of Visual Perception*, 60–61, quoted in Smith, *The Wisdom of Ancient Cosmology*, Kindle loc. 8211–8219. See also Smith, *Cosmos and Transcendence*, chap. 7.

5. See Smith, *The Wisdom of Ancient Cosmology*, Kindle loc. 8211–8219.

6. Quoted in Smith, *Physics and Vertical Causation*.

7. Smith, *Physics and Vertical Causation*.

8. Ibid.

9. Gilson, *The Spirit of Medieval Philosophy*, chap. 9, "Christian Anthropology."

10. Michael J. Behe, *Darwin Devolves: The New Science About DNA That Challenges Evolution* (HarperOne, 2019), 276–277.

11. Bertrand Russell, *Religion and Science* (Oxford University Press, 1997), 243.

12. See "Gödel's Incompleteness Theorem: The #1 Mathematical Discovery of the 20th Century," Perry Marshall, https://www.perrymarshall.com/articles/religion /godels-incompleteness-theorem/.

13. Hao Wang, *A Logical Journey: From Gödel to Philosophy* (Cambridge, MA: MIT Press, 1996), 57. This and other quotes about Gödel, unless otherwise stated, are from Héctor Rosario, PhD, "Kurt Gödel's Mathematical and Scientific Perspective of the Divine: A Rational Theology," Department of Mathematics, University of Puerto Rico, Mayagüez Campus, December 9, 2006, https://anantarama.files.wordpress.com/2018/04 /aissq-2006-godelstheology-rosario.pdf.

14. Freeman Dyson, *From Eros to Gaia* (Penguin Books, 1993), 161. (Freeman Dyson was Professor of Physics at Princeton's Institute for Advanced Study.)

15. Rosario, "Kurt Gödel's Mathematical and Scientific Perspective of the Divine," 1.

16. See the appendix "Gödel's Theorem" in Barr, *Modern Physics and Ancient Faith*.

17. Douglas R. Hofstadter, *Gödel, Escher, Bach: An Eternal Golden Braid* (Basic Books, 1979), 84.

18. Roger Penrose, Hawking's coauthor on black hole physics, recognized this connection and wrote about it. His book *The Emperor's New Mind* (1989) links Gödel to Turing and establishes the noncomputable nature of creativity. See Dembski, Luskin, and Holden, eds., *The Comprehensive Guide to Science and Faith*, Kindle loc. 445.

19. See Smith, *Physics and Vertical Causation*.

20. Wigner, quoted in Barr, *Modern Physics and Ancient Faith*, Kindle loc. 255.

21. Marston Morse, quoted in Robert A. Nowlan, *Masters of Mathematics: The Problems They Solved, Why These Are Important, and What You Should Know about Them* (Sense, 2017), 161.

22. Heisenberg, *Physics and Philosophy*, 32, quoted in Stephen Duguid, *Nature in Modernity: Servant, Citizen, Queen or Comrade* (Lang, 2010), 245.

23. Thomas S. Kuhn, *The Structure of Scientific Revolutions*, a book about the history of science, was a landmark event for several reasons. Notable among these was its challenge of the status quo view of "science" as the "objective," impartial, unbiased, and independent judge of "reality." Kuhn, in his impeccable research, showed by contrast that the cause of scientific revolutions and new "paradigm shifts" was not sheer "science" and "reason" but a mixture of intuition, imagination, and the atmosphere of the society in which the revolution occurred.

24. Smith, *The Wisdom of Ancient Cosmology*, Kindle loc. 7975–7981.

25. Heisenberg, *Physics and Philosophy*, 55.

26. Modris Eksteins, *Rites of Spring: The Great War and the Birth of the Modern Age* (Houghton Mifflin, 2000), 31.

27. Edward Feser, *Aristotle's Revenge*: *The Metaphysical Foundations of Physical and Biological Science* (Editiones Scholasticae, 2019), 1, 546. J. P. Moreland, *Scientism and Secularism: Learning to Respond to a Dangerous Ideology* (Crossway, 2018), 55–69; J. P. Moreland, *Christianity and the Nature of Science: A Philosophical Investigation* (Baker, 1989), 108–133.

28. Iain McGilchrist, *The Divided Brain and the Search for Meaning: Why Are We So Unhappy?* (Yale University Press, 2012), 9.

29. Ludwig Wittgenstein, *Culture and Value*, ed. G. H. von Wright and H. Nyman, trans. Peter Winch (University of Chicago Press, 1984), 5e, quoted in Iain McGilchrist, *The Master and His Emissary: The Divided Brain and the Making of the Western World* (Yale University Press, 2018), Kindle loc. 157.

30. Sylvain Cappell, quoted in "Do Numbers Exist? A Philosophical Question," October 14, 2016, http://ifsa.my/articles/do-numbers-exist-a-philosophical-question.

31. Barr, *Modern Physics and Ancient Faith*, Kindle loc. 256.

32. Roger Penrose, *Shadows of the Mind*: *A Search for the Missing Science of Consciousness* (Oxford University Press, 1994); Ernest Nagel and James R. Newman, *Gödel's Proof* (Taylor & Francis, 2012).

33. Smith, *Physics and Vertical Causation*.

34. See chaps. 22, 23, and 24 in Barr, *Modern Physics and Ancient Faith*, for a physicist's insightful explanation of human uniqueness.

35. Barr, *Modern Physics and Ancient Faith*, Kindle loc. 26.

36. Raymond J. Seeger, "Heisenberg, Thoughtful Christian," *Journal of the American Scientific Association* 37 (December 1985): 231–232, https://www.asa3.org/ASA/PSCF/1985/JASA12-85Seeger.html.

37. John D. Barrow, *The Constants of Nature: From Alpha to Omega — The Numbers That Encode the Deepest Secrets of the Universe* (Knopf Doubleday, 2009), 26, quoted in Dr. Joshua M. Moritz, "Max Planck and the Mind Who Is the Matrix of All Matter," Aish, September 14, 2022, https://aish.com/max-planck-and-the-mind-who-is-the-matrix-of-all-matter/2.

38. Moritz, "Max Planck and The Mind Who is the Matrix of all Matter."

39. Aquinas, *Summa Theologiae*, I, q.10, a.5.

40. Originally a statement by Friedrich Nietzsche.

41. Nagel, *Mind and Cosmos*, 92, quoting Roger White, "Does Origins of Life Research Rest on a Mistake?" *Noûs* 41, no. 3 (2007): 453–477, quoted in Dembski, Luskin, and Holden, eds., *The Comprehensive Guide to Science and Faith*, Kindle loc. 309.

42. Sir James Jeans, quoted in William D. Gairdner, *The Book of Absolutes: A Critique of Relativism and a Defence of Universals* (McGill-Queen's University Press, 2008), 89.

43. Hao Wang, *A Logical Journey*, 318, and Palle Yourgrau, *A World without Time: The Forgotten Legacy of Gödel and Einstein* (Basic Books, 2005), 104–105.

44. Ibid., 152.

45. Ibid..

46. Heisenberg, *Physics and Philosophy*, p. 11 of the appendix.

47. Quoted by Fiona Ellis, "God, Naturalism, and the Limits of Science," in Gillian Straine, ed., *Are There Limits to Science?* (Cambridge Scholars, 2017), 17.

48. Heisenberg, *Physics and Philosophy*, 46.

49. Max Planck, *Scientific Autobiography and Other Papers* (Williams & Norgate, 1950), 184.

50. Max Planck, "Religion and Natural Science," in *Scientific Autobiography and Other Papers*, 187. See also Moritz, "Max Planck and The Mind Who is the Matrix of all Matter."

51. For a development of these ideas, see Frenkel, *Love and Math*.

52. Mario De Caro, "Varieties of Naturalism," in Koons and Bealer, eds., *The Waning of Materialism*, 366. See also Lindberg, *The Beginnings of Western Science*.

53. Heisenberg, *Physics and Philosophy*, 175–176.

54. Alfred North Whitehead, *Science and the Modern World* (Macmillan, 1953), 54.

55. Albert Einstein, "Physics and Reality," in *Ideas and Opinions*, 292. Originally published in *The Journal of the Franklin Institute* 221, no. 3 (1936).

Chapter 9: Which Story Do I Inhabit?

1. *Genesis* in Hebrew means beginnings; *apocalypse* in Greek means revelation.

2. John Berger, *Keeping a Rendezvous* (Knopf Doubleday), Kindle loc. 172.

3. Terence E. Fretheim, *God and World in the Old Testament: A Relational Theology of Creation* (Abingdon Press, 2005), Kindle loc. 143–144.

4. L. Michael Morales, *Who Shall Ascend the Mountain of the Lord? A Biblical Theology of the Book of Leviticus* (nterVarsity Press, 2015), Kindle loc. 39.

5. *New Spirit-Filled Life Bible: Kingdom Equipping Through the Power of the Word* (Thomas Nelson, 2013), 36. See also James Strong, *A Concise Dictionary of the Words in the Greek Testament and The Hebrew Bible* (Logos Bible Software, 2009), 112, no. 7650. For *sheba* see Strong, no. 7651.

6. Brown-Driver-Briggs Hebrew and English Lexicon, BibleSoft, https://biblehub.com/hebrew/7650.htm.

7. Donald W. Mitchell, "Catholic Theology of Creation: Nature's Value and Relation to Humankind," *Claritas: Journal of Dialogue and Culture* 4, no. 2 (October 2015): 70–74, https://docs.lib.purdue.edu/claritas/vol4/iss2/18/.

8. I take the opportunity here to thank the author Liam O' Flynn, *Writing with Stardust: The Ultimate Descriptive Guide for Students, Parents, Teachers, and Lovers of English*

(CreateSpace, 2013) for so many of the terms I have used in these pages to describe landscapes and skyscapes.

9. Words of the consecration formula during the Mass: see *The Roman Missal*, 3rd typical ed. (United States Conference of Catholic Bishops, 2011), 639.

10. Augustine, *Confessions*, 3, 6, 11, quoted in *Catechism of the Catholic Church* (VLibreria Editrice Vaticana, 1997), 79.

11. John H. Walton, *The Lost World of Genesis One: Ancient Cosmology and the Origins Debate* (InterVarsity Press, 2009), 72–106.

12. This argument is from Morales, *Who Shall Ascend the Mountain of the Lord?*, Kindle loc. 39–44. Morales develops it in his book *Cult and Cosmos: Tilting toward a Temple-Centered Theology* (Peeters, 2014).

13. See Scott Hahn and Curtis Mitch, ed. *The Book of Genesis: Commentary, Notes, and Study Questions: Ignatius Catholic Study Bible, Revised Standard Version 2nd Catholic Ed.* (Ignatius Press, 2010), 19.

14. Terence E. Fretheim, *God So Enters into Relationships That ... A Biblical View* (Fortress Press, 2020), Kindle loc. 29.

15. Terence E. Fretheim, *The Suffering of God: An Old Testament Perspective* (Fortress Press, 1985), Kindle loc. 37.

16. N. T. Wright, *Surprised by Hope: Rethinking Heaven, the Resurrection, and the Mission of the Church* (HarperCollins, 2008), 111, 115.

17. N. T. Wright, *Interpreting Scripture: Essays on the Bible and Hermeneutics* (Zondervan Academic, 2020), 250.

18. The dimension of the supernatural that we will refer to most frequently in future chapters will be grace: "Sanctifying grace is an habitual gift, a stable and supernatural disposition that perfects the soul itself to enable it to live with God, to act by his love" (CCC 2000). For an explanation, see Adolphe Tanquerey, *The Spiritual Life: A Treatise on Ascetical and Mystical Theology* (TAN Books, 2000), pt. 1.

19. G. K. Chesterton, *The Collected Works of G. K. Chesterton*, vol. 1 (Ignatius Press, 1986), 88.

20. See G. K. Beale, *The Temple and the Church's Mission: A Biblical Theology of the Dwelling Place of God* (InterVarsity Press, 2004).

21. Josephus, *The Jewish War*, bk. 3, trans. H. St. J. Thackery, Loeb Classical Library (Harvard University Press, 1957), 7.7, 403, quoted in Walton, *The Lost World of Genesis One*, 80.

22. Josephus, *Antiquities of the Jews*, 3.132, quoted in T. Desmond Alexander, *From Eden to the New Jerusalem* (Kregel), Kindle loc. 73.

23. Josephus, *The Jewish War*, 5.2, 10–14, quoted in Desmond, *From Eden to the New Jerusalem*, Kindle loc. 73.

24. T. Desmond Alexander, *From Paradise to the Promised Land: An Introduction to the Pentateuch*, 3rd ed. (Baker Academic, 2012), 131. G. K. Beale, "Eden, the Temple, and the Church's Mission in the New Creation," *Journal of the Evangelical Theological Society* 48, no. 1, (March 2005): 5–31, 16; Iain Provan, *Discovering Genesis: Content, Interpretation, Reception* (Eerdmans, 2016), 57; Gordon J. Wenham, "Sanctuary Symbolism in the Garden of Eden Story," in Proceedings of the Ninth World Congress of Jewish Studies (World Union of Jewish Studies, 1986), 19; Meredith G. Kline, *Kingdom Prologue* (Gor-

don-Conwell Theological Seminary, 1989), 54; and Beale, *The Temple and the Church's Mission*, 54.

25. From the essay by the cultural critic Moyshe Shtarkman, "'From Eternity to Eternity': Thoughts and Considerations in Honor of Passover," trans. Ross Perlin, Yiddish Book Center, April 15, 2016, https://www.yiddishbookcenter.org/language -literature-culture/yiddish-translation/eternity-eternity-thoughts-and -considerations-honor; first published in April 1960 in the journal *Folk un velt* (Nation and world).

26. Josephus, *The Jewish War*, 5, 212–218, quoted in N. T. Wright, *Paul and the Faithfulness of God* (Fortress Press, 2013), Kindle loc. 101.

27. Quoted in Wright, *Paul and the Faithfulness of God*, 101.

28. H. W. Nibley, "What Is a Temple?," in T. G. Madsen, ed., *Temple in Antiquity: Ancient Records and Modern Perspectives* (Religious Studies Center, Brigham Young University, 1984), 22. Nibley writes, "We can summarize a hundred studies of recent date in the formula: a temple, good or bad, is a scale-model of the universe."

29. Taylor, *A Secular Age*, chap. 2, Kindle.

30. Thomas Aquinas, among others, recognized the presence of sacramentals among our Jewish forefathers. See Walter Farrell, OP, *A Companion to the Summa* (Sheed and Ward, 1942), 256–258.

31. Fretheim, *God So Enters into Relationships That*, Kindle loc. 22.

Chapter 10: Breaking the Code to Understand the Divine Strategy

1. G. K. Chesterton, *Daily News*, September 15, 1906, quoted in Kevin L. Morris, *The Truest Fairy Tale*, 137.

2. Irenaeus, *Against Heresies*, 3.22.3, quoted in Hans Urs von Balthasar, *The Scandal of the Incarnation: Irenaeus Against the Heresies: Selected and Introduced by Hans Urs von Balthasar*, trans. John Saward (Ignatius Press, 1990), Kindle loc. 980.

3. See Council of Trent, session 5, "Decree on Original Sin," in Denzinger and Rahner, eds., *The Sources of Catholic Dogma*, 246.

4. C. S. Lewis, *The Four Loves*, chap. 6, par. 21, in Root and Martindale, eds., *The Quotable Lewis*, Kindle loc. 682.

5. The classic statement of this point, though not developed in apocalyptic terms, is E. P. Sanders, *Paul and Palestinian Judaism: A Comparison of Patterns of Religion* (Fortress Press, 1977), 474: "For Paul, the conviction of a universal solution preceded the conviction of a universal plight." See also 442–447, quoted in John Behr, *John the Theologian and His Paschal Gospel* (Oxford University Press), Kindle loc. 132. "Universal solution" does not mean "universal salvation" but rather the means by which salvation is made possible for all humans.

6. Nicholas Cabasilas, *The Life in Christ*, 6.91–94 (ET 6.12 modified), quoted in Behr, *John the Theologian and his Paschal Gospel*, Kindle loc. 244.

7. Nick Bott, "Adam," in John D. Barry et al, eds., *The Lexham Bible Dictionary*. (Lexham Press, 2016).

8. Lewis, *The Four Loves*, chap. 6, par. 21, in Root and Martindale, eds. *The Quotable Lewis*, Kindle loc. 681.

9. Aquinas, *Summa Theologiae*, III, q.9. See also Dominic Legge, OP, *The Trinitarian Christology of St Thomas Aquinas* (Oxford University Press, 2017), Kindle loc. 172ff. "He combined both the divine nature and the human into the only holy perfection of himself; (for there is one Lord Jesus Christ, and not two; the same God, the same Lord, the same King)," in "The Creed of Epiphanius," quoted in Denzinger and Rahner, eds., *The Sources of Catholic Dogma*, 10.

10. See Jewish author Alfred Edersheim, "The Upbringing of Jewish Children," chap. 7 in *Sketches of Jewish Social Life in the Days of Christ* (London: Pardon, 1876).

11. Arnold Toynbee and David Churchill Somervell, *A Study of History*, vol. 2 (Oxford University Press, 1987), 267.

12. See Aquinas, *Summa Theologiae*, I, q.46, a.4.

13. N. T. Wright, *The Day the Revolution Began: Reconsidering the Meaning of Jesus's Crucifixion* (HarperCollins, 2016), Kindle loc. 181.

14. Wright, *The Day the Revolution Began*, Kindle loc. 181.

15. Ex 3:12, 18; 4:23; 5:1–3; 7:16; 8:1, 20; 9:1, 13; 10:3, 24–26. Wright, *The Day the Revolution Began*, Kindle loc. 182.

16. Words of the minor doxology in the Holy Sacrifice of the Mass, which is the mystical enactment of the passion.

Chapter 11: Deeper Magic

1. Wright, *The Day the Revolution Began*, Kindle loc. 64.

2. Ibid., 181.

3. Ibid.

4. N. T. Wright, *Simply Christian: Why Christianity Makes Sense* (HarperCollins, 2006), Kindle loc. 109–110.

5. Wright, *The Day the Revolution Began*, Kindle loc. 191.

6. Søren Kierkegaard, *Works of Love: Kierkegaard's Writings*, vol. 16, ed. and trans. Howard V. Hong and Edna H. Hong (Princeton, NJ: Princeton University Press, 1995), Kindle loc. 99.

7. Ibid., Kindle loc. 99–101.

8. N. T. Wright, *The Lord and His Prayer* (Society for Promoting Christian Knowledge, 1996), 9.

9. See Jeffrey S. Siker, *Jesus, Sin, and Perfection in Early Christianity* (Cambridge University Press, 2015), Kindle loc. 1102.

10. Joseph de Maistre, *Considerations on France*, ed. Richard A. Lebrun (Cambridge University Press, 1994), 46.

11. Jesus, as the incarnate Second Person of the Trinity, is a divine Person with two natures, human and divine. For the basis of this certainty in the teachings of the Church, especially in the Council of Trent, see Ludwig Ott, *Fundamentals of Catholic Dogma* (Herder, 1954), 180–193.

12. I am grateful for this insight expressed by Christopher J. Wiles in his article "'Death Working Backwards:' Narnia, Deeper Magic, and Easter."

13. C. S. Lewis, *The Lion, the Witch & the Wardrobe*, quoted in Wiles, "Death Working Backwards."

14. C. S. Lewis, *God in the Dock: Essays on Theology and Ethics* (Eerdmans, 1970), pt.

1, chap. 9, par. 3, 4, and 8.

Chapter 12: You Are a Shadow of Your Future Self

1. C. S. Lewis, *The Problem of Pain*, chap. 10, par. 4, p. 178, in *The Quotable Lewis*, Kindle loc. 478.

2. G. K. Beale and David H. Campbell, *Revelation: A Shorter Commentary* (Eerdmans, 2015), 471.

3. Peter J. Leithart, *Revelation 12–22*, ed. Michael Allen and Scott R. Swain, International Theological Commentary (Bloomsbury T&T Clark, 2018), 352.

4. Wright, *The Day the Revolution Began*, Kindle loc. 113.

Chapter 13: The Heavenized Planet Earth

1. de Maistre, *Considerations on France*, 46.

2. Wright, *The New Testament and the People of God*, 217. The Second Temple era was the postexilic epoch, from 516 BC to AD 70, during which the Second Temple of Jerusalem existed.

3. Peter J. Leithart, *Revelation 1–11*, ed. Michael Allen and Scott R. Swain, International Theological Commentary (Bloomsbury T&T Clark, 2018), 12.

4. G. K. Beale, "Eden, the Temple, and the Church's Mission in the New Creation," *Journal of the Evangelical Theological Society* 48, no. 1 (March 2005): 5–31, quoted in Alexander, *From Eden to the New Jerusalem*, Kindle loc. 73.

5. Siker, *Jesus, Sin, and Perfection in Early Christianity*, Kindle loc. 1102.

6. See Scott Hahn, *A Pocket Guide to the Bible* (Our Sunday Visitor, 2008).

7. N. T. Wright, *Climax of the Covenant: Christ and the Law in Pauline Theology* (Biddles, 2004), 150.

8. Scott W. Hahn, *The Kingdom of God as Liturgical Empire: A Theological Commentary on 1–2 Chronicles* (Baker Academic, 2012).

9. See Wright, *The Day the Revolution Began*, Kindle loc. 356–364.

10. Wright, 117.

11. N. T. Wright, *Simply Jesus* (HarperCollins, 2011), Kindle loc. 11. See also Wright, *How God Became King: The Forgotten Story of the Gospels* (HarperCollins, 2012).

12. Wright, *The Kingdom New Testament*.

13. See Wright, *How God Became King*.

14. Wright, *The Day the Revolution Began*, Kindle loc. 180.

Chapter 14: Your Forever Home

1. Heisenberg, *Physics and Beyond*, 210.

2. McGilchrist, *The Master and His Emissary*, Kindle loc. 125.

3. T. Desmond Alexander, *The City of God and the Goal of Creation* (Crossway, 2018), 15–16.

4. See Peter J. Leithart, *Theopolitan Reading* (Theopolis Books, 2020), chap. 5. Also see Leithart, *On Earth as in Heaven: Theopolis Fundamentals* (Lexham Press, 2022), pt. 3, the section "Garden in the Wilderness"; and Alexander, *From Eden to the New Jerusalem*.

5. Leithart, *Revelation 12–22*, 400–401.

6. See Alexander, *From Eden to the New Jerusalem*, Kindle loc. 25, 27, 74–79, 96–118.

7. Leithart, *Theopolitan Reading*, Kindle loc. 96–97.

8. Fretheim, *God and World in the Old Testament*, Kindle loc. 24.

9. Ibid., 24.

10. Dietrich Bonhoeffer, *Creation and Fall*, 66, quoted in Fretheim, *God and World in the Old Testament*, Kindle loc. 86.

11. Bonhoeffer, *Creation and Fall*, 67, quoted in Fretheim, *God and World in the Old Testament*, Kindle loc. 415.

12. See Paul Shepard, *The Others: How Animals Made Us Human* (Shearwater Books, 1996).

13. During renovations at the Gubbio church of San Francesco in 1872, diggers found the skeleton of a large wolf under a slab near the church wall.

14. Alexander, *From Eden to the New Jerusalem*, Kindle loc. 157.

15. See chap. 4 "A Visit to Relationton," in Spretnak, *Relational Reality*.

16. John Ruskin, *Works of John Ruskin: The Stones of Venice* (Wiley, 1886), 222.

17. See Lars Spuybroek, *Textile Tectonics: Research and Design* (NAi010, 2011), 48–61, quoted in Matthew Huber, "The Eco-Gothic," Christoph Eckrich, Spring 2019, https://christopheckrich.com/The-Eco-Gothic#_ftn10.

18. Worringer, *Ceaseless Melody of the Northern Line*, quoted in Huber, "The Eco-Gothic."

19. See Slattery, chap. 9, "Men with Music, Artistry, and Drama in Their Souls," in *Heroism and Genius*.

20. Leithart, *Theopolitan Reading*, Kindle loc. 96–100.

21. G. K. Beale and Benjamin L. Gladd, *The Story Retold: A Biblical-Theological Introduction to the New Testament* (Intervarsity Press, 2020), 490.

22. See for instance Alexander, *From Paradise to the Promised Land*.

23. Owen Barfield, *Saving the Appearances: A Study in Idolatry* (Harcourt, Brace & World, 1965.), 94.

24. See chap. 6 in Alexander, *From Eden to the New Jerusalem*.

Chapter 15: The Vision of the Future Civilization in Which Humans Thrive

1. Geert Keil and Nora Kreft, eds., *Aristotle's Anthropology* (Cambridge University Press, 2019), 26.

2. "The Church teaches that every spiritual soul is created immediately by God — it is not 'produced' by the parents — and also that it is immortal: it does not perish when it separates from the body at death, and it will be reunited with the body at the final Resurrection" (CCC 366).

3. See Alexander, *From Eden to the New Jerusalem*, Kindle loc. 163ff.

4. Leithart, *Revelation 12–22*, 370.

5. Irenaeus of Lyon, *Adversus Haereses*, 4, 20, 7, quoted in James G. Bushur, *Irenaeus of Lyons and the Mosaic of Christ: Preaching Scripture in the Era of Martyrdom* (Routledge, 2017), Kindle loc. 98–99.

6. Ian Boxall, *The Revelation of Saint John*, Black's New Testament Commentaries (Continuum, 2006), 301.

7. Ibid., 301.

8. Miroslav Volf and Ryan McAnnally-Linz, *The Home of God: A Brief Story of Everything* (Brazos Press, 2022).

9. Volf and McAnnally-Linz, *The Home of God*. See also Jn 14:23, 17:22–23.

10. "Tabernacled," in Thomas Newberry and George Ricker Berry, *The Interlinear Literal Translation of the Greek New Testament* (Logos Bible Software, 2004).

11. Leithart, *Revelation 12–22*, 350.

12. Ibid., 352.

13. Ibid.

14. *The Poems of Gerard Manley Hopkins*, ed. Robert Bridges (Digireads.com, 2018), Kindle loc. 4.

15. Volf and McAnnally-Linz, *The Home of God*, 13.

16. G. K. Beale, God *Dwells among Us: Expanding Eden to the Ends of the Earth* (InterVarsity Press, 2014), 48–49.

17. William J. Dumbrell, *The End of the Beginning: Revelation 21–22 and the Old Testament* (Lancer, 1985); Richard Bauckham, *The Theology of the Book of Revelation* (Cambridge University Press, 1993), 48; and Beale, *The Temple and the Church's Mission*, 365–369.

18. Jurgen Moltmann, quoted in Thomas F. Torrance and Richard W. A. McKinney, *Creation, Christ, and Culture: Studies in Honour of T. F. Torrance* (T&T Clark, 1976), 129.

19. Volf and McAnnally-Linz, *The Home of God*, 13.

20. St. John Damascene, *Orthodox Faith*, 2.11, quoted in Volf and McAnnally-Linz, *The Home of God*, 211.

21. Hahn, *The Kingdom of God as Liturgical Empire*, 35.

22. Sigmund Mowinckel, *The Psalms in Israel's Worship*, vol. 1 (Abingdon, 1962), 81, quoted in Fretheim, *God and World in the Old Testament*, 335. The psalms powerfully express this certainty: see for instance Ps 22:3; 96:1 and 9; 97:1 and 6; 98:4; 99:1; 100:1; and 117:1; 119:171–172; also the prophet Isaiah: Is 42:10–12.

23. Hahn, *The Kingdom of God as Liturgical Empire*.

24. Walton, *The Lost World of Genesis One*, 83–84.

Chapter 16: Your Deepest Longings

1. C. S. Lewis, *The Last Battle*, in *The Chronicles of Narnia* (HarperCollins, 2001), 760.

2. E. M. Forster, quoted in Surabhi Banerjee, *E. M. Forster: A Critical Linguistic Approach* (Allied, 1995), 156.

3. Pythagoras, quoted in Donald A. Hodges, *A Concise Survey of Music Philosophy* (Routledge, 2017), 109.

4. St. John Henry Newman, *The Idea of a University* (Doubleday, 1959), 111–112.

5. C. S. Lewis, *The Last Battle*, in *The Chronicles of Narnia*, 760.

6. Slattery, *Heroism and Genius*, Kindle loc. 4923.

7. C. S. Lewis, *The Weight of Glory: And Other Addresses* (HarperCollins, 2009), Kindle loc. 30.

8. C. S. Lewis, *The Problem of Pain* (HarperOne, 2009), 96.

9. Beale and Campbell, *Revelation: A Shorter Commentary*, Kindle loc. 471–472.

10. See similarly Jer 2:13; Ps 36:8–9; Jl 3:18; Jn 4:10; 7:38.

11. Lewis, *The Problem of Pain*, 96.

12. Leithart, *Revelation 12–22*, 442.

13. Volf and McAnnally-Linz, *The Home of God*, 11.

14. Lewis, *The Problem of Pain*, 97.

15. de Maistre, *Considerations on France*, 46.

16. C. S. Lewis, *Perelandra*, chap. 17, pp. 216–217, in *The Quotable Lewis*, Kindle loc. 552.

17. John Eldredge, *All Things New* (Thomas Nelson, 2017), Kindle loc. 5.

Chapter 17: Trailblazer for a New Civilization

1. "*La vie, c'est une grande aventure vers la lumière.*" Paul Claudel, quoted by Hans Scholl, leader of the White Rose anti-Nazi student movement in a letter six days before he asked to enter the Catholic Church. Shortly after, he was guillotined. Quoted in Graham Collier, *What the Hell Are the Neurons Up To? The Wire-Dangled Human Race* (AuthorHouse, 2011), 39.

2. See Joshua Becker, "What to Do When a Distraction Becomes a Lifestyle" Becoming Minimalist, https://www.becomingminimalist.com/distractions/.

3. Dante Alighieri, *Paradiso*, trans. Stanley Lombardo (Hackett, 2017), l. 144.

4. John Phillips, *Exploring Genesis: An Expository Commentary* (Kregel, 2009), 40.

5. *Entre la lampe et le soleil*, quoted in Paul Gifford and Brian Stimpson, eds., *Reading Paul Valéry: Universe in Mind* (Cambridge University Press, 1998), 41.

6. John Ruskin, *Praeterita*, vol. 35 of *The Works of John Ruskin*, ed. E. T. Cook and Alexander Wedderburn (London, 1903–1912), 286, quoted in Peter Davidson, *The Last of the Light: About Twilight* (Reaktion Books, 2015), Kindle loc. 68.

7. Davidson, *The Last of the Light*, Kindle loc. 61.

8. G. K. Chesterton, *William Blake* (1920), 131–132, quoted in Morris, *The Truest Fairy Tale*, 155.

9. G. K. Chesterton, "Reading the Riddle," in *The Common Man*, quoted in Morris, *The Truest Fairy Tale*, 68.

10. Chesterton, quoted in Morris, *The Truest Fairy Tale*, 27.

11. Oscar Wilde, *The Picture of Dorian Gray* (Wordsworth, 1992), 105.

12. G. K. Chesterton, *The Everlasting Man*, pt. 2, chap. 3, quoted in Morris, *The Truest Fairy Tale*, 186.

13. My translation from the Septuagint.

14. Hans Georg Gadamer, *Truth and Method* (Bloomsbury Press, 2004), 485. My remarks on the connection between beauty and light are from 482–487, and I thank Peter Leithart for introducing me to the philosopher's ideas in his essay "Gadamer on Light and Beauty," Theopolis, May 1, 2012, https://theopolisinstitute.com/leithart_post/gadamer-on-light-and-beauty/. The quotations from Gadamer are taken from Leithart's article.

15. Gadamer, *Truth and Method*, 486.

16. Gadamer, 484.

17. Fr. Thomas Dubay, *The Evidential Power of Beauty: Science and Theology Meet* (Ignatius Press, 1999), Kindle loc. 20. The quotation from Dostoyevsky is: "The terrible thing is that beauty is not only fearful but also mysterious. Here the devil is struggling

with God, and the battlefield is the human heart." Fyodor Dostoevsky, *The Brothers Karamazov: A Novel in Four Parts with Epilogue*, trans. Richard Pevear and Larissa Volokhonsky (Farrar, Straus and Giroux, 2002), 108.

18. Psalm 57:8, my translation from the Greek Septuagint.

19. Hahn, *The Kingdom of God as Liturgical Empire*.

20. Frank-Lothar Hossfeld and Erich Zenger, "Psalms 3: A Commentary on Psalms 101–150," in Klaus Baltzer, ed., *Hermeneia — A Critical and Historical Commentary on the Bible*, trans. Linda M. Maloney (Fortress Press, 2011), 119.

21. Aberjhani, "A Poem for a Poet," Connect Savannah, January 6, 2011, https://www.connectsavannah.com/savannah/a-poem-for-a-poet/Content?oid=2134308.

22. Joseph Pearce, *Literature: What Every Catholic Should Know* (Ignatius Press; Augustine Institute, 2019), 3. See also Alan Kreider, *The Patient Ferment of the Early Church: The Improbable Rise of Christianity in the Roman Empire* (Baker Academic, 2016); Rodney Stark, *The Rise of Christianity: How the Obscure, Marginal Jesus Movement Became the Dominant Religious Force in the Western World in a Few Centuries* (HarperCollins, 1997); Slattery, *Heroism and Genius*.

23. Richard J. Neuhaus, "Creating a Culture of Life" (lecture, Toronto, Canada, October 26, 2002) quoted in Slattery, *Heroism and Genius*.

24. My translation from Léon Bloy, *Le Désespéré* (Paris: Nouvelle Librairie A. Soirat, 1887), 128.

25. Novalis, *Schriften*, 3, 523–524, quoted in Frederick C. Beiser, *Enlightenment, Revolution, and Romanticism: The Genesis of Modern German Political Thought, 1790–1800* (Harvard University Press, 1992), 274.

26. Novalis, *Christendom or Europe*, quoted in Frederick C. Beiser, ed., *The Early Political Writings of the German Romantics*, trans. Frederick C. Beiser (Cambridge University Press, 1996), 78.

27. Quoted in Christopher Partridge, *The Re-enchantment of the West*, vol. 1 (Bloomsbury Academic, 2004), 8. The phrase was coined by Friedrich Schiller.

28. Novalis, *Schriften*, 2, 45, no. 105, quoted in Beiser, *Enlightenment, Revolution, and Romanticism*, 232.

29. Friedrich Nietzsche, *The Will to Power* (n.p.: Jovian Press, 2018).

30. G. K. Chesterton, *A Short History of England*, chap. 8, quoted in Morris, *The Truest Fairy Tale*, 171–172.

31. "*tsâphâh*" in James Strong, *A Concise Dictionary of the Words in the Greek Testament and The Hebrew Bible*, 2, 100.

32. From V. Sander, *St. Seraphim of Sarov*, trans. Sr. Gabriel Anne (SPCK, 1975), 15–16, as quoted in Roger Pooley and Philip Seddon, *The Lord of the Journey* (Collins, 1986), 151.

33. Lewis, *The Last Battle*, chap. 16, in Root and Martindale, eds. *The Quotable Lewis*, Kindle loc. 248.

Acknowledgments

1. Pope John Paul II, Homily for the Inauguration of His Pontificate, October 22, 1978, Vatican.va, par. 5.

ABOUT THE AUTHOR

William J. Slattery, Ph.D., S.T.L., born in Ireland, was ordained by Pope St. John Paul II to the priesthood in St. Peter's Basilica in 1991. A specialist in modern and postmodern worldviews, he has worked on three continents. He is the author of several books, notably *The Logic of Truth* and *Heroism and Genius*. He is a professor at the Franciscan University of Steubenville and chaplain at Damascus while continuing to write, lecture, and give retreats in North America and Europe.